France
today

UNOTT

France today

Introductory studies

Sixth edition

Edited by
J.E. Flower

Routledge
London and New York

First published in 1971 by
Methuen & Co. Ltd
Second edition 1973
Third edition 1977
Fourth edition 1980
Fifth edition 1983
Sixth edition 1987

Reprinted 1990 by
Routledge
11 New Fetter Lane
London EC4P 4EE
29 West 35th Street
New York NY 10001
© 1971, 1973, 1977, 1980, 1983 and
1987
Methuen & Co. Ltd

British Library
Cataloguing in Publication Data
France today: introductory studies.—
    6th ed.—(University paperbacks;
    415)(9   1. France—Civilization
    —1945—   I. Flower, J.E.
    944.083′8   DC33.7
    ISBN 0-415-05138-X

Library of Congress
Cataloging in Publication Data
France today.
    (University paperbacks; 415)
    Includes bibliographies and index.
    1. France—Civilization—1945–
    I. Flower, J.E.   (John Ernest)
DC415.F73   1987   944.08
86-23824
ISBN 0-415-05138-X

Printed and bound in Great Britain by
Richard Clay Ltd, Bungay, Suffolk

6003625920

Contents

Foreword to the sixth edition

Only just before I began to write this foreword France experienced one of the most turbulent periods of internal unrest in recent years. The terrorist attacks which caused such havoc in Paris in the autumn revived just before Christmas with the attempted assassination of the former minister Alain Peyrefitte; racial violence continued to gather momentum with the burning of several appartment blocks housing immigrant workers and their families in areas of northern Paris; widespread strikes by railway and *métro* workers disrupted the winter holiday period. And in late November nearly half a million young people from all of France converged on the capital to march in protest against reforms in higher education proposed by the Loi Devaquet. The spectre of 1968 was soon evoked. Although not as militant and with limited union support only, what was a peaceful and well-ordered demonstration nonetheless developed pockets of violence: barricades were erected, cars burned and at least one student killed. The proposals have been withdrawn and consultation promised, but the activities of the CRS and of the Minister of the Interior (who accused journalists and television of misrepresenting events) have not eased a situation that will remain tense for some months to come. More significantly, the government's behaviour has been interpreted by some, especially on the Right, as weakness; by others it has been seen as a sign of common sense (and presidential strength) on the part of Mitterrand who made little attempt to disguise his approval for the way in which the students conducted themselves. Abroad too there have been problems – the government's negotiations over hostages and suggestions of arms deals in the Middle East, and a set-back over New Caledonia. And behind it all lies the unprecedented and sometimes uneasy *cohabitation* between a socialist President and a right-wing government due to last for another 16 months.

Like its predecessors this new edition of *France Today* attempts, as far as schedules allow, to provide an up-to-date and informed view of the most significant developments within modern French society. I should like to take this opportunity to thank Eric Cahm most warmly for his contributions on political parties in previous editions and to welcome Malcolm Slater in his place. My thanks go as well to all other contributors, to the publishers for their continuing support and to Pat Shears for her copy editing and compilation of the index.

John Flower
Paris, January 1987

One

Social structures

Andrée Shepherd

Introduction

French society today can no longer be neatly divided into the traditional units of ruling class, middle class, working class and peasantry. During the last hundred years in particular, wars and revolutionary movements, shifts of population and developments in industry, science and technology, have all helped to create a kind of uniformity and standardization which makes any clear-cut divisions of this nature difficult. This trend has also been emphasized by the evolution of the more traditional institutions of society – the Church, the family, the educational system and even military service. French society has changed and is still changing, a fact which has been recognized in a number of important administrative reforms – an attempt to break down excessive centralization and encourage the development of regions as more autonomous units, the spreading of social and cultural services and changes in social legislation. Much remains to be done, however, and the economic crisis weighs on the future.

Population

Today France has just over 55 million inhabitants including some 4.5 million foreigners. With low birth and death rates, and with immigration now virtually at a standstill, the population is still increasing but at a much slower rate. By the year 2000 it is expected to reach only 56 to 58 million. During the last forty years French governments have been in favour of large families – the *Code de la Famille* was first drafted in 1939 though not put into effect until after the Second World War, and more recently still there have been large-scale press campaigns to encourage French people to have more children. However, in spite of government incentives (in the form of increased benefits and allowances for families with three or more children), the birth rate has fallen to 1.8 (which is below replacement level), and family-forming habits seem to have settled into a stable pattern: people marry later, divorce more (one in six marriages ends in divorce) and have two rather than three children, or less. Except perhaps in working-class and immigrant groups, large families are very much a thing of the past. With increasing numbers of women at work (often in low-paid, insecure and part-time jobs), there seems to be little chance of a reversal of recent trends, and the present balance between the 23.5 million economically active (out of which, in 1985, 2.3 million were unemployed) and the 30 million or so dependent members of the population is unlikely to improve. One in every three people is still under twenty and almost one in five over sixty: with longer education, earlier retirement and steadily increasing unemployment, there is bound to be a mounting burden on health, social and educational services.

A large proportion of the population lives in towns – 39.9 million in 1985 compared with 17.5 million in 1911 – with the migration from countryside to town continuing at a faster rate than ever before. But what is more significant still is the fact that the population is becoming tripartite: 16 million in towns proper, 20 million in suburbs and *grandes banlieues* (expected to increase to 25 million in the next twenty years), and the remaining one-third spread over a countryside of about 500,000 sq. km. This growing suburbia is creating new challenges and new problems. The architectural horror of Sarcelles north of Paris, for example, brought with it fresh social problems. The very existence of this type of dormitory-suburb, catering for vast numbers of industrial and office workers, has had unexpected consequences, one of which is a growing tendency to introduce the continuous working day, which only ten years ago would have been anathema to French workers used to one- or two-hour lunch breaks. But the solution may be elsewhere: these distant suburbs may, for example, be developed into viable economic units. From 1956 to 1965, Sarcelles grew from 8400 to 30,000 inhabitants: a *grand ensemble* with no life of its own. Socio-cultural facilities have gradually changed it into a proper town. Sarcelles 1986, with its (now stable) population of some 54,000 inhabitants, regional commercial centre, schools, town library and cultural centre, industrial development zone and municipal bus service, no longer relies on Paris, although it is only nine miles away. A few miles to the west the new town of Cergy Pontoise is still expanding around new factories, office blocks and schools in an attempt to avoid previous mistakes, but with only limited results. Together with the other eight New Towns in France – five of them in the Paris area – Cergy Pontoise suffers from a too rapid growth rate and a closeness to the capital. Another problem is the change in the overall plan, especially in the development of the Paris area: originally the five New Towns were supposed to be large autonomous units, close to but not too dependent on Paris. They are now seen as an integral part of a restructured greater Paris, a megalopolis of 14 million inhabitants by the year 2000.

The massive exodus of French people from the land towards the expanding towns has meant a radical change in the distribution of the population between agricultural and other activities: over the last thirty years, the number of people employed in agriculture has decreased from 25 per cent to 8 per cent of the active population today, while the professionals and *cadres* grew from 9 per cent to 20 per cent. This points to a large-scale reorganization of the socio-economic structure. A direct comparison between agriculture and industry (still strong, with 34 per cent of the population in blue-collar jobs in 1980) leaves aside the most important sector of activity, known as the tertiary sector – transport, distribution and services. Today, this 'non-productive' sector (which accounts for over 57 per cent of the active population) is larger than the other two put together and still growing apace: most of the new jobs are in non-manual occupations and are filled by an increasing proportion of women. Industrial growth is greatly impaired by the effects of the economic crisis, with large-scale redundancies resulting from restructuring in all the major industries. A further factor is the regional imbalance between the hard-hit areas in the North and in Lorraine and the still developing Rhônes-Alpes area. A continuation of these trends because of further technological change, mechanization and rationalization may be expected to lead to a society in which only a minority will be directly involved in production, with the majority occupied in administrative and servicing activities. In such a situation there may be a number of consequences. The division between manual and non-manual workers could become more marked, leading to a greater proletarianization of a smaller manual working class, the increasing marginalization of the unemployed (many of them young people) and growing social unrest. With a large number of workers facing redundancy, unless extensive retraining facilities are developed quickly, the wealth created by automation will only heighten the problem of inequality and a new class of 'unemployables' will emerge.

Country v. town

Where have all the peasants gone?

France used to be described as a nation of small farmers; as F.C. Roe once put it, a 'garden in which millions of peasants dig, plough, hoe and weed from sunrise to sunset'. This is undoubtedly no longer true, as the widely-used phrase 'the death of the peasantry' indicates. But this does not mean that the countryside has become a desert: moving away from agriculture has not necessarily meant moving out of the countryside. Many former farmers have only moved a short distance away to the nearest market town in search of a job, or even continue to live in their village and commute to work. Many families are now earning only part of their income from the land. The husband may, for example, remain a farmer but a supplementary (and regular) income is provided by his wife who has become a nurse or a teacher, or by his sons and daughters who work as secretaries, shop-assistants or factory workers. This may not be by choice but rather out of necessity, since small family farms are no longer viable economic units. Many small farmers and agricultural labourers are among the poorest in the French community, while the regrouping of

land, modernization of farming methods and judicious recon-
version to intensive fruit, cereal or meat production have
enabled the few (who may also draw high profits from the
Common Market) to become very wealthy indeed. Whether or
not they are still deriving their income from the land, villagers
can no longer be sharply distinguished from the rest of the
population in their way of life. In the 1960s they became bitter-
ly aware of the fact that, far from being protected by the
Welfare State, they had not joined the consumer society and
were not receiving their fair share of the national income in
spite of the fact that they were doing more than their fair share:
harder work, longer hours, lack of cultural facilities and
modern conveniences were their lot. This is no longer the case
and, increasingly, village, suburb and town dwellers alike
watch television, own a car and do their Saturday shopping in a
neighbouring hypermarket. They may not all have a bathroom
and indoor toilet, but they have a deep-freeze (well-stocked
with home-produced as well as pre-packed food) and a
washing-machine. In the last twenty years, country life has in
fact become an attraction for former town-dwellers who now
return to the land at weekends, or even turn what was originally a weekend cottage (a *résidence secondaire*) into their permanent home. The farming community has become a minority
on its home ground and village life has often been transformed
out of recognition by these 'neo-villagers' who have sometimes captured key positions on local councils.

Generalizations are of course dangerous: historians and
sociologists have repeatedly demonstrated through case
studies that the contrast between town and countryside within
a given area is less striking than the often extreme regional differences. The great plains of the Paris basin with their rich
crops of wheat and intensive farming, the mixed-crop farming of Brittany or the Rhône valley, the vine-growing areas
and the mountain deserts of central France present widely differing problems and prospects. The healthy areas seem to be of
two kinds: the capitalist type of intensive farming; and the
more traditional type of mixed farming, which, by increasingly involving co-operative enterprise, fulfils the need for
skilful crop rotation and the division of labour. Future prospects are certainly favourable given certain conditions: namely

concentration on products in high demand (fruit, vegetables, high quality wine); sufficient organization (co-operatives); and well-planned marketing. In some favoured areas like the Côte d'Or, the agricultural labour force (vineyard labour) earns salaries comparable to those of the Dijon factories nearby. In less prosperous areas, like Brittany, however, some poultry farmers are worse off than industrial labourers. A large firm may deliver day-old chicks and chicken food and impose precise planning. After nine weeks the chickens are collected for slaughtering. The farmer is a home-labourer paid to work according to conditions laid down by the firm. He may own his poultry farm, but this is probably a liability as he is usually tied down by debts and is entirely dependent on the firm employing him. Some poultry farmers have managed to organize themselves into co-operatives, but these are exceptions. For the majority, proletarianization has reached the countryside in a brutal form, and even in the richer Rhône valley there are increasing tendencies for the farmers to contract with freezing and canning firms like the American firm Libby's. All too often, the farmers' share in the profits is a minor one, and agricultural incomes vary even more than industrial ones.

In the last thirty years or so, a certain amount of government planning has been introduced to improve the lot of rural communities, very often in answer to growing unrest and insistent demands by younger farmers who first began to organize themselves in the early 1950s around a Catholic youth organization, the JAC (*Jeunesse agricole chrétienne*). From Bible meetings and socials to study groups on accountancy and farming techniques, they developed a growing awareness of their lack of formal schooling and absence of cultural facilities. They soon openly entered the trade union arena, led by Michel Debatisse who had coined the phrase 'the silent revolution of the peasants' to describe their aim. The main farmers' union, the FNSEA (*Fédération nationale des syndicats d'exploitants agricoles*), was controlled by the older, richer, conservative farmers. But its moribund youth section, the CNJA (*Centre national des jeunes agriculteurs*) could be revived. They took it over and gradually captured key posts in the trade-union movement, while using their position as a platform to advocate new policies. They claim that peasant unity is a myth, that there are rich and poor farmers whose interests are different. They admit that the rural exodus is normal – most of the small family farms are not economically viable – but they want it to be 'humanized' by the provision of proper training facilities. They do not deny the importance of maintaining prices (the French farmers' lobby is a powerful one in the EEC), but wish to give greater importance to structural reforms (land and marketing). Finally they question the sacred principles of property ownership and individualism: 'The fishermen do not own the sea. Why do we need to own the land?' They have started implementing their own proposals by renting rather than owning their farms, by establishing group enterprises for marketing and shared production, by introducing computerized farm management, by supporting the government agency set up for buying land and letting it in order to prevent speculation and by encouraging the regrouping of land (parcelled as a result of equal inheritance laws dating back to Napoleon). The movement has not always been peaceful, however, and there were notorious riots in Brittany in 1961, for example, when ballot boxes were burned. Michel Debatisse himself has now become an establishment figure, while the *jeunes agriculteurs* have found younger, more militant leadership. Constant campaigning of the government has been effective; greater concentration and specialization has also had some benefit; agricultural schools and training have been developed, new regional investments are co-ordinated through the EPR (*Etablissements publics régionaux*) created in 1972, government grants are given to young farmers willing to settle in depopulated areas, loans for equipment are now easier to obtain, and the old-style co-operatives have federated into vast units and modernized their methods. There are also industries contracting out work over large areas of countryside. This *saupoudrage industriel*, as it is called, provides regular work for women at home or winter occupation for the whole family. This is the case with watch-making in the Jura, textiles in the Loire, footwear around Cholet and cutlery in the Lozère, though it can and does lead frequently to the exploitation of cheap labour, and may not survive the deep-rooted industrial restructuring which is at present on the way.

Finally, the extension of tourism may also help bring a new lease of life to areas which are often beautiful but deserted (mountainous areas in particular). But the development of the tourist potential must provide new jobs (as ski instructors or in hotels in the mountains) if the local youth is to stay in the village and earn a proper and regular wage, while in the coastal areas those responsible for development must beware of ecological – and architectural – disasters. The growth of the tourist industry, if properly controlled by local communities rather than by capitalist sharks, may help provide extra income and facilities for country folk while answering the need of town-dwellers for open-air leisure activities and rest – thus further bridging the gap between the 'two nations'.

Paris and the French desert

And yet, it remains traditional to underline both the contrast between town and country and the divorce between Paris and the provinces – a metropolis in 'the French desert'. Taine put it in a nutshell as long ago as 1863:

> There are two peoples in France, the provinces and Paris, the former dines, sleeps, yawns, listens; the latter thinks, dares, wakes and talks; the one dragged by the other like a snail by a butterfly, now amused now worried by the capriciousness and audacity of its leader.

As the focus of national life in France, Paris is unrivalled and the Parisian has a somewhat haughty attitude towards anybody who does not belong there. This is somehow surprising to outside observers who happen to know that while one in every five Frenchmen lives in Paris or the Paris region, relatively few have been established in the capital for more than a generation, and one in five Parisians is a foreigner. In spite of the pressure of life in the capital, the constant rush and noise (1 million commuters spend two or more hours travelling to and from work every day), the still desperate housing situation, and the very high cost of living, the prestige and desirability of life there were unaltered until recently. Stifled by cars which encroach even on the pavements, much of the old Paris is being demolished and replaced by tall tower blocks, or tastefully renovated at high cost, thus driving the original slum inhabitants into the distant suburbs. With the extension of the underground outwards and the creation of fast RER lines, there has been a definite move towards the outskirts of the city – a phenomenon which is true of all the large towns – and since 1968 the number of provincials moving into the capital has consistently been smaller than the number of Parisians moving away.

Just as it is a social centre, so, too, is Paris an intellectual one: with its thirteen university campuses and its flood of students it contrasts sharply with quieter provincial university towns. But is prestige necessarily matched by excellence? Certainly it appears to be so. In a centralized and fiercely competitive system, a Paris appointment is often seen as promotion for teachers, as indeed for most Civil Servants; and students compete for places in the *grandes écoles* which are still more often to be found in the Paris conurbation than outside. Paris used also to be considered the world's cultural capital. It is still a very lively but expensive centre. Many of the new films can now be seen in provincial towns for half the price of an *exclusivité* on the Champs Elysées or the Boulevards, but while the decentralization policy for the arts and the increasing number of summer festivals have made culture available to more provincials than ever before, it is often at such a high price that many lower-paid people are effectively debarred from enjoying it.

With industry the situation is similar and, in spite of efforts to decentralize, the city is bursting at the seams. Tax rebates are awarded to industries moving outside the Paris area. Thus, between 1968 and 1975, half a million new jobs were created in provincial cities. But the general underdevelopment of the provinces (communications in particular are poor though improving) counteracts government incentives. While Paris itself, with its 2.3 million inhabitants, lost 11 per cent of its population between 1968 and 1975, the greatest increases in population were in other areas of the *Ile de France* (the Paris conurbation) which grew from 9.2 to 9.9 million, and includes five New Towns. Recent years have also seen the fostering of provincial conurbations to serve as poles of attraction, such as the Rhône-Alpes region, with the already enormous Lyon complex (well over 1 million inhabitants) and much publicized expansion of the Winter Olympics town of Grenoble. Only five towns have 500,000 (Lyon, Marseille, Lille, Bordeaux, Toulouse); another ten have over 300,000. Compared with the size of the Paris conurbation, this shows a lack of balance greater than in Britain.

Efforts to fight the growing suffocation of Paris have been extended by a policy of regionalism, which is still causing a great deal of controversy. Regionalism is a positive effort to adapt to the requirements of contemporary life and needs. It involves the formation of viable and autonomous economic units, rather than a negative rejection of the arbitrary division into *départements* and a resulting return to historical provinces. The ninety-five departments have thus been grouped into twenty-two economic regions, the eight largest towns have been singled out as *métropoles d'équilibre*, and the first regional councils were elected in March 1986. But real industrial decentralization is proving difficult. Too many Paris-based firms are setting up one or even several factories in the provinces while retaining their *siège social* in Paris. As a result, decisions are often taken in Paris without enough direct knowledge of local conditions. The system of regional development has now been diversified, to include both the *métropoles d'équilibre* and the *villes moyennes* (50,000 to 80,000 inhabitants), helped by better road and rail communications between towns (like the Lille-Paris-Lyon-Marseille TGV and the TGV-Atlantique now under construction), and by greater specialization of each industrial centre to avoid costly competition within one region. However, the *question régionale* still remains, with its political, economic and cultural undertones, and is especially used in political and electoral manoeuvring. Regional cultures and languages, which the introduction of compulsory schooling and the imposition of the French language had helped to destroy, are being revived in the South and in Brittany. Nationalist, political or religious minorities act as pressure groups, attempting to restructure local communities. This quest for local, regional roots may be part of a search for identity in a mass society in which so many local and traditional features have been ironed out.

Young and old, men and women

In the early 1960s, the cult of youth invaded advertising, fashion and the entertainment and holiday industries. And *les jeunes* were the basis of France's faith in its political and economic future. This faith was shaken by the explosion of May 1968 when young workers and students were suddenly seen as a threat to the establishment. Until then rebellious minorities had largely been ignored by the wider public. Even pop culture was tame. It was the reign of '*les copains* walking hand in hand' and listening to Françoise Hardy and Johnny Halliday on their transistor radios – nothing resembling the wild English or American crowds. They were on the whole conforming to accepted patterns of behaviour. The more culturally aware formed the audience for Georges Brassens, Juliette Gréco and other upholders of the poetical or the political tradition of the *chansons*; the more politically minded were militant in innocuous-looking *groupuscules* torn by infighting.

Rebellious youth was brought to the fore in May 1968 – untamed university and secondary school students, unorganized union militants all defying the establishment. They questioned authority in all its manifestations and won some concessions. Although student unrest now seems to have receded, protest will continue to simmer under the surface as long as educational reforms are not properly implemented, and this will take years, thousands of new teachers and millions of francs. The youth of the 1960s has now reached adulthood and entered a labour market dominated by unemployment, often facing reactions of hostility and fear from older generations. The statistics of youth unemployment point to a crisis situation.

Today, in spite of the successive youth employment schemes (*Pacte national pour l'emploi*), over 40 per cent of the unemployed, among whom two-thirds are women, are under twenty-five. Worse still, according to the *Agence nationale pour l'emploi* (ANPE), 35 per cent are still unemployed after six months, the jobs they find are often temporary (*emplois intérimaires*), and unqualified school-leavers only represent a small proportion of those who gain admission to one of the government schemes – a situation which the Socialist government (1981–6) tried to remedy with special measures for the sixteen-to-eighteen age group. A hard core of unqualified young unemployed is slowly emerging and it is hardly surprising that suicide and criminal rates are increasing. But accusations of apathy, rejection of adult values or downright laziness are misguided for a number of reasons. These accusations both ignore educational and social disparities (a university graduate has three times more chance than an unqualified school-leaver of finding a first job), and fail to acknowledge the fact that most young people still share the same values as their elders. Recent opinion polls and government reports alike paint a more positive picture: most young people do not reject their own family and wish to have one of their own; they want to work and are worried about their prospects in a society which only offers them insecure and uninteresting jobs with no prospects of obtaining further qualifications. Work, therefore, is no longer the central value in their life since it will bring them neither satisfaction nor social recognition: their questioning of traditional hierarchical models, of repetitive fragmented tasks, their demand for greater autonomy and a sense of purpose are aspirations they share with many adult workers. They did not invent the consumer society, they were born with it and want to join it – though it may be true to say that they prefer spending their money on going out dancing or buying stereo equipment rather than a colour television or a new settee. And their life-styles often imply different values, rather than a rejection of all values: cohabitation before marriage may be read as the sign of a search for marital harmony and true respect for marriage itself.

One reason for the tension between young and old may be that adults fear the approach of old age. While earlier retirement is welcomed by those for whom work has been synonymous with physical strain, repetitive tasks, noise and long hours, those who find fulfilment in their job are often loath to retire. Nevertheless, there are already signs that retirement no longer means relinquishing an active social life: pensioners have their own clubs (*clubs du troisième âge*), travel, take up university courses and enjoy leisure activities – all the more so when they receive a decent pension and have not been worn out by a life of toil. Moreover, the pensioners of today are the last pre-war generation of workers; the grandparents of tomorrow will have spent their active life in the prosperous 1950s and will probably not have the same value systems. Society must adapt to the new distinction between the 'younger pensioners' whose needs are psychological as well as economic, and the 'very old' (*le quatrième âge*) for whom isolation and health will remain the main problems.

Women, both young and old, are claiming their place in French society. Fairly recently, legislation granted them formal equality with men: joint choice of the matrimonial home (1965), freedom to work, open a bank account and own property without the need for the husband's consent (1965), equal pay (1972), protection from sex discrimination (1975), birth control (contraception and abortion Acts of 1974 and 1975), divorce reform (1975). Yet French women, who represent 40 per cent of the workforce, constitute a majority in unskilled industrial jobs, while in white-collar occupations they rarely rise to a position commanding responsibility and initiative. As a result, they remain lower-paid (in the proportion of 2 to 1 for the lowest wages, of 1 to 7 for the highest), and are twice as likely to become unemployed. Such inequalities were officially recognized in 1981 with the appointment of a Minister for Women's Rights – a post which however did not survive the Socialist defeat at the 1986 general election.

Some observers are quick to point out that, paradoxically, women may have lost more than they gained by leaving their home for the world of work: the subordinates of men at work, they have also lost 'control' over the home since the domestic tasks are shared – though often unequally – and they may well have the worst of both worlds. Yet most women, except perhaps the unskilled labourers, claim that having a job has meant an overall improvement in their lives, and many young mothers choose to continue working after the birth of their first child. Thereafter, however, economic and practical difficulties may force a choice between outside employment and the birth of a second or third baby. But for over 3 of the 9 million women at work, there is little freedom of choice: they are single wage-earners, many of them with dependent children. Though still a minority in militant trade union, political or cultural organizations, they are beginning to assert themselves. Opinion is divided as to the social consequences of these continuing trends.

Social classes

The general improvement in the standard of living, the development of hire-purchase and changing patterns of consumption in the (relatively) affluent society have caused a blurring of former class distinctions. The family car and the television set have entered working-class homes, holidays are no longer the privilege of the rich and even home ownership is spreading, though it is still less common than in England. Could this mean a destruction of class barriers and the end of the struggle for control and power which were the hallmark of pre-war French society, with its powerful working class and strong Communist Party? The language of the class struggle may have changed; but it does not necessarily mean that a classless society is emerging.

Wealth and income

Between 1950 and 1980, the purchasing power of the average annual wage has more than trebled and the introduction, in 1968, of the index-linked minimum wage – the SMIC (*Salaire minimum interprofessionnel de croissance*) – has helped to reduce the gap between high salaries and low wages: a gap which is still greater in France than in any other European country except Italy. In 1981, a comparison between the top and bottom 10 per cent of the salaried workers showed a ratio of 1 to 15: over 34,000 francs (about £3000) a month for *cadres supérieurs*, less than 2200 francs (about £200) for unskilled manual workers – a ratio which, according to the INSEE (*Institut national de la statistique et des études économiques*), was still the same in 1985. Even more serious perhaps is the fact that, since 1976, the growth of wages has not kept pace with the cost of living. Low-paid workers are among the new poor and below them, and excluded from the consumer society, we find the 'submerged' – the unemployed, the old, the immigrants and the handicapped who barely survive on social security. For these people, a new expression has been coined – 'le quart-monde' (the Fourth World).

At the other end of the social scale, the wealthy *grande bourgeoisie* still possesses considerable power and influence, particularly in the *Chambre des députés* (the legislative assembly) and in the Civil Service, especially, for example, in the Foreign Office. The economic rule of this class remains undisputed, though the frequency of mergers and takeovers by foreign firms causes signs of strain to appear. In the educational, social and cultural spheres, its influence is less marked. State education, which is anti-clerical and fairly democratic (but perhaps more a formal than a real democracy), has almost completely escaped its grasp; but it still controls élite recruitment through private education and the prestigious *grandes écoles*. There is an ever-widening gap between the very rich and the very poor, but if we exclude the two extremes, we may agree with Peter Wiles's comment in his survey of the distribution of disposable income per household carried out for the OECD: 'France is more equal than she thinks.'

The working class

The traditional condition of the working class has changed considerably in the last fifty years. The growth of unionization, the system of social security and the increased mechanization of industry leading to an overall higher level of training and skill, have certainly improved the lot of the workers. However, some problems remain; others are heightened. There is in particular a sense of insecurity at a time when many industries are under threat: mining, as in Britain, is declining; the car industry is shaken by regular crises; bankruptcies have caused regional disasters; even in more advanced sectors like the aircraft industry, rationalization has led to large-scale redundancies.

Class consciousness seems to have remained somewhat sharper than in Britain, in spite of the electoral decline of the Communist Party which lost half its voters in five years and polled less than 10 per cent of the vote in 1986. A certain language or jargon and an analysis based on the class struggle are being kept alive by the labour movement, although the staunch unionists form a minority of the workers, and the commitment of workers to their unions seems to be changing: the very militant are probably becoming more politically conscious and active, while those on the fringe of union activity only snatch a limited amount of time and energy from their main commitment to a better standard of living. The search for security is a key word for the working class, who now prefer the monthly-paid status to the hourly-paid insecurity of the past. For many of them, secure employment can no longer guarantee the maintenance of a newly-acquired standard of living now under threat. As the shorter working week spreads, those with safe jobs will be able to satisfy their new cultural and leisure requirements, though time thus gained is too often wasted commuting to distant suburbs.

The new middle classes

The new extended middle classes are not a purely French phenomenon. But there are some specific French characteristics: the number of minor Civil Servants (*petits fonctionnaires*), who often earn less than manual workers, do a repetitive and often tiring type of office work, and yet consider their position as promotion, mainly on account of the 'image' (white collar worker) and the security (no fear of redundancy and guaranteed retirement pension) which such posts offer.

It must be remembered that the French Civil Service includes, besides administrative workers, other sections of the working population like teachers and post-office workers. The social status of teachers is certainly higher than in Britain, though large numbers of supply teachers (a quarter of the total number) have low pay and no security of employment. Teachers are generally held to belong to the very French category of *cadres*, which forms a new middle class largely corresponding to the growth of the service sector. The *cadres* are distinguished from managers because they are salaried workers, not employers. They may be responsible for a large section of a factory or administration (*cadres supérieurs*) or only a smaller group of workers (*cadres moyens*). In some industries, they represent 3 per cent of the salaried workers only (mining), in others 12 per cent (mechanical and chemical industries), and even 18 per cent (power) or 19 per cent (oil). They enjoy a high standard of living, due to the relative security of their jobs, but they too are increasingly suffering from unemployment and inflation. Their number has been estimated at around 1.5 million and it is still rising. They mainly enjoy a better education, are more numerous in large towns and differ from the traditional bourgeoisie by their more reckless way of life with a tendency not to save but rather to consume.

Social mobility: a myth or a reality?

It is generally acknowledged that it takes three generations for the gradual change from the worker/peasant class to post-graduate or professional status to be achieved. But formal education, which plays such an important role in this, is not always attainable: scholarships and grants are scarce and in most cases insufficient to ensure reasonable chances of success. Of course, the unification of syllabuses, the *tronc commun* for all children between eleven and fifteen, and centrally-organized examinations, though criticized for being overdone, are to some extent helping to standardize things. But inequalities remain, between those who are deemed capable of following the three-year *lycée* courses leading to the *baccalauréat* (*cycle long*) and the others, who join technical schools for shorter courses of study, enter apprenticeship, or drift out of school with no qualification at all only to join the dole queue. Although all the *lycées*, in theory, cater for anybody according to ability, they do in fact have different clienteles. The best *lycées classiques* are still largely a preserve of the bourgeoisie while the others, because of geographical distribution and lack of prestige, get more working-class and fewer brighter children. Access to the very top of the social structure remains the privilege of the very few: recruitment to the administrative élite (executive class of the French Civil Service) may be considered to be predominantly incestuous. However, there is considerable mobility around the middle of the occupational scale: investigation into the family background of the *cadres moyens* shows their extremely varied social origins, but this is also the case for the manual workers and the unemployed: mobility is not always upwards.

Institutions: stability and change

In May 1968, after ten years of stable Gaullist rule, France woke up in turmoil. The country came to a standstill, the regime itself was threatened. Everything seemed to be called into question: parliament and political parties, trade union bureaucracies, the educational system, the mass media, bourgeois culture. With the breakdown of normal communications – press, radio, television – came what has been called an 'explosion of the word'. Everybody talked to everybody else, in university lecture theatres and cafés and on the streets (this was of course more true of large towns than villages, of Paris rather than the provinces, of young people than of old). For a short while, there was an impression of liberation from the constraints of normal life, an awakening, for people normally held down by routine. Theatre companies, journalists, writers, television personalities who visited the occupied factories and universities, were struck by the overwhelming response of their audiences. People became aware of the censorship of the government-controlled radio and television, of the cultural desert in which they were kept. But romanticizing is of no avail: the wave of excitement was followed by a Gaullist landslide victory. The staying power of institutions had proved stronger than the wind of change.

The stability of the basic institutions of the State was not at stake; and the electoral victory of the Socialists in 1981 did not mean a radical departure from the past. The government did not attempt to change the 'Gaullist' Constitution of the Fifth Republic and was content to introduce reforms within the existing framework. Nor did it lead a frontal attack against the Church in the form of a straightforward nationalization of private schools which are often 'Catholic' schools, nor an attack against the Army by abolishing conscription or altering defence policy. The institutions closer to economic and social life were, of course, modified, but not out of recognition. Nationalization itself was not new – cars (Renault), banks (Crédit Lyonnais), railways and cigarettes were already nationalized. The reform of the judiciary and the symbolic transfer of the guillotine to a Paris museum have not meant a radical transformation of the system: the Home Secretary, faced with the continuing problem of terrorist bomb attacks and insecurity, repeatedly asserted confidence and pride in his police force. Social and education policy tried to reduce inequalities, but the school and university system were not lastingly modified, and the survival of the family as a basic element in the social fabric continued to be encouraged by government incentives. Policy changes are to be expected after the return of a right-wing government, but institutional continuity is unlikely to be affected.

And yet, consumer groups and lobbies of all kinds are sprouting everywhere, organizing protest, putting pressure on Civil Service and local authorities, on trade union and political bureaucracies. Over the last eighteen years, a new consciousness seems to have developed, however diffuse. It is revealed through many initiatives and practices which are growing at local level, close to the grass roots; just as if the French, realizing the rigidity of their institutions, were constantly trying to find ways of bypassing bureaucracies in a constant battle against an abstract enemy – the 'administration'. Thus, unofficial strikes and claims for workers' control over production and organization of work (*autogestion*) are sometimes given equal weight with more traditional wage claims, all the more so in a trade union like the CFDT (*Confédération française et démocratique du travail*) which is less centralized than the vertically-structured CGT (*Confédération générale du travail*). Grass-roots militancy has also developed within political parties: the Socialists are often faced with minor revolts from their rank and file, while the right-wing parties hold regular ' summer schools' hoping to develop a new image among the young by extending the activities of their local branches outside election periods. Christian associations openly debate problems of doctrine, young magistrates and judges criticize the judicial system, conscripts demand new rights of association, and discipline has been transformed beyond the wishes of many teachers and administrators in the *lycées*. More say in decision-making is the order of the day, even though 'participation' tends to be quickly formalized, and therefore anaesthetized in the process.

This may be painting too bland (or too fractious?) a picture: activists will remain a minority in a population which is above all trying to survive economically and snatch as many crumbs as possible from the cake of affluence. The fabric of society is being changed, but this does not necessarily mean a lack of continuity.

The best example is perhaps the family: its death has been prophesied; some people deplore the loss of many of its former functions while others attack it for curbing the development of its individual members. And yet the French family is going strong. When asked about ideal family size many people say they would like to have three or more children, and yet they only have one or two. This contradiction may be partly explained by factors like poor housing and economic difficulties which bring them down to earth. Young parents are not willing to have larger families at the expense of a standard of living which has been painfully attained through the added source of income of the increasingly numerous working wives and mothers. Indeed, as a result of the number of working mothers, there are twice as many places in *crèches* for young children in France as in England. Young people seem to favour 'juvenile cohabitation' rather than marriage and a large-scale survey carried out by the INED (*Institut national d'études démographiques*) shows that 44 per cent of the couples who married in 1976–7 had lived together before marriage as against 17 per cent in 1968–9. At the same time their decision to have children is usually linked with the decision to legalize the union and illegitimate births are only 10 per cent of all births.

Close ties still exist everywhere between the small family unit (parents and children), and the extended family (grandparents, uncles, cousins and so on) – ties which have survived the move of the children to the city. Parental authority, respect and politeness are on the whole more sternly enforced than in England, though all this is being eroded in urban communities. In this respect, French society seems nearer to Irish than to English society, though just how far this is due to a common Roman Catholic tradition is difficult to ascertain. Kinship links remain important in all social groups: they are useful when you look for a job, or a home; grandparents look after children after school and at holiday time; and with the widespread search for cultural roots, they recover a role they had lost in most western societies – transmitting to the younger generations the traditions and language of their own family past, thus helping to bridge the gap between young and old, between peasant origins and urban living.

Another unifying element between social groups, conscription, is still enforced, and young men face twelve months of military service. Until the Second World War, this period *sous les drapeaux* used to create a real melting pot, some kind of initiation rite in which young men from varying backgrounds shared. It still remains a meeting ground, but offers less social mixing. Great numbers of students used to obtain several years' delay, but the law is trying to enforce early military service for all young men of eighteen, and attempting to reduce the number of exemptions from military service. However, students still tend to serve their time as teachers in ex-colonial countries or, if they serve in the armed forces, very often do so as NCOs, and in any case do not mix well because of their age and different interests. So the rift between the educated and uneducated is no longer bridged as it once was by this common experience of army life. Conscription itself provokes bitter controversy, and the Socialist election promise to reduce the length of military service to six months was never fulfilled.

Some new or forthcoming changes, however, must not be minimized. The most momentous is probably 'decentralization' (the Act came into force in March 1982), hailed by the Socialists as 'a quiet revolution' (*une révolution tranquille*), an attempt to bring decision-making closer to the people affected by these decisions – hence greater democracy. Inevitably it was denounced by their opponents as a divisive measure and a wasteful manipulation of committees and personnel, since the local and regional assemblies would need brains trusts and advisers to help them perform their new functions. The *préfet* was the eye of the Home Secretary in each *département*; he has become a *commissaire de la république*, the local representative of the executive. Will he be a mere delegate, or the new referee over problems which will no longer need to be referred to Paris? Time, and decisions over financing, will decide.

Decentralization may help defuse the Corsican time-bomb; may bring a new lease of life to regions like Brittany, the Jura, or the Dordogne, for which distance from the Paris Ministries meant files sometimes 'getting lost' on their way through the red-tape of administration, and in any case long delays. If fully implemented despite Civil Service resistance and powerful lobbies, the Act will certainly have meant diversification – a departure from the long tradition of Jacobin centralization.

Leisure and culture

For three years there were in France two Ministries in charge of leisure and cultural activities: the *Ministère de la Culture* which was responsible for the development of libraries and museums, music, theatre and the cinema, and the *Ministère du Temps libre* which dealt with problems connected with leisure: the timing of holidays to avoid the August mass migration and its consequences for both the tourist industry and the economy; the development of the tourist potential of the country areas to counterbalance the dominant choices of seaside or mountain holidays; the diversification of State subsidies to enable the less affluent members of the community to enjoy a holiday away from their urban or village homes; the balancing of work and leisure (*aménagement du temps de travail*). The reversal to a single *Ministère de la Culture* in 1984 implied a change of emphasis and perhaps a recognition that, for the unemployed and those on early retirement schemes, 'enforced leisure' was a burden rather than a conquest. But the concern with holidays and leisure still remains a leading issue in French society today. The pressure of urban living, longer life expectancy and earlier retirement, rising unemployment (hence the slogan *travailler moins pour travailler tous* – 'shorter hours mean jobs for all') combined with the return of a Socialist government committed to fulfilling the task started by the Popular Front in 1936 which was for a shorter working week (forty hours, now reduced to thirty-nine with the aim being a thirty-five hour week) and an annual paid holiday for all (increased from four to five weeks).

Holidays

The French seem obsessively to live for *les vacances* – eleven months of noise, work and stress, of scrimping and saving for an annual spending spree. Two-thirds of the population regularly migrate south and west in the summer while farmers account for nearly half of those who remain behind. Half the holidaymakers rush to the seaside and the sun. The spectacular success of such institutions as the *Club Méditerranée*, with its thatched-hut villages built around the Mediterranean as well as in more exotic places like Tahiti, Mexico or China, is a witness to this trend. But the majority of holidaymakers either stay with friends or relatives (35 per cent), go camping (23 per cent), or rent a flat or a cottage (*gîtes ruraux*). Among the less affluent, schoolchildren often go away without their parents, staying with grandparents or in *colonies de vacances* (holiday camps) – the social security system partly footing the bill. Disadvantaged children from the towns frequently have only the streets and some adventure playgrounds for their holidays, and confrontation with the police for their excitement – a problem which, after the long hot summer of 1981 (with the news-catching 'rodeos' with stolen cars in a Lyon suburb), the government tried to tackle with special holiday camps or day outings.

When they can afford it, families go away together with organizations like *Villages-Vacances-Familles*, *Les Maisons Familiales*, *Vacances-Loisirs-Familles* and so on, which offer family accommodation, communal catering and leisure activities for all ages. A more recent trend is the distribution of holidays over a (longer) summer and a (shorter) winter period. Even skiing holidays, still a preserve of the urban upper-middle class (only 8 per cent of the population can afford them), are in a minor way open to the underprivileged. This is through the system of *classes de neige* whereby primary schools from town areas can in turn send one or more classes to the mountains for a month, complete with teacher and skiing equipment, to combine normal teaching in the morning with outdoor activity in the afternoon. This is still far too sporadic to be effective in any general way, and too expensive for all children concerned to be able to go, but it does point to a future when what used to be the privilege of the better-off may be available to many more.

Pastimes and leisure

Besides holidays proper, leisure activities of all kinds develop in all social groups – the advent of a 'civilization of leisure' has even been prophesied. People often say they would prefer a longer weekend to a bigger pay packet: time is too often 'wasted' in the mad rush to earn a living ('on perd sa vie à la gagner') and increasingly, the French insist on 'choosing' how to divide their life between work-orientated and leisure activities (*le temps choisi*), or increasing the amount of time to be devoted to non-work (*le temps libéré*).

Pastimes vary greatly depending on social class and education. Gardening has become a national pastime for rich and poor alike; one Frenchman in three now mows his lawn, grows vegetables or flowers, and may even decorate his garden with plastic gnomes or reproduction nymphs. Radio, television and newspapers are part of most people's daily lives, though they were only mentioned by a tiny minority as being among their 'favourite pastimes' in a recent IFOP (*Institut français d'opinion publique*) survey, while reading and sports vied for the lead followed by music, needlework, do-it-yourself (*bricolage*) and gardening. 'Sports' of course means different things for teenagers and adults, for workers and professionals. Football and cycling are the popular sports and are more often watched than actively practised, with the ritual *Tour de France* taking over from cup matches in July on television. Elite sports like tennis, horse-riding, sailing and wind-surfing are becoming accessible to increasing numbers of young people through the multiplication of municipal clubs and investments. However, cultural activities outside the home remain largely the preserve of the middle and upper classes: few people frequently attend concerts (7 per cent) or go to the theatre (12 per cent), though one person in five still goes out to the cinema at least once a week – the highest percentages being among the *cadres* and Parisians. More films are watched on the family television than on the screen, however, and the number of films hired from video clubs doubled between 1983 and 1985.

There is certainly greater demand for cultural activities now than ten or twenty years ago, as the success of classes for classical or modern ballet dancing, learning languages, pottery, playing the guitar and other instruments has demonstrated. However, the dream of a popular culture bridging class differences remains, at present, a pious dream. The gap between the cultured and the deprived (rural communities, the working class) seems likely to remain for quite a long time. Formal education at present is insufficient, and adult education sadly underdeveloped. Industrial workers may be alienated for a number of reasons: work on a machine; closed community living; lack of time and facilities or the poor quality of the mass media, for example. This alienation causes a reversion to what one such worker calls 'illiteracy' when he compares the reading and writing abilities of adult factory workers to that of their children still in junior schools. But the role of associations of all kinds in developing an awareness of cultural needs has led to initiatives – both private and public – for extending cultural activities to an ever-growing audience, and the dominance of Paris is beginning to be challenged.

Decentralization of culture

There are 1200 *Maisons des jeunes et de la culture* (youth and arts centres) in France, with some 600,000 members (half workers, half schoolchildren and students). They are subsidized partly by the State, partly by local and regional councils, and each centre is administered by a permanent head (who nearly always has experience outside the educational profession) and by a house council elected by the young members themselves. Very often the centre is the only meeting-place for young people in a small town, apart from the local café, and is used for amateur dramatics, film shows, lectures, concerts, dances, and other indoor leisure activities; it also serves as a base from which to organize outings, holidays and so on. A high proportion of the worker members of the *Maisons des jeunes* are active trade unionists, and their members in general are among the most literate young people apart from students. Recently they have been under attack for being hotbeds of politicization of youth, and for wasting public money through bad administration. Not surprisingly both charges have been denied, but action has been taken against them. Under the pretext of decentralization, State subsidies have been reduced by 13 per cent, and more financial responsibility has been placed on local councils who thus became direct employers of the staff. The consequences of this are tighter control over cultural policy by the local councils (generally Right of Centre) and a tendency to demand that what is supposed to be a public service should also be economically viable.

The *Maisons de la culture* were created by André Malraux in order to give a single 'home' to all the arts, where culture would be represented with its many facets, and where various types of audience could meet under one roof. The fifteen *Maisons de la culture* created since 1961 in provincial cities (except for Créteil and Nanterre near Paris) have helped the development of a variety of cultural projects and practices. They have three principal missions. The first is creativity (*création*), the presentation of new high-quality productions often undertaken by permanent theatre or ballet companies (Grenoble and La Rochelle), by teams of film-makers (Le Havre) or musicians (Amiens), and sometimes with the collaboration of specially-invited and well-known artists. The second is cultural dissemination (*diffusion*) and outside companies, itinerant exhibitions and orchestras are welcomed. The third is cultural *animation*, an encouragement for all forms of cultural activity, especially those which favour confrontations and exchanges between actors, designers, musicians and their public, thereby encouraging cross-fertilization and experiment. Though the *Maisons de la culture* have developed into lively arts centres transforming life in their city, they are plagued by a shortage of funds and often have to curtail their own most adventurous projects and instead invite well-known companies on tour in order to boost the bookings. Unfortunately the development of a real cultural policy is bound to be inhibited by the need to make a profit.

The *Maisons de la culture* regularly welcome the regional theatre companies, themselves formed as a result of the decentralization policy for the arts and also fighting for survival. When Jean Vilar's *Théâtre National Populaire* in Paris (founded in 1951) was forced to close down through lack of government subsidy in 1972, Roger Planchon (who had gathered together his company in Lyon during the early 1950s) inherited the title of *national* theatre for his *Théâtre de Villeurbanne*. This may have been a victory for decentralization but it also meant the disappearance of the stronghold of popular theatre in élitist Paris. In the provinces, nineteen *Centres dramatiques* sprang up, with financial support from both government and local councils: the *Comédie de l'Est* (Strasbourg), ... *de l'Ouest* (Rennes), ... *du Centre* (Bourges), and so on. Their policy is to serve both the town where they are based and the surrounding rural community by regular tours, and their 'consecration' comes when they are invited to Paris for a season. Their aim is obviously to reach out to a working-class audience, and they partly succeed: some 30 per cent of the audience of Planchon's *Théâtre de Villeurbanne* is *populaire*. But the public reached is mainly skilled workers, foremen and the like – perhaps because the ordinary workers have fewer contacts with the trade union bureaucracy that handles the bookings. There is now an increasing realization that the theatre must go out to people in their normal surroundings; the general difficulties then are how to combine artistic quality with mobility, and to ascertain what degree of effort can be demanded of the audience. Much more specific is the financial problem.

In 1981, only 0.5 per cent of the national budget went to support the arts. In 1977, State help to the *Centres dramatiques* increased by only 7 per cent, even though a 25 per cent increase had been written into the contracts. The same year, the prestigious *Centre Beaubourg* opened, absorbing in running costs almost half the total State budget allotted to the arts. Mitterrand's choice of a well-known personality of the arts, Jack Lang, as his Minister of Culture, and a government commitment to a larger share of the national budget undoubtedly helped to make culture available to all and may even encourage the new government in the same direction. Whether this is a democratic phenomenon or a new form of twentieth-century bourgeois patronage remains to be seen, however. Debates on what exactly is meant by 'the explosion of culture' have been revived in the wake of the spectacular success of the *Centre Beaubourg* whose futuristic and metal architecture in the historic heart of the city attracts millions of visitors from all countries and backgrounds. Provincials and foreigners discover Paris from the top of the escalators encased in glass across the west façade; Parisians young and old visit the Public Information Library, the *Cinémathèque*, the Museum of Modern Art's permanent collection, one of the many temporary exhibitions, the Centre of Industrial Creation or the Experimental Music Department (IRCAM) directed by Pierre Boulez. Everything cultural is under one roof, with permanent fairground activity outside: is it culture made available to the masses, a catalyst for artistic development, or a supermarket of culture? In its nine years of existence, the *Centre Beaubourg* has become a leading landmark on the tourist route from the Eiffel Tower to Notre-Dame.

Bibliography

Ardagh, J., *The New France* (revised edition). Harmondsworth, Penguin Books, 1970. A very comprehensive study. See Chapters IV, on farmers; VI, on provincial life; IX, on daily life; X, on youth, as the most relevant to social structure.

Bauer, G. and Roux, J.M., *La Rurbanisation ou la ville éparpillée*. Paris, Le Seuil, 1976. On the invasion of rural areas by the urban overspill which thus creates the new 'rurban' phenomenon.

Biraben, J.N. and Dupaquier, J., *Les Berceaux vides de Marianne*. Paris, Le Seuil, 1981. Analyses the failure of government incentives to increase the French birth rate.

Canacos, H., *Sarcelles ou le béton apprivoisé*. Paris, Editions Sociales, 1979. The mayor of Sarcelles and his fight against 'sarcellitis' – the malaise which became associated with the concentration of high-rise flats.

Chombart de Lauwe, M.J. and P.H. *et al.*, *La Femme dans la société, son image dans les différents milieux sociaux*. Paris, Editions du CNRS, 1977. A comprehensive survey: women at home, at work, at university; the evolution over the last fifty years.

Données Sociales. INSEE (Institut national de la statistique et des études économiques), Paris, 1986. Statistical information on all aspects of social life, with an analysis of the main trends and reports on social surveys and consumer studies.

Dossiers et documents. Paris, *Le Monde*, ten issues per year. A supplement to the well-known daily newspaper, gathering together recent articles concerning social, political and economic problems. A very useful tool for the student who wants to keep up-to-date with the evolution of French society. Recent issues include: *Les Jeunes et l'emploi* (May 1982); *La Société française* (Feb. 1986); *Les Villes nouvelles* (June 1986).

Dupeux, G., *La Société française, 1789–1970*. Paris, Colin, 1972, and London, Methuen, 1976. See its analysis of the population structure and migrations in particular.

Esprit, L'armée et la défense (Numéro spécial). Paris, October 1975. In particular B. Kitou's inside view as a conscript, and the analysis of the 'malaise de l'Armée'.

Le Roy Ladurie, E. and Vigne, D., *Inventaire des campagnes*. Paris, J.C. Lattès, 1980. The first part traces the history of the 'peasantry', the second presents the *paysans* in a series of live interviews. Both informative and enjoyable reading.

Mallet, S., *La nouvelle classe ouvrière*. Paris, Seuil, 1963, and Nottingham, Spokesman Books, 1976. On the changes in working-class life and consciousness.

Mendras, H. (ed.) *et al.*, *La sagesse et le désordre: France 1980*. An excellent collection of articles including social and institutional aspects of contemporary France.

Nicolas, J.P., *La pauvreté intolérable*. Paris, Erès, 1985. The life of a family on public assistance.

Potel, J.Y. (ed.), *L'Etat de la France et de ses habitants*. Paris, La Découverte, 1985. A wide-ranging survey covering society, politics, the economy and the geography of France and including maps and statistics.

Reynaud, J.D. and Grafmeyer,Y. (eds), *Français, qui êtes-vous?* Paris, La Documentation Française, 1981. A collection of articles on social classes, the industrial world, the institutions and intellectual life, with useful statistics. Most informative.

Roudy, Y., *A cause d'elles*. Paris, Albin Michel, 1985. The Socialist Minister for Women's rights presenting her work.

SOFRES, *Opinion publique 1986*. Paris, Gallimard, 1986.

Sue, R., *Vers une société du temps libre*. Paris, PUF, 1982. The changing patterns of leisure.

Syndicat de la Magistrature, *Justice sous influence*. Paris, Maspero, 1981. An examination of the judicial system by judges who analyse its evolution and discuss the balance between social control and individual liberty.

Vaughan, M., Kolinsky, M. and Sheriff, P., *Social Change in France*. London, Martin Robertson, 1978.

A very comprehensive collection of government *Reports* was published in 1982, the result of surveys carried out by commissions appointed to study the state of the country at the time of the Socialist return to power in 1981. Well-informed, comprehensive, programmatic as well as analytical. They are all published by *La Documentation Française*, together with many other books and reviews, among which are *Les Cahiers français*, five issues per year, each devoted to a particular subject: for example *La Fonction publique* (nos 194 and 197), *Le Monde urbain* (no. 203), *La Décentralisation* (no. 204). These publications are available from *La Documentation française*, 29–31 quai Voltaire, Paris, which also houses a well-stocked documentation library.

Two

Political parties
Malcolm Slater

Introduction

A basic outline of political parties in France would be, on the Left

'the Communists': *Parti communiste français* (PCF)

'the Socialists': *Parti socialiste* (PS)

and on the Right

'the Gaullists': *Rassemblement pour la république* (RPR)

'the Giscardians' or, as they themselves would increasingly prefer, 'the Liberals': *Union pour la démocratie française* (UDF)

'the National Front' (or some more value-ridden description): *Front national* (FN).

The background to this outline is firstly, that in 1981 the Socialists captured the presidency when François Mitterrand narrowly beat Valéry Giscard d'Estaing in the second-round run-off on 10 May, and that a few weeks later the nation confirmed this choice by electing to the National Assembly a Socialist majority which for nearly five years, in conjunction with smaller parties, supported the policies and guaranteed the survival of a government consisting overwhelmingly of Socialists; and secondly, that although Mitterrand's term of office was for seven years, the end of the five-year Parliament in 1986 led to the replacement of the Socialist majority by a right-wing majority supporting a new government which had then to 'cohabit' with President Mitterrand.

Policy programmes

What policy programmes did the parties put to the electorate
in March 1986, after five years of Socialist government? Clearly, it is at election times that the parties are at their most
salient, and the average voter has the best chance to be aware
of the difference, not just between Right and Left, but also
between individual parties, large and small. Electoral choice
is a complex process, often with a high degree of irrationality,
but obviously the established parties play an important part
in this process, by dominating the institution which makes the
choice necessary (Parliament), by having a virtual monopoly of candidate selection, and by indulging in political
marketing.

French political parties in the run-up to the March 1986 elections tried to differentiate themselves from their rivals in the
major policy spheres, with basic preoccupations in mind. The
Socialists were campaigning on their record, their former allies
the Communists were attempting to recover waning support,
the National Front tried to exploit fears, and differences of emphasis within the RPR-UDF 'parliamentary opposition' of
1981–6 often surfaced despite their joint 'Platform for government' signed in January 1986. A summary, albeit simplified, of
their different approaches in major areas, follows.

Industry and jobs

The PS wanted to maintain the level of nationalization in
the economy, which it had significantly raised in 1982, but
it placed less emphasis than before on State planning, and promised more incentives for risk capital and modernization of
small and medium firms. The PCF accused the nationalized
industries of merely conforming to capitalist economics, and
repeated its call for recovery based on mass domestic consumption of French products. While the Left were proud of industrial 'democratization' in the form of increased job security
and participation in firms' decision-making processes, the
RPR-UDF urged the privatization of all sectors of the economy
except public services. The Right wanted to reduce the role of
trade unions, and to allow firms greater freedom to make

workers redundant, negotiate wage rates and take on part-time and temporary staff.

General economic policy and taxation

The Socialists wanted to fight inflation by continuing their policy of economic austerity (*la rigueur*) involving minimal rise in real incomes. The Right plumped for economic growth (despite the risk of increased inflation), incentives for personal savings, and the raising of thresholds for income and inheritance tax. The Socialists' new wealth tax was to be significantly increased by the PCF, and abolished by the Right. The proposals of all parties on taxation appeared to be a sop to their 'natural' electorates, rather than a clearly thought-out attempt to improve an outmoded system and counter widespread tax evasion.

Social policy and education

The Left's pride in increased tenants' rights and rent controls introduced by the *loi Quilliot* was countered by the Right's promise of a judicious relaxation of housing controls and a bigger role for market forces.

With regard to welfare and social security the Left's slogan of 'national solidarity' fostered by State action competed with the Right's emphasis on individual responsibility, which would allow cuts in State spending.

The failure of the *loi Savary* in 1983–4 to convince the public of the merits of a unified State sector of education which would also closely supervise independent schools meant that the field was open to the RPR-UDF to urge greater freedom of parental choice and of individual schools' action by reducing centralization.

Media

Faced with the media explosion, the Socialists in power adopted a 'mixed economy' approach, making dominant press ownership illegal (despite the problems this involved) but ending the State monopoly of radio and television and allowing private television channels, and local stations and cable networks. Any reaction of the Right towards deregulation was bedevilled by the problem of 'who pays?' and a desire to prevent the influx of too many foreign, in particular American, programmes.

European co-operation

The PCF continued its hostility to a 'capitalist' EEC, but the other parties were in favour. The Socialists even talked of a 'two-speed' Europe in which a group of member states wanting more rapid progress on specific issues would move independently to these goals. The UDF since its creation in 1978 has followed the lead of one of its constituent groups in being strongly pro-European, and the RPR under Chirac has abandoned the hostility of its Gaullist heritage to give pragmatic approval.

Defence

The PCF, as other parties, wanted to maintain a French nuclear deterrent, but said that multilateral disarmament should be sought as well. The Socialists in power added some degree of flexibility in military matters by introducing a tactical nuclear capability and a rapid intervention force; they also emphasized greater European co-operation on defence matters, and this was echoed by the RPR which abandoned its policy of France as a 'sanctuary' to be defended. The UDF went several stages further in calling for French participation in a European combat aircraft and arms procurement in general.

Impact of the Front national

In fact, the neat model of the 1978 and 1981 elections where four main parties (or, in the UDF's case, group of parties) competed for support as distinct entities or as Left or Right coalitions, was complicated in 1986 by two relatively new phenomena – the FN and Raymond Barre. The FN began to gain significant electoral support in the 1980s on a tough policy of abrogation of many of the social reforms of the Giscard and Mitterrand presidencies and even a dilution of the right to strike. But in two particular areas, law and order and immigration, the FN made most impact on the electorate.

The Left, faced with increased international terrorism and rising crime rates, tried to make the police more effective while less repressive and to find alternatives to custodial sentences. The RPR-UDF proposed not to re-establish the death penalty which the Left in power had abolished, but to introduce long irreducible prison sentences for serious crimes. The FN was much more uncompromising: reintroduction of the death penalty for murderers and international drug traffickers, and 'shock' prison sentences for petty criminals.

The Left regularized the position of illegal immigrants in 1981 and talked of giving voting rights to immigrants (the PS for local elections, the PCF for all); and the Socialists proposed automatic naturalization for immigrants after five years – even, claimed the FN, for illegal immigrants or those convicted of crimes – in an effort to integrate immigrants into the community. The RPR-UDF wanted strict control of immigration, in agreement with countries of origin, and expulsion of illegal immigrants and those convicted of crimes. The FN agreed with the latter, but added the category of the unemployed to the list, in an effort to 'reverse the flow of immigration': an entry visa would be required by any visitor from the traditional countries of origin, to stop 'false tourists', and priority would be given to 'French people' where housing and welfare provisions were concerned.

Raymond Barre

Raymond Barre, former Prime Minister under Giscard between 1976 and 1981, while heading the 1986 UDF list in his electoral home base of the *département* of the Loire (chief city – Lyon), had more and more in the 1980s distanced himself from the UDF. Barre's reputation rested firstly on his plain speaking on economic matters – the unpopularity he earned as Prime Minister turned by the mid-1980s to admiration for his 'realism' – and secondly on his uncompromising stance concerning institutions.

Barre is notorious for having stirred up within the RPR-UDF, as the 1986 elections approached, the basic question of whether the victorious Right should form a government when there was still a Socialist President in the Elysée. Barre's argument against such 'cohabitation' was two-fold: either a government of the Right would have to compromise with President Mitterrand, thus reducing the possibility of its applying the policies on which it was elected, or it would apply these policies in spite of the President, thus robbing the latter of the powers which the Constitution (particularly in its practice over nearly thirty years) gives him, and effectively ending the Fifth Republic. Since Barre did not want the latter – very few French people do – his solution to his own conundrum was that President Mitterrand should resign in 1986, as de Gaulle had done in 1969, and that Barre would become President.

On other aspects of the political institutions, all parties appear to favour reduction of the presidential term of office to five years, without necessarily agreeing on the implications of this and its consequences for the nature of the regime. Far-reaching constitutional reforms of this nature depend on an elusive, not to say impossible, concertation between the parties; but one reform was regarded as much more urgent in 1986 – the abandonment of the proportional electoral system introduced by the Socialists in 1985, and a return to the single-member system in operation from 1958. The Right favoured this, even though a future strong PS with the support of something approaching 40 per cent of the electorate would benefit from it.

Proliferation of parties

The scheme of political parties in France, however, is complicated not only by the phenomena of the FN and of Raymond Barre, but also by the existence of many minor parties. The single-round proportional system in the 1986 election did not reduce the incidence of minor parties which in a two-round system would be eliminated on the first round. It simply meant that they were presented to the electorate either as no-hope lists, sometimes of minor parties in combination, or as adjuncts of the major parties trying to extend the range of their appeal.

In the March 1986 legislative and – for the first time – direct regional elections, voters had a wide range of electoral lists from which to make their choice, giving a clear indication of the proliferation of French political parties. As an example, Table 1 shows the range of choice open to voters in Paris (the *département* of the Seine) and the success of each list of twenty-three names, including two 'stand-in' candidates (*suppléants*).

Of course, the name of what may generically be called a 'party' is not always helpful in definitional terms. Of the five main parties in the mid-1980s only two were called '*parti*'. Sometimes this appellation is eschewed in favour of a word with more rousing connotations, like '*Front national*', '*Nouvelle action royaliste*', '*Lutte ouvrière*', or '*Initiative 86*'. Similarly, the Gaullist party in its various guises has always been an '*union*' or a '*rassemblement*'. Use of the term '*mouvement*' may foster the impression that there is a wider basis of sympathy for political aims waiting to be mobilized, as in '*Mouvement des radicaux de gauche*' or '*Mouvement pour un parti des travailleurs*' (though this had been the *Parti communiste internationaliste* from 1981 to 1985). Yet '*parti*' can refer to what are clearly groups limited in membership, in appeal (*Parti humaniste* – see Table 1), or in territorial concern (*Parti pour l'organisation d'une Bretagne libre*); and parties can often spring up at the whim of a single person.

A 1982 count identified some seventy-five parties, clubs and movements across the whole political spectrum, but small groups often disappear by amalgamation. In May 1985, the *Parti démocrate*, *Clubs avenir centre gauche*, *Europe environnement*, *Rassemblement fédéraliste européen*, and several members of the *Parti démocrate français* went to make up the '*Union républicaine et démocrate – Parti réformiste*'. In November 1985, the new '*Troisième Voie*' was an amalgam of three extreme Right groups: *Parti des forces nouvelles*, *Jeune garde*, and *Mouvement nationaliste révolutionnaire*. Parties can also disappear on being dissolved by the authorities; this happened in forty-four cases between 1958 and 1962, sixteen on the extreme Right, thirteen on the extreme Left, and fifteen separatist or 'liberation' movements.

Table 1

% of votes received	
35.0	*RPR pour Paris – liste d'union présentée par le RPR, le CNI, Unité Radicale, UNIR, le Parti démocrate français
31.9	*Liste pour une Majorité de progrès avec le Président de la République présentée par le Parti socialiste, le MRG et d'autres formations démocratiques
11.8	*Liste UDF pour Paris
11.1	*Liste de Rassemblement national présentée par le Front National et Jean-Marie Le Pen
4.6	*Liste présentée par le Parti communiste français
2.6	*Liste la France en tête avec Marie-France Garaud
1.4	*Les Verts Paris Ecologie
0.4	*Liste Lutte Ouvrière
0.3	Ecologie et Humanisme
0.3	Liste du Mouvement pour un Parti des Travailleurs
0.2	*Liste Alternative 86 Paris
0.2	Initiative 86 – Entreprendre et réussir la France de l'an 2000 – Paris 'Initiative' avec Gérard Touati
0.1	Parti Humaniste
0.03	Liste Maurice Mercante – croissance + 10 pour cent
0.02	Mouvement pour l'organisation des états en micro-démocraties
0.02	Liste 'Pour une économie libérée'

*voters had also the choice of one of these lists to elect 42 regional councillors

Party identity

Even if the plethora of minor groups is ignored, the student of French politics will meet an abundance of initials created by two common phenomena of French political parties; firstly their tendency to change their names much more frequently than is the case in Britain or the USA, usually to emphasize to the public that they have a new image. The Socialist party was called *Section française de l'internationale ouvrière* (SFIO) from 1905 to 1969 and the *Parti socialiste* (PS) from 1971. During the 1969–71 hiatus, it was referred to as '*le nouveau parti socialiste*' which was a description rather than a title. The PCF was originally (1920–36) called *Section française de l'internationale communiste*. The Gaullist party has assumed various titles:

1946　　　*Union gaulliste*.

1947–53　*Rassemblement du peuple français* (RPF) (during 1953–8 Gaullists in Parliament after the dissolution of the RPF called themselves *Républicains sociaux*).

1958　　　*Union pour la nouvelle république* (UNR).

1967　　　*Union des démocrates pour la cinquième république* (UDVᵉ).

1968　　　*Union pour la défense de la république*, then *Union des démocrates pour la république* (UDR).

1976　　　*Rassemblement pour la république* (RPR).

Secondly, parties and groups frequently co-operate just for election periods under umbrella titles established only weeks before. Examples have been in the elections of:

1986　　　*Alternative 86*, comprising the *Parti socialiste unifié* (PSU), *Ligue communiste révolutionnaire*, *Parti pour une alternative communiste*, *Fédération de la gauche alternative*, and assorted ecologists, regionalists and trade unionists.

1981　　　*Union pour la nouvelle majorité* linking the RPR and UDF.

1978　　　*Union pour la démocratie française* mainly comprising the *Parti républicain* (PR), *Centre des démocrates sociaux* (CDS), and *Parti radical*. This co-operative venture of course survived the election for which it was originally intended.

1973   *Union de la gauche socialiste et démocrate* linking the PS and *Mouvement des radicaux de gauche* (MRG); these two parties co-operated closely in all subsequent elections.

1973   *Union des républicains de progrès* (URP) comprising UDR, *Républicains indépendants* (RI) and some Centrists.

Development of parties and political groups

It must not be forgotten that parties in the sense of permanent and centralized organizations did not appear on the French political scene until the beginning of the twentieth century, whereas a durable parliamentary Republic was established in 1875 and universal masculine suffrage in 1848. But a very limited suffrage before then meant that 'parties' (in the sense of loose groups) in Parliament had no incentive to organize or appeal to the electorate, as was the case in Great Britain, and political activity outside the *pays légal*, as Guizot called it, was restricted to clubs, often existing clandestinely. This fact, together with the massacre or exile of thousands of insurgents who had taken part in the Paris Commune of 1870–1, meant that even after the establishment of the Third Republic in the 1870s, Socialists in France were divided over aims and methods, and a Socialist party (the SFIO) was not founded until 1905.

In other parts of the political spectrum, parliamentary politics was traditionally organized through loose groups of local worthies (*notables*) whose electoral clientelism was limited to their own constituency and who felt little need of a national party organization, with the constraints which this implied. Thus it was not until 1901 that the Radicals created a *Parti républicain radical et radical-socialiste*; it survived in the 1980s as a shadow of its former self under the new official name of *Parti radical-socialiste*, though people always referred to it simply as the *Parti radical*. This phenomenon of a loosely-organized group with minimal parliamentary discipline and electoral co-ordination was still evident until the 1960s. In

1962, Valéry Giscard d'Estaing formed a pro-de Gaulle group of *députés* of the *Centre national des indépendants et paysans* (CNIP) into the *Républicains indépendants* (RI), but it was not until 1966 that he decided to organize it as a party in the sense of a nation-wide organization dedicated to disseminating a doctrine, recruiting members and maximizing electoral support. It became the *Parti républicain* (PR) in May 1977.

In fact, as late as the 1950s, the French scene reflected almost perfectly Maurice Duverger's analysis of the distinction between the old established *parti de cadres*, like the ones just described, and the newer phenomenon of the *parti de masse* such as the SFIO and PCF, more suited to parliamentary democracy in the second half of the twentieth century because of their higher membership, tighter organization, clear policy alternatives based on a distinct doctrine, and their high level of political activity outside election periods. But this analysis needed to be refined in the light of the emergence of a Gaullist party in the 1960s and a new *Parti socialiste* in the 1970s which perceived their functions in a different light and could best be called a *parti d'électeurs*, that is, a party which tried to appeal to the widest possible electorate. The consequences of this development were, firstly a more even geographical spread of the electoral support for a specific party, and secondly a reduction in the extent to which party programmes were inspired by ideologies, though these remained a source of slogans used to mobilize support, justify allegiance and attack adversaries. In the run-up to the 1986 parliamentary elections, one of the PS's themes was to try to strike horror in voters' minds by slogans such as '*Au secours, la droite revient*', and '*Dis-moi, jolie droite, pourquoi as-tu de si grandes dents?*', while a more self-confident RPR preferred the simple optimism of '*A demain*' (with a picture of Chirac and local candidates against a clear blue sky), and '*Prenons une France d'avance*'. In fact, the RPR and PS in the 1980s have the characteristics both of a *parti de masse* and a *parti d'électeurs*.

Party appeal

All parties now have to appeal to a wider circle than their 'natural' or traditional supporters. Aware of its waning support, the PCF adopted less ideologically specific slogans calling for an *'Union du peuple de France'* (at its 22nd Congress in 1976) and *'Rassemblement populaire majoritaire'* (25th Congress, 1985). Conscious of the mobilizing force of the word 'Socialism', the RPR – UDF was led in the mid-1980s to use 'Liberalism' as a counter, even though this created problems of interpretation in such a wide-based coalition before and after the March 1986 elections. Moreover, the distinction must be made between the anti-interventionist emphasis of continental liberal tradition and the preference for State-sponsored social reform characteristic of British liberalism.

In more concrete terms, political parties in France can hope to enlarge their appeal through the press and television, but they also exploit the relatively high propensity of French people to buy paperbacks by publishing political manifestos and sometimes 'blueprints for society' (*projets de société*) in this easily-digested format. Early examples were the Radical Party's *Ciel et Terre* in 1970 (which must necessarily be taken as the most comprehensive electoral promise of all time!), *Changer de cap* (PCF, 1971), *Changer la vie* (PS, 1972), *L'enjeu* (UDR, 1975); and more recently *Libres et responsables* (RPR, 1984), *Réflexions pour demain* (R. Barre, 1984) and *Pour la France* (FN, 1985). Opinion polls confirm the suspicion that television is the main influence on electoral behaviour, followed by newspapers, radio, magazines, and meetings, leaflets and posters. But 'conversations' and opinion polls themselves, over which the parties have in law no control, also figure on the list.

Party organization

The major political parties in France tend to have remarkably similar organizational structure. The basic geographical framework of party organization, as in so many aspects of French administrative life, is at the level of the *département*, and usually called a *fédération*; these normally have at least some full-time staff and co-ordinate groups at the local level, whether *comités de base* (Rad.) or *cellules* (PCF) grouped into *sections* (PCF and most other parties). The focus of membership activity in organizational terms is the national delegate conference held typically every two years, and called *Congrès* (PCF, CDS, UDF, Rad.), *Congrès national* (PS, Fédération anarchiste) or *Assises nationales* (RPR). Parties can of course call special conferences when necessary – the PS had a *Congrès extraordinaire* at Créteil in January 1981 to confirm Mitterrand's presidential candidature; and the parties sometimes hold mini-conferences on matters of the moment in the intervals between full party conferences.

The conference elects (or rubberstamps the appointment of) a consultative body, sometimes referred to in the press as the 'parliament' of a party, called *conseil national* (RPR, PR, UDF), *conseil politique* (CDS), *comité central* (PCF) or *comité directeur* (PS, CNIP, MRG), above which is the central policy-making group, the 'government' of the party: *bureau national* (MRG, CDS), *bureau politique* (PCF, Rad., PR, UDF, RPR, CNIP, FN) or *bureau exécutif* (PS), sometimes with a smaller core of leaders, a *secrétariat* (PCF, PR) or *commission exécutive* (RPR). The party leader, with whom of course the party will be associated in the mind of the public, is a *président* (RPR, UDF, CDS, Rad.), or *premier secrétaire* (PS); a *secrétaire général* can be the leader (PCF) or the number two to a president.

Party membership

Membership of French political parties is always difficult to assess with accuracy, since parties tend to inflate figures to prove their own popularity. In 1986, party claims were: *Fédération anarchiste* 1000, PSU 7000, PCF 608,543 (at the 25th Congress 1985), PS nearly 200,000, Radicals 15 to 20,000, CDS 49,350 ('we try to lie less than the others'), PR 100,000, UDF 'direct members' 25,000, RPR 900,000, FN 60,000. These figures, however, are in contradiction with the more objective estimate of academic commentators who put the total membership of French political parties at about 1 million. Accuracy concerning party membership is possible only in relation to increasing or decreasing trends over, say, five-year periods. The major problem, of course, is to determine what constitutes membership. Parties which emphasize the possession of a membership card tend to ignore the concomitant requirement of a valid contribution payment record throughout the year, and their claims may rely too much on the number of cards sold, or given away, at mobilizing events such as the long-established *Fête de l'Humanité* (PCF, annually on the second weekend in September), the more recent *Fête de la Rose* (PS) or *Fête des bleus-blancs-rouges* (FN). In fact, even among French people who identify positively with one particular party, that is, whose interest goes potentially beyond merely voting reasonably consistently for a party, the desire to join or financially support that party is not strong, as the following table shows (the figures add up to more than 100 because of multiple replies).

Question: Parmi les choses suivantes, quelles sont celles que vous seriez prêt à faire pour le parti politique auquel vont vos préférences?

	%
Parler de son programme autour de vous	32
Assister à une réunion organisée par ce parti	33
Adhérer à ce parti	16
Participer à une manifestation organisée par ce parti	11
Lui donner de l'argent	6
Distribuer des tracts ou vendre des journaux de ce parti	6
Aucune de celles-ci	29
Sans opinion	7

Source: SOFRES, December 1983

Party youth movements

Youth movements are an obvious way in which parties can influence the political education of young people, as well as mobilize their energies at election times. Thus there is the *Mouvement de la jeunesse communiste* (PCF) of which the *Union des étudiants communistes* is a part, *Mouvement de la jeunesse socialiste* (PS), *Mouvement des jeunes radicaux de gauche* (MRG), *Mouvement des jeunes démocrates-sociaux* (CDS), *Mouvement des jeunes giscardiens* (PR, but obviously hitched to the political fortunes of Valéry Giscard d'Estaing) and the *Front national des jeunes* (FN). But some parties have no separate youth organization as such: the *Parti radical* because it is too small and not very youth oriented and the RPR because of its predecessor's experiences with its youth movement, the *Union des jeunes pour le progrès* (UJP), which caused problems because it could not decide whether it was a force for dynamic independent thought or a breeding ground for future party leaders; it could not stomach Chirac's alleged distortion of 'pure' Gaullism, and survived into the 1980s only as a minuscule isolated group.

Mobilization of party faithful at another level can take the form of periodic meetings of the leaders of the *fédération* in each of the 96 *départements* in metropolitan France (though not all parties have an organization in every *département*), of parliamentarians in 'journées parlementaires', and of sitting members and candidates, actual or potential, in an 'université de printemps' or 'université d'été', more often than not held in a salubrious part of southern France.

Parliamentary candidature

Candidature in parliamentary elections is open to every citizen fulfilling certain legal conditions, but was progressively monopolized by political parties from 1958 to 1981 when a single-member constituency system operated; and this tendency was compounded in 1986 by the system of proportional representation requiring a list of at least four people, which presupposed some coincidence of viewpoint and led to a reduction in the number of candidates not readily identifiable by party. The typical candidate will emerge directly from the party, regarding candidature as a further step in commitment or in a political career. This is particularly so on the Left, where a PS candidate must have three years' party membership behind him, and about one-third of PCF candidates will be full-time party members – which explains why the proportion of 'new' candidates tends to be smaller for the PCF than for any other party. But a strongly entrenched 'independent' local politician is sometimes able (frequently on the Right, very occasionally on the Left) to negotiate, or tactically oblige, endorsement by a party with which he or she has the closest political affinities. Party central leaderships have played an increasingly important part in the Fifth Republic in approving candidatures arising at local constituency (or, in 1986, *département*) level, sometimes by mediating between rival personalities and their supporters, for example between a local contender and a total outsider indulging in what is called '*parachutage*'.

Financial aid

The question of the financial support which parties need for their activities, particularly at election times, has caused considerable problems. Parties receive contributions from members, but the level is far from adequate: it is supplemented by the handing over by *députés* of some of their salaries. In 1985, a *député* received, as well as free research and secretarial help, official postage and telephone expenses, rail and internal air travel, 33,458.97 francs monthly, of which only 55 per cent was subject to tax. Of this, PS *députés* gave 8380 francs to the party, those of the UDF 5000 francs and those of the RPR 3500 francs. PCF *députés* give all their salary to the party, which then pays them an allowance – 9000 francs per month in 1985. Apart from these sources, the Right benefits from business support, direct and indirect; the Left has had to rely mainly on 'consultancy fees' on contracts with the local authorities which it controls. Both are reputed to make considerable money from, for example, spurious market studies for which big retailing chains are obliged to pay to obtain local planning permission for supermarkets. And it is usually accepted that a large proportion of a special fund controlled by the Prime Minister's office (361.6 million francs in 1985) will find its way into the coffers of the appropriate party.

At present, if a candidate receives 5 per cent of votes cast, the State repays costs incurred in printing ballot papers, the propaganda sheets which are sent to voters with ballot papers, and the posters put on official hoardings outside polling stations. The money involved is not insignificant (531 million francs in 1981) but proposals to give State financial aid to the parties themselves to cover adequately the whole range of their activities have always run into difficulties. Giscard in his reforming mood raised the question in 1974 and again in 1978, but recognized the problems: which 'parties' would qualify? Would there have to be a stricter legal framework, including of course a definition of a political party? On what basis would money be distributed – percentage of votes received at parliamentary elections? The parties themselves, as one would expect, are generally in favour of official funding, but doubts about the destination of money given to the PCF will always be a problem; and sceptics point to the Italian and West German examples, where a system of State financial aid has not put a stop to secret funding.

Intra-party relations

The organizational structure of parties can lead to significant variations in the degree of internal democracy. The constitution (*statuts*) of the new PS in 1971 was based on a determined effort to move away from the 1945–69 period which allowed domination of the former SFIO by a small group under the leadership of Guy Mollet. The composition of the *comité directeur* is a direct reflection of the proportion of support at the party conference for general policy motions proposed by different factions (*courants*) within the party. On the other hand, delegates to the 1984 Grenoble Conference of the RPR merely confirmed Chirac's decision rather than debated a proposal to change the party's organizational structure. In the PCF, in keeping with the doctrine of 'democratic centralism', the party conference elects the *comité central*, but there is only a single list of candidates already drawn up by the *bureau politique*.

Moreover, internal democracy in the PS of the kind described stops at the *comité directeur*. When this body comes to elect the smaller *bureau exécutif*, it does this by voting for lists, and the new leadership is composed of those names on the list which receive the most votes; in this way, a faction can be 'majoritaire' in the sense of participating in the highest decision-making body of the party, or be excluded from it.

For example, the faction called *Centre d'études, de recherche et d'éducation socialistes* (CERES), a left-wing ginger group within the party, allied in 1971 with the faction around Mitterrand, to give the latter the leadership. But CERES was not happy with the increased importance within the PS from 1974 of a 'modernist' faction led by Michel Rocard. Rocardism represented a technocratic approach to socialism, rejecting explicit doctrinal references, especially Marxist ones. The Mitterrandists followed the pragmatic line of 'le socialisme du possible'.

The PS in power tried to minimize the centrifugal tendencies of the factions in an effort to present a united front. The factions continued to put forward their own motions to party conferences, but composite motions (*motions de synthèse*) were hammered out and carried overwhelmingly. Issues sometimes cut across factions, for example, the schools question of 1983–4; and some PS *députés*, feeling that existing factions were insufficiently attuned to changing circumstances, created a new forward-looking *transcourant* group in 1985, though the suspicion was that it was a vehicle for the political ambitions of Laurent Fabius. Pulling in the opposite direction, a small extreme left faction 'Socialisme maintenu' appeared in 1984–5, opposed to any move of the PS towards a social democratic position. CERES, always a vigorous PS faction, also attacked the '*social-libéralisme*' represented by Michel Rocard, but then in April 1986 adopted a milder stance and the new name of 'Socialisme et République'. A CERES minority opposed to this move created a faction within a faction, and merely served to underline the democratic (some would say fissiparous) nature of the PS.

An examination of individual French political parties shows they are not monolithic blocs, any more than parties in other countries, yet the extent of intra-party strife does appear to be quite significant. In 1972 the Radical Party split and its left wing broke away, soon afterwards taking the name of *Mouvement des radicaux de gauche* (MRG). In the 1980s the MRG was wracked by the dilemma of whether to revert to the search for a united Radical 'family', or whether to convert close electoral co-operation with the PS into outright amalgamation. In the PR, a pro-Barre group of thirty leading members including eighteen *députés*, and calling itself 'Contrat libéral', appeared in 1985 and had to be reminded of the need for 'loyalty' and 'discipline'. The PR of course forms part of the UDF which would find it very difficult actually to federate its constituent parties.

Party leaderships are often in acute conflict with local branches: in 1986 FN dissidents in the *département* of Bouches-du-Rhône accused the local leadership of operating an old pals' network (*politique du copinage*), and left to create a *Front d'opposition nationale*; and the whole Radical Party membership (200) of the *département* of Puy-de-Dôme resigned from the party on the grounds that its incorporation into the UDF had taken it inexorably to the Right. The composition of party lists for the March 1986 elections provoked much local ill temper: the FN national leadership was accused of authoritarianism, and PS members did not like the inclusion of individual candidates and groups to its Right, at the expense of its traditional working-class base. Earlier, the change to proportional representation for the 1986 elections caused strong resentment in those PS *fédérations* whose parliamentary representation would be reduced.

The most dramatic manifestation of intra-party conflict in the 1980s was in the PCF. In an effort to emerge from the long period of opposition which had begun in 1947 (usually referred to as a 'political ghetto') the PCF in the 1960s and 1970s adopted a less uncompromising stance and showed signs of ideological flexibility. But the close co-operation with the PS which produced a joint policy programme to be applied when the Left came to power was abruptly halted in 1977. This heralded a period of internal dissension hardly muted by the 1981–4 participation in a Left government. Relations between the leadership and the grass roots were strained, and at the 25th Congress in 1985, the leadership stressed the party's constitution in an effort to stamp out factions, but some prominent people left the party or were ousted from the *bureau politique*.

Inter-party relations

Relations between parties in France are focused on the need in a multi-party system to maximize chances of electoral success, however slim these may be in reality, by co-operation with other parties. Even parties which have been dominant at a given time – the Gaullist party in the 1960s, the PS in the early 1980s – cannot ignore the fact that the circumstances which gave them this advantage may not endure in the longer term.

The post-war party system in France is best seen as a concretization in party terms of six main 'political families'. This term implies a tradition of shared memories, attitudes and beliefs which may predate the parties themselves: thus there was a body of thought and doctrine appearing at different points in history for each of Communism, Socialism, Radicalism, Christian Democracy, Liberalism, and (more recently, of course) Gaullism, before the existence of the respective party.

Inter-party relations during the Fifth Republic can be understood by reference to a 'snapshot' of the party system at three representative times:

A	Nov. 1962	PCF	SFIO	Rad.	MRP	RI	UNR	
B	Mar. 1977	PCF	PS + MRG	Rad.	CDS	PR	RPR	
C	Mar. 1986	PCF	PS		UDF		RPR	FN

Elections in 1958 to the new Fifth Republic Parliament had continued the post-war pattern of a National Assembly in which the six political families mentioned were represented. But whereas this six-party configuration was preserved after the election in November 1962 of a second Parliament, a new phenomenon also appeared which has profoundly affected inter-party relations since that date. This was '*le fait majoritaire*', that is, the existence in the National Assembly of a majority group of *députés* willing to give support to the government's policies – a government party, or closely co-operating group of parties, owing its majority position to the fact that voters were impressed by the past record of the President and the government appointed by him, or on the other hand preferred, as in 1981 and 1986, opposition policies. This *alternance* (peaceful transfer of power after elections) of the 1980s, which made parties more 'respectable' in that an election could now mean a change of party or coalition of parties in power and not just a reshuffle of the previous governing coalition, nevertheless took a long time to materialize. The majority in 1962 comprised the UNR and the RI led by Giscard; the Christian Democrat MRP was also very briefly associated, until de Gaulle alienated them by his anti-European utterances. The existence of this right-wing majority obliged the remaining parties to reassess their position. The MRP dissolved itself in 1966 to become the *Centre des démocrates sociaux* (CDS), dropping explicit allegiance to reformist Catholicism, but preserving its pro-European leanings and hoping to keep alive a separate Centrist identity at a time of increasing bipolarization of the party system between Right and Left. Bipolarization was fostered by the new method of electing the President, first applied in 1965, by a two-round system where only the two best-placed candidates went through to the second round, and by the requirement from 1966 that a candidate in the first round of parliamentary elections, to be permitted to stand again in the second round, must receive a number of votes equal to 10 per cent of registered voters – raised to 12.5 per cent in 1976.

It was particularly on the Left that adjustment to the new reality of a majority in Parliament was necessary if it was itself to constitute an eventual majority, but changes were slow to appear. The PS and PCF found it easy to continue with electoral co-operation, begun tentatively in 1962, whereby the candidate with fewer first-round votes withdrew and urged his or her supporters to back the other party's candidate. This rational tactic allowed both parties to maximize their parliamentary representation in elections between 1965 and 1981, but co-operation on actual policy was a different matter. The strategy which eventually bore fruit in 1981 was begun in embryonic form by Mitterrand's presidential bid as the candidate of all the Left in the 1965 elections. It was Mitterrand who realized that the Left must accept that:

the new Fifth Republic regime was entrenched in public opinion;
the presidency was the locus of power in this regime;
a majority in sociological terms could be converted into a parliamentary majority only if the non-communist Left first united, and then acted in close political and not just electoral conjunction with the PCF.

To try to unite the non-communist Left, Mitterrand in 1965

linked the SFIO, his own group of political clubs and the Radical Party, but this attempt foundered in the aftermath of the 'events' of May–June 1968. The Radical Party then pursued its own course, and split into two in 1972. It was not until 1971 that the non-communist Left was effectively united in the new *Parti socialiste*. Relations between Socialists and the PCF, which had been characterized during the 1960s by 'two steps forward, one step back', took a major step forward in 1972 when the Joint Programme for Government was signed by the PS, the PCF and soon afterwards the MRG, and the 'Union de la gauche' began actually to mean something. This development, together with the progressive incorporation between 1969 and 1974 of the Centre (CDS) and the rump of the Radical Party into the governing right-wing majority, gave the party system a distinct bipolar appearance in the mid-1970s – in line B in the table on p. 50 the division between the two 'poles' of Right and Left would come between MRG and the Radical Party.

However, perfect bipolarization was impossible so long as Left and Right were not solid coalitions. Not only was the Giscardian wing of the Right loosely structured and lacking a coherent policy – and the establishment of the UDF in 1978 did nothing to change this – but its relations with the Gaullists were far from harmonious during Giscard's presidency. This was especially true after 1976 when Chirac decided he could no longer continue as Prime Minister, and transformed the Gaullist party into the RPR as a vehicle for his presidential ambitions. Chirac refused to let the RPR be 'giscardised'; and when Paris was finally allowed to have a mayor in 1977 he soundly beat Giscard's candidate in the election for the post.

On the Left, the *Union de la gauche* suffered a setback in 1977 by failure to update the 1972 Joint Programme for Government, and the PCF, unwilling to accommodate a shift in the centre of gravity (*rééquilibrage*) within the Left, resumed hardline criticism of its Socialist partners. When in 1981 the dimension of joint participation in government became available, it should have marked the supreme achievement of the Left's objectives, but instead it merely served to underline the divergent perceptions and strategies within the Union. The PCF indulged in *participation sans soutien*, and this only until

1984. In any case the PS parliamentary landslide in June 1981 allowed it to constitute a majority on its own. So the *Union de la gauche* was dead and buried by 1986 in national terms though some jointly administered local councils survived the 1983 municipal elections setback. It had since 1962 taken the form of joint opposition and joint government, but had never been put to the supreme test of joint parliamentary majority, a test which the Right passed with difficulty in 1976–81 and faced again after 1986. The new one-round proportional system for the 1986 elections in fact removed the problem of whether the *Union de la gauche* could survive in its original and most rudimentary form – a PS-PCF agreement for candidates to stand down and give fellow candidates of the Left a better chance in the second round of parliamentary elections. On the Right, this absence of *désistement réciproque* for parties' mutual benefit also meant that the question of the relationship between the RPR-UDF and the FN was not posed in stark terms.

The political fortunes of the extreme Right in France were at a low ebb after 1945, but decolonization and especially the Algerian war (1954–62) gave a boost to virulent anti-system, which from 1958 meant anti-de Gaulle, nationalism; however, Jean-Marie Le Pen, as the leader of one of the extreme Right factions – among which fusion and fission were rife – received only 0.76 per cent of the votes in his 1974 presidential bid. In 1981 he was unable to collect the 500 signatures legally required for a presidential candidature (raised from 100 in 1976) and the FN received only 0.18 per cent of the total vote in the parliamentary elections. But by making race and immigration an electoral issue – or as Le Pen would have it, by 'saying out loud what everybody thought in their hearts' – support climbed to 11 per cent in the 1984 European elections. People voting for the FN were much more likely to be swayed at the moment of their choice by issues such as immigration, and law and order, than those voting for other parties; the RPR's move towards the UDF's 'liberal' stance and its abandonment of hardline language on these issues left room for the FN to flourish.

The RPR and UDF however were sufficiently confident of electoral victory to exclude the possibility of post-1986 collaboration with the FN. They signed an agreement in April 1985 with which the CNIP, the *Parti libéral* and the *Parti démocrate français* were associated. This became the 'Plateforme commune de gouvernement' to be applied after electoral victory, which in the end was quite narrow. In fact, constraints on RPR–UDF cooperation remained strong: the subordinate position of the UDF in the arrangement, their smaller number of *députés* after 1986, their ill-feeling over the number of ministerial portfolios allotted to them in the Chirac government, and the possibility of a separate Barrist parliamentary group being formed of RPR and UDF *députés*. The post-1986 party system, therefore, revealed elements of bipolarization, in that a shaky coalition on the Right faced a party on the Left – the PS – which had the prospect of benefiting without recourse to other groups from the next manifestation of *alternance*; and elements of a multi-party system with the presence of two parties – the PCF and the FN – whose exclusion from the major 'poles' reinforced their anti-system tendencies.

Limits to party influence

In fulfilling their traditional function of 'intermediaries' between governors and governed, political parties in France, as elsewhere, aggregate interests, channel demands and draw up policies. Yet much political action takes place either outside political parties or involving them only marginally. Some elements of this exclusion arise from factors specific to France:

The particular circumstances of the first decades of the Third Republic, proclaimed in 1870, militated against the formation of a broad party of labour. Political action in defence of the economic interests of labour has been undertaken as much by trade unionism as by the parliamentary Left.

Groups in the French second chamber predated the foundation of political parties, and there are still groups in the Fifth Republic Senate not identifiable with a party.

During the nineteenth century, political clubs kept alive republican humanism associated with the 1789 Revolution. They still undertake political education and, especially in opposition, doctrinal renewal – functions which are not always performed well by the parties themselves.

The phenomenon, not exclusively French, of broad-based nationalist movements has also militated against political parties – Bonapartism, particularly in its plebiscitary phase under the Second Empire, and in more recent times Pétainism (1940–44) and Gaullism.

In his bid to re-establish the authority of the State, de Gaulle made a deliberate attempt to reduce the role of political parties in the new Fifth Republic regime: the President of the Republic was to be elected not by the two Chambers of Parliament as before, but by a much larger 'collège' (from 1965, of course, by the whole people); single-member constituencies were to reduce the salience of parties in electoral choice; the upper Chamber, peopled by largely non-party *notables*, was renamed the Senate and its role was increased.

Moreover, political parties which played a crucial role in France, if not in establishing representative democracy, at least in defending it under the Third and Fourth Republics, have not always found it easy to come to terms with participatory democracy in the second half of the twentieth century. The 'participation' which was a central element of de Gaulle's political thought has always occupied a very minor place in the policy programme of the Gaullist party. Advocacy of the self-management (*autogestion*) of units of economic – and by implication political and cultural – activity was halfheartedly undertaken by the Left in the 1970s, though it survived in the Rocardian faction of the PS. Directly elected regional councils and a measure of administrative decentralization had to wait until the 1980s. Parties would also be bypassed if on presidential initiative large issues of public concern were opened up to direct consultation of the people by referendum. De Gaulle did this successfully in 1962 and tried it unsuccessfully in 1969, but the notion is far from dead. The FN would want it on the question of capital punishment for terrorists and international drug dealers, and even Mitterrand briefly toyed with the idea in 1984 in the aftermath of the schools reform fiasco.

A further measure of how political parties are far from all-pervading is that politicians, particularly on the Left, are at pains to show awareness of a '*société civile*', which is best understood as those non-State economic, social and cultural forces which give life to a society through their own initiative, outside spheres where the State has monopoly action or maintains a bureaucracy. Commentators have suggested that located within, or arising from, this civil society are countervailing forces (*contre-pouvoirs*), including the expanding phenomenon of '*associations*' not all of which are explicitly political, which serve to limit the power of the State. Political parties in France may find it increasingly difficult to reconcile their desire to foster or exploit or supplant these forces, with their close involvement in the institutions of the State.

Role of parties in the system

It is this close relationship which, as the Fifth Republic developed, allowed political parties to recover the influence of which the framers of the 1958 Constitution tried to deprive them. It was accepted that parties would dominate the National Assembly, as traditional defenders of representative democracy, and parties came into their own again in three ways: firstly, the unforeseen emergence of a parliamentary majority, and the coincidence of this with a presidential majority, if necessary by dissolving the National Assembly and holding new elections as in 1981; secondly, the growth of bipolarization which made electoral choice between policy programmes or presidential candidates the determinant of political decisions; and, thirdly, the close relationship between political parties and the presidency.

While it is true that the original Gaullian concept of a non-party President lingers (some people in 1965 thought somebody like Albert Schweitzer could take over from de Gaulle, and the equivalent line of thought in the 1980s produced names like Bernard Tapie or Yves Montand), the parties have become indissociable from political power by offering what they did before 1958 – a path to the highest political office. Because this office is the directly elected presidency, every party in France has to be in the basic sense a *parti d'électeurs*. The phenomenon can be looked at in two ways.

Firstly, one can speak of the presidentialization of political parties. Public acceptance in the 1962 referendum of a directly elected presidency meant that politicians recognized as serious potential candidates ('*présidentiable*') gained in stature within their party. The formal structure, or at least the leadership composition, of a party tended to be modified (e.g. UDR in 1967, PS gradually during the 1970s) to give support to its *présidentiable* and, more importantly, to increase his or her general popularity; the obvious reason was that, to win a second round run-off, candidates need much wider support than the traditional electorate of a single party. Thus Pompidou needed the support of some Centrists in 1969, Giscard of some Gaullists led by Chirac in 1974, and Mitterrand of Communists in 1981. A party needs a candidate of stature, but a serious candidate needs more than a party. Moreover, having more than one *présidentiable* can be a source of weakness for a party, for example Mitterrand and Rocard in the PS in 1981 (and others in the mid-1980s) and Giscard and Barre in the UDF.

The second aspect of the close association of a political party with the presidency is when a presidential strategy is successful and a party's candidate becomes President. Already under Giscard the decisive role of the parties in presidential action was being felt – the President needed the Gaullist party and Ministers were in the Government as representatives of their party; also, party nepotism and administrative clientelism began to take root. So it might have been thought, when the 1981 elections produced a Socialist President *and* a PS majority in the National Assembly, that the Socialist party would be in a position to determine the major orientations of policy. But while it is true that the composition of the Left governments reflected the various factions of the PS and parties co-operating with it, the *Parti socialiste* was never allowed to impose its will on the President or the government. Mitterrand made this clear when addressing the new ministers in May 1981: 'tout en restant fidèles à vos communs engagements, vous cessez d'être les représentants de vos partis, vous êtes les représentants de la France'. The party leadership was not allowed to assume a mediating function between the government and the PS parliamentary group, and its hope of having permanent joint working parties with Socialist ministers never materialized. There was acrimony in 1985 when both Jospin as party leader and Fabius as head of the government claimed to be in charge of the Socialists' campaign for the forthcoming elections.

In the final analysis, the PS in power was subject to the institutional logic of the Fifth Republic. Mitterrand's electoral triumph in 1981 was on the basis of his '*110 Propositions pour la France*' worked out by his own team, not the party leadership, though obviously there was cross-membership; and his message to the PS 'victory' conference at Valence was 'Président de tous les Français, je ne saurais être l'homme d'un parti'. When people spoke of a 'PS State' in 1981–6, as they had of a 'UDR State' in the late 1960s, they were saying no more than that there was a dominant political party which had successfully adjusted to a novel situation. French political parties have largely recovered from the subordinate position to which the Fifth Republic regime as initially conceived had consigned them, but in the context of a constantly evolving constitutional and political system, the role, perceived function and mutual relations of political parties in France are far from settled.

Bibliography

General

Chapsal, J., *La vie politique sous la Ve République*. Paris, PUF, 1984. Provides a historical narrative on Fifth Republic politics

Duhamel, A., *La république giscardienne*. Paris, Grasset, 1980 and *La république de Monsieur Mitterrand*. Paris, Grasset, 1982. Provide a readable account of the political background between 1974 and late 1981, and could be supplemented by the more recent

Bauchard, P., *La guerre des deux roses – du rêve à la réalité, 1981–85*. Paris, Grasset, 1986 and

July, S., *Les années Mitterrand*. Paris, Grasset, 1986.

In English, the following introductory books are suggested:
Hayward, J.E.S., *Governing France – the one and indivisible republic*. London, Weidenfeld & Nicolson, 1983.

Slater, M., *Contemporary French Politics*. London, Macmillan, 1985. Description and analysis are accompanied by texts in French and linguistic exercises.

Wright, V., *The Government and Politics of France*. London, Hutchinson, 1983.

Parties

Books which are relatively easy to read and digest from the point of view of content are

Adereth, M., *The French Communist party – a critical history 1920–84*. Manchester, MUP, 1984.

Bell, D.S. (ed.), *Contemporary French Political Parties*. London, Croom Helm, 1982.

Borella, F., *Les partis politiques dans la France d'aujourd'hui*. Paris, Le Seuil, 1981.

Charlo, J., *The Political Parties in France* (56-page booklet published by the Ministry of Foreign Affairs in 1986 and available from embassies).

Lancelot, A., *Les élections sous la Ve République*. Paris PUF, 1983.

Petitfils, J.-C., *L'Extrême-droite en France*. Paris, PUF, 1983.

Tartakowsky, D., *Une histoire du PCF*. Paris, PUF, 1982.
Books which are useful, but which may be of greater conceptual difficulty are

Charlot, J., *Les partis politiques en France*. Paris, A. Colin, 1986.

Du Roy, A. and Schneider, R., *Le roman de la rose*. Paris, Le Seuil, 1982, on the *Union de la gauche*.

Juquin, P., *Autocritiques*. Paris, Grasset, 1985. By a former member of the PCF *bureau politique*.

Kergoat, J., *Le parti socialiste*. Paris, Le Sycomore, 1983.

Nay, C., *Le Noir et le Rouge*. Paris, Grasset, 1984 on Mitterrand's political career.

Petitfils, J.-C., *La démocratie giscardienne*. Paris, PUF, 1981.

Robrieux, P., *La secte*. Paris, Stock, 1985 on the PCF.

Rollat, A., *Les hommes de l'extrême-droite*. Paris, Calmann-Lévy, 1985.

Roucaute, Y., *Le parti socialiste*. Paris, Huisman, 1983.

Roussel, E., *Le cas Le Pen – les nouvelles droites en France*. Paris, J.C. Lattès, 1985.

Touchard, J., *La gauche en France depuis 1900*. Paris, Le Seuil, 1981.

and the following journals

Pouvoirs no. 20 (1982): La gauche au pouvoir;
Pouvoirs no. 28 (1984): Le RPR;
Revue française de science politique. vol. 36 no. 1 (Feb. 1986) includes articles on French political parties.

Other media

French-speaking radio stations can usually be received adequately on long wave and are a source of information on the current political scene (all times quoted are local times in France)

France-Inter   (1829m – 164kHz) the early morning weekday news has a guest, though not always a politician, at 7.40 a.m. At 7.20 p.m. on weekdays a political debate or phone-in programme is the long-established pattern, though the precise weekly format may be changed from time to time.

Europe 1   (1648m – 182kHz) the early morning weekday political coverage is at 7.25 and 7.40 a.m., with an interview at 8.20 a.m. On Sundays at 7.00 p.m. is the well-tried formula of *'Club de la presse'* where a politician is interviewed by a panel of journalists – one can subscribe to their free service of the *'Phrases significatives'* of each broadcast – Service de Presse d'Europe 1, 26 bis, rue François 1er, 75389 PARIS CEDEX 08.

RTL   (1271m – 236kHz) the early morning weekday political comment is at 7.43 a.m., with an interview at 8.10 a.m.

Three

Trade unions

Richard McAllister

Introduction

The last act of the outgoing Socialist government before the March 1986 legislative elections was to enable the working week to be more flexible. This was noteworthy not just as part of the famous 'U-turn' in economic policy of the 1981–6 government, and not just because the PCF had broken most of the records by the number of amendments it had put down to the proposed legislation. The main trade union confederations demonstrated clearly that they were not of the same mind as each other about it.

A similar lack of unity was evident on the streets of Paris for the May Day parades after the elections which returned the Right to power. Despite the fact that this was both the centennial May Day and the fiftieth anniversary of the Popular Front government of 1936, lack of numbers as well as lack of enthusiasm were notable; and, in contrast say to 1976, the main union confederations paraded separately.

The elections themselves had produced a notable 'first' in French political life. For the first time, none of the main trade union confederations had given official, explicit instructions to its members on how to vote. The reasons varied, from on the one hand, a desire to distance a confederation from the expected electoral disaster of its ally party (the PCF), to, on the other, a desire to establish a confederation as an '*interlocuteur valable*' with the incoming government. In France, such disunity, combined with effective weakness, verbal and occasionally physical militancy have reinforced each other. These features have been evident in all the relations in which the trade unions are involved: with each other; with political parties and government; with management; with their rank and file. This chapter seeks to examine why this has been so, and what the prospects are now.

Background

When Giscard was elected President in 1974, one of the first things to be commissioned was a report on reform of enterprises, the Sudreau Report. It traced the origins of the 'crisis of confidence between the social partners' back to the d'Allarde decree and the *loi Le Chapelier* of 1791. The latter, in particular, had prohibited members of any trade or profession from combining on the basis of their 'supposed common interests'. Reform of this situation was a long time coming, grudgingly given and limited: the recognition of unions (significantly, *syndicats*) by the law of 1884 did not give them the freedom to operate within individual plants, and most public services (including the railways) were prohibited initially from unionizing. The right to organize union sections in the workplace did not finally arrive until a law of December 1968, in the wake of the 'Events'.

Divisions were apparent almost immediately after the passing of the 1884 law. Indeed, despite changes of name and on occasion of stance, it is remarkable how closely the original lines of division match those of much later times: revolutionary and reformist; 'confessional' and secular. Right from the start, the divisions between the main strands of Socialism in France found their echo in the industrial organizations. The strategy of political action – the need to conquer the machinery of State to better the workers' lot – was represented by the Marxist *Fédération nationale des syndicats*, founded in 1886. A different aproach, seeking originally to 'domesticate' the labour movement, the 'self-help' and self-improvement strategy, was represented by the *Bourses du travail*, combining employment-exchange with educational and friendly society functions. These formed a national federation in 1892. The *Confédération générale du travail* (CGT), founded in 1895, was to become the most important national organization. It preached industrial action; but, although it commanded the loyalties of the majority of the militant working class in the period up to the First World War, it has never succeeded in uniting all the main unions. Almost as if following the Leninist precept ('split, split and split again!') it has itself split three times – in 1921, 1939 and again in 1948. Yet another contrasting strain was 'social-Catholic' in origin, pre-dating, in the *Cercles ouvriers* of the 1870s, the actual legalization of unions; but given a powerful push by the Papal Encyclical *Rerum Novarum* of 1891. This urged Catholics to become actively involved in the problems of workers.

At various points during the last century, a greater degree of unity in the trade union movement has seemed possible; but at each point it has been overwhelmed by the forces making for disunity. Lack of unity was no surprise in the swirling tides of the generation that followed the Paris Commune. But it seemed that, when the different strands of French socialism came together in 1905 to form the *Section française de l'internationale ouvrière* (SFIO), this might lead in turn to greater unity in the trade union movement. It did not do so because the CGT at that time was dominated by revolutionary syndicalists who believed that a revolutionary general strike was essential and despised those who became embroiled in parliamentary charades. The other principal occasion when unity seemed possible was the electoral victory of the coalition of the Left, the Popular Front, in 1936. For three years, indeed, the CGT was reunited: but the 'Muscovite' allegiance of its leading Communists was clear (not for the first or last time) in their support of the Nazi-Soviet pact in 1939, and again a split occurred.

The Second World War brought great repression and suffering to all trade unionists, and this, together with the important part played by a number in the Resistance, helped to recreate a sense of solidarity. Once again, it proved short-lived. The Fourth Republic was only two years old when cold war tensions once again caused a split which has so far proved enduring.

The main divisions in the French trade union movement date from this period. Since then, there have been three large confederations, as well as two other important bodies and a host of minor ones. The biggest (thought the extent of its dominance has never again reached its apogee at the Liberation) was, and continues to be, the CGT. Its two main rivals were the *Confédération générale du travail-force ouvrière* (CGT-FO) and the *Confédération française des travailleurs chrétiens*(CFTC). The CGT has been, thoughout its post-war history, very closely allied indeed to the French Communist Party (PCF). It has always retained token non-Communists in certain positions, but the key offices are nowadays virtually monopolized by PCF members. It was precisely to counter this obedience to the PCF line – and behind it, it was usually thought, the Moscow line – that the CGT-FO was set up in 1948. It was mildly Socialist, and reformist in outlook and tactics. The CFTC was much older: its roots were in the social-Catholic tradition of the nineteenth century already mentioned; but it was actually set up in 1919. Although both Catholics and Protestants could be members, it was of course predominantly Catholic. As time went by, it generally became more radical; in doing so, it exchanged the earlier suspicion felt towards it by other unions (that it was 'yellow', a creature of the *patronat*) for the suspicion of many Church leaders that it was a tool of Communist and Socialist revolution – even if an unwitting one. As this strain grew, it gradually lost its Church links, and these ended finally in 1964. It then split; the great majority marking the shift by a change of name to that which it bears today; *Confédération française démocratique du travail* (CFDT). Only about a tenth opted to retain the 'Christian' formula and the old name CFTC, thus creating another, minor, breakaway confederation.

In addition to the 'big three', certain other organizations should be mentioned. Next largest is a trade union federation which is specific to a particular sector, and thus not affiliated to a confederation: the *Fédération de l'éducation nationale* (FEN), which has grown rapidly in line with the expansion of education since 1945. Next in importance is the *Confédération générale des cadres* (CGC), founded in 1944, representing precisely those 'cadres' of its name – managerial, technical and scientific personnel who disliked the political affiliations of the other confederations and wished to defend their status and income differentials. There are other minor groups as well –the

Confédération des syndicats indépendants, the *Confédération des syndicats autonomes*, and so on.

The fragmentation and division of the French trade union movement goes hand in hand with its weakness, which is still marked. It is both a cause and an effect of that weakness, whose various aspects we shall examine later. Nor is this sort of fragmentation uncommon in western Europe. There are united trade union movements in Britain and West Germany for example; but in Belgium, Holland, Italy, Spain, Switzerland, the situation is more like that in France.

Such division is but one aspect of deep political cleavages. These may be based on any or all of social, ideological, or geographical factors. In such a situation the political Left is almost always split too (though this is less true of Holland), and this holds whether or not there are close organizational links between parties and unions. In France a number of factors in the general environment of the trade unions have tended to heighten or sharpen divisions between them. The most important appear to have been: the revolutionary tradition; the religious factor, and the pattern of economic development of the country over the last century and a half.

The tradition of seeking fundamental change through revolution is well known. In both the late eighteenth and the nineteenth centuries, the lessons to be derived from seeking social change by revolutionary means have been much contested in France. This was no less true of the blood-bath of the 1871 Paris Commune than of earlier episodes, and sharpened the divide within the working class between reformists and revolutionaries. Likewise with the religious question: despite the existence of 'progressive' Catholicism, religion was regarded as fundamentally reactionary by much of the Left. In France, religious practice has for long been regionally differentiated; and has been strong in, among other places, several of the parts of the north and east which have also become main industrial centres. The religious question dominated political debate in the first years of the present century, and has helped sustain a major division within the trade union movement since.

The pattern of economic development in France has also enhanced and sustained division within the trade union movement. Although rapid economic change occurred patchily in most countries, it was particularly patchy in France, and the places most affected by the new developments – including the development of an industrial working class – were often physically far removed from each other. Local conditions, too, were very diverse: again, not conducive to the growth of a unified and powerful mass movement with a sense of common cause underpinned by similarity of experience and relative ease of communication. The main industrial concentrations were around Paris, and in the north and east; there were patches (for example in mining areas) elsewhere. The result was a ghetto mentality: the industrial working class was aware of being in a minority; and in addition, often worked in relatively small plants and factories harder to organize than large units; and local conditions, including wage-rates most notably, differed strikingly until quite recently.

Recent economic changes have been numerous, but their effects somewhat ambiguous. By the mid-1970s, it was clear that twenty-five years of rapid economic growth were coming to an end. During that period, France had become a much more industrial country and, in some ways, more of a mass society than ever before. By the late 1970s, however, the talk was of de-industralization. The high growth period was itself marked by one major explosion, in the tradition of '*drame révolutionnaire*' – the Events of May–June 1968. This produced quite considerable changes in industrial attitudes – on both sides of industry. The period also saw the rise to a dominant position in the economy of a number of large firms: some already nationalized, such as Renault; some originally not, but nationalized under Mitterrand (such as Rhône-Poulenc); and some remaining in the private sector (Peugeot-Citroën). Questions not merely of ownership, but of how firms should be run, came more to the fore. France from this period has become much more urbanized, and has experienced a very large growth of salaried employees. Despite this, in general the number of trade unionists has declined; French trade unionism remains numerically weak as well as organizationally divided. And despite the many changes under the Fifth Republic, the influence of the more distant past continues to weigh heavily.

The trade unions and ideology

The influences of ideological differences upon the French trade union movement appear to be many and varied, but are in practice hard to evaluate. Two points stand out. The first is that it is not always the *same* beliefs or ideologies which have been prominent. The second is that there has always been an element of ideological competition: a tendency for some groups to indulge in leapfrogging with others in the escalation of demands (a phenomenon not limited to the unions), and for other groups to distance themselves deliberately from this process. An interesting question, but a hard one to answer, is whether ideology has had any 'independent' effect on members or non-members of trade unions in France: whether it can be said to have attracted or repelled them, or to have shaped their perceptions of the world and how they relate to it.

The ideologies that have had prominence have changed; or a particular trade union grouping has sometimes changed its ideological attachment. Revolutionary syndicalism, the belief in a great general strike to bring about massive societal change, though it remains present, is now the belief of rather few (though often influential) people. It was the original credo of the CGT at the end of the nineteenth century; and it was especially influential around 1900–10. It was not a single, self-consistent doctrine but rather a reflection of an attitude and a mood. Thus its most famous expression, the Charter of Amiens adopted by the CGT Congress of 1906, talked about improving the workers' lot in essentially reformist ways, but added that complete emancipation required the expropriation of the capitalist class; this would be brought about by a general strike which would establish the *syndicats* no longer as mere 'resisters' but as the basis of the new social order. Revolutionary utopianism was therefore very much part of the credo too.

These years were perhaps the high-water mark of revolutionary syndicalism. But in 1908, a sharp increase in unemployment was followed by severe repression of the syndicalist movement by the authorities. In the very next year, 1909, the CGT leadership was taken over by one of the hardiest perennials ever of the French trade union movement,

Léon Jouhaux. He remained its general secretary from 1909 to 1947, when, logically for one of his views, he transferred his allegiance to the CGT-FO. It was he who converted the CGT to a much more reformist approach.

This approach, however, had been directly challenged by the Russian Revolution of 1917 and events immediately following it. A growing body of opinion looked to the Soviet model of a successful revolution: others favoured continuing along a parliamentary road to Socialism. This divide showed itself first in the political parties, leading to the setting up of the PCF at the Tours Conference in 1920. But its effects did not stop there, for the Leninists of the PCF believed that the trade unions required the lead of a revolutionary political party with a high degree of class consciousness; and that these unions should be subordinate to the party which should infiltrate and control them, since, left to their own devices, they would concentrate only on the narrow sectional interests of their members and could achieve little. This view was totally opposed to that of the social democrats and reformists: the conflict came to a head in the violent 1921 Lille Conference which culminated in the expulsion of the Communists. At this point the Communists were in the minority, and set up their own organization, the CGTU (*Confédération générale du travail unitaire*).

This episode has left a deep legacy of hatred between Communists and non-Communists, within both parties and the unions. Only on certain occasions since were the PCF and CGTU willing or able to associate closely with non-Communists on the Left, notably during the 1930s when the Soviet Union, alarmed at the rise of Fascism and National Socialism, was prepared to back the Popular Front. But the events, first of the 1930s – deep economic depression, and the fight against Fascism – and then of the Second World War, served to increase the appeal of the Communists. Their excellent organization helped them in the Resistance: in turn, their excellent Resistance record gave them a dominant position in the immediately post-war trade union movement. At the CGT 1946 Conference, the Communists could count on about 80 per cent of the vote to go their way.

For a short while all seemed workable: Jean Monnet's proposals for planning looked to trade union involvement; even De Gaulle's Bayeux speech had looked to increased functional representation. It did not last long. The tensions of the cold war period reached very directly into French politics: after the expulsion of the Communist members of government in 1947, the CGT called a wave of strikes which were widely described as 'insurrectionary' and certainly seemed aimed to bringing government and the economy to its knees. Non-Communists within the CGT became more and more alarmed; an unease increased by the Prague coup of February 1948 which confirmed the worst fears of many about Moscow-inspired methods. Once again there was a split; but this time, with the Communists firmly in the majority, it was most of the non-Communists who left CGT to set up the CGT-FO in 1948. The bitterness of this period marked relations between the two groupings for a long time thereafter, even though the seriousness of subsequent conflicts was generally not as great. The new union, CGT-FO, sought to distinguish itself from the CGT by concentrating directly on issues of 'relevance' to its membership, rather than honing them for the wider political struggle, or, indeed, as CGT did, taking up cudgels on behalf of the non-unionized in an effort to widen its constituency. In its turn, CGT-FO was also very much a child of the cold war: it was widely reported to have not only the (domestic) support of SFIO, but that of US unions and the CIA as well.

The third main confederation had, as we have seen, a very curious history. The CFTC drew much of its membership from the lower middle classes and from women; it was rather despised by the other confederations, yet its membership was greater than that of CGT-FO for much of the time. Post-war, its original ideological position may be described as 'liberal-Catholic'. As with other French trade unions, however, it claimed for itself independence of all political parties, and, with the shift to the Right of the Christian democratic MRP and of economic policy, CFTC took its distance. The final victory of its Reconstruction group led to the split and formation of CFDT in 1964. From that point on, as we shall see, events (and 'the Events') took over: the CFDT went through an 'ultra-radical' phase, before swinging rather more recently to trying to find a middle way between social democracy and Marxism.

Its successes during the 1970s and 1980s owe not a little to the influential General Secretary of the period, Edmond Maire, to whom we shall return.

The fact that a number of different ideologies and perspectives are catered for in the unions might be thought conducive to overall numerical strength. The opposite is the case. France is virtually at the bottom of the European league in the proportion of the workforce unionized. In Switzerland, that proportion is about 90 per cent; the EEC average is some 43 per cent, with West Germany, Italy and the UK all near or above the 40 per cent level. In France the figure has been falling, steadily if not dramatically, to about 23 per cent. Thus, despite the range of ideology, there is a real problem about the 'representativeness' of trade unions in France which, when added to the hostile instincts of the *patronat*, especially at plant level, has made for prickly and difficult relations between the two sides.

Organization and record

The picture that emerges then, is one of underdevelopment and weakness. French trade unions have had an uphill struggle to be taken seriously by the *patronat*, by government, and by the mass of workers. There have been surges in their numerical strength: after the First World War, after the Popular Front victory of 1936; following the Second World War, and following the Events of 1968: but there have also been relapses.

The unions have usually been regarded by employers as unreliable partners: as unable to make a settlement stick with the shop-floor and even as unable to control strike action. The Sudreau Report commented on the tendency of the grass roots to 'spontaneous' action. The trade unions as such have generally been seen as being only one of a number of channels for contact, negotiation and management of industrial relations – and, depending upon the situation in the particular factory or plant, by no means always the preferred one. There are also the *délégués du personnel*, finally confirmed in law in 1936. In addition, there are the *comités d'entreprise* (or works councils) set up after the Second World War in all undertakings with a staff of fifty or more. The *délégués* have generally been the more effective 'grievance' channel; the *comités* (chosen by the staff from among candidates usually nominated by the unions), which deal with welfare and social activities and are supposed also to act as a channel for information and advice between management and workers, have usually been less effective. Unions have also had to vie with each other to obtain the status of 'most representative' union. This status confers important rights (of negotiation and representation), is conferred by the State, and may be – and has been – challenged in the administrative courts.

The organization of trade union activity in France is both territorial and functional. Most main bodies are confederations, with a decentralized and usually rather weak structure. The CGT, for example, has both a geographical structure (*unions locales*, *unions départementales*) and a professional (or occupational) structure (*sections syndicales d'entreprise*, *syndicats*, *fédérations nationales*) together making up the *confédération*.

The total membership of French trade unions is small, almost certainly between 3 and 4 million. All confederations have habitually claimed more adherents than their paid-up membership. The CGT probably has less than 1 million paid-up members and the numbers fell each year from 1977 to 1985, mainly in response to the perceived 'wrecking tactics' of the Communists over the 'united-left' negotiations and the 1978 legislative elections. The CFDT's membership is estimated at from 800,000 to 900,000; it grew substantially following its radical stance in the Events of 1968. That of CGT-FO is about the same; it also has grown, partly as its 'moderate' stance of co-operation with management found some echoes among the more reformist and innovative sections of the *patronat* during the 1970s. FEN probably has about 0.5 million members and CGC between 300,000 and 500,000.

All the organizations suffer from limited financial resources and consequently limited numbers of paid headquarters staff. At 'confederal' level, CGT and CFDT each have headquarters staffs of only between one and two hundred: FO well below a hundred. Constituent organizations, with small budgets of their own, also support very small staffs. There is heavy reliance upon unpaid 'militants' at local level, which in turn decreases the control between the various levels. Nor do the confederations have the kind of substantial strike-funds to support a prolonged strike, and one result is a marked preference for token one-day stoppages, work-to-rule, go-slow and rotating lightning-strikes, affecting one plant after another unpredictably. Action at the plant level is very often unsuccessful, even if spectacular (occupations, locking-in of management and so on). Negotiations frequently have to be referred to much higher and usually national level if they are to succeed.

Such has been the tradition. There is also evidence of change. Characteristically, that change seemed to require the extraordinary catalyst of the Events of May–June 1968 to set it in motion.

The Events and their aftermath

It is generally agreed that the Events took most people, and certainly much of the union leadership, by surprise. The CGT was especially alarmed at the outbreak of 'spontaneity' (demands for a transformation of work-relations and so on) and sought to alter and limit demands and to channel them into the traditional mould – rates of pay and hours, benefits and so on. Although they succeeded in doing this to some extent, in other ways the Events did signal a long period of reflection and reconsideration, on all sides, of the role of trade unions and their relationships both with employers and with the activities of the State.

From the point of view of the union leaderships, the grievances that had appeared at the time of the Events were not novel. They felt left out in the cold by government economic policy; victims of a 'reform' of the social security system in 1967 in which they had not been involved and which appeared to combine higher contributions with unchanged or diminished benefits. Unemployment was rising, and real wages were held down in the name of 'competitiveness' and the wider 'financial rigour' by which France in the late 1960s sought to build a substantial balance of payments surplus which could be turned – literally – into gold; transported to the vaults of the Bank of France, hence forcing the 'Anglo-Saxon profligates'

– the United States and Britain – to mend their ways. The protests began at the grass roots; they were not directed by union leaderships. They were directed, most of all, at antiquated social relationships, rigid and outdated attitudes especially of management. Much of what happened, too, was in imitation of the students – the occupation of factories in particular – even though no united front between students and workers was established.

At the time, it was claimed that the general strike peaked with some 9 million involved. Though this was almost certainly an exaggeration, the government was badly shaken and at one time looked as if it might fall. But the longer chaos continued, the stronger the reaction to it became, as the massive Gaullist victory in the election a month later proved.

The main forces involved differed sharply in their reactions at the time, and in their attitudes afterwards. The CGT, along with the PCF, declared that a revolutionary situation 'did not exist'. Regardless of the ability of the government to 'defend the Republic' by military means (de Gaulle was absent, endeavouring to reassure himself on this point, at the height of the crisis) it was fairly clear that there could be no 'revolutionary situation' if the CGT and PCF declared that there was not. The CGT settled for accommodation in the Grenelle agreements – mainly involving an across-the-board 10 per cent pay increase and a one-third rise in the minimum wage (SMIC – *Salaire minimum interprofessionnel de croissance*), which also served to reduce differentials. They had no intention of seeking 'transformations' of work-relationships which might take the edge off class antagonism and alienation. For all this, Georges Séguy, then General Secretary of CGT, was heckled and booed for his acceptance of the Grenelle agreements. Not a few of the rank and file were seeking – realistically or not – much wider changes of outlook and regarded Grenelle as a betrayal.

This was truest in the CFDT, which was quite deeply affected by the Events, confirming the more radical course announced by the 1964 split. At its 1970 Congress, it linked the call for collectivization of the means of production and exchange to more novel demands which distinguished it from the other confederations. These were calls for democratic planning (as opposed to merely 'technocratic') and *autogestion* (workers' self-management). It was in the years immediately following the Events that the CFDT seemed most hostile to the existing order. Under Edmond Maire, its General Secretary from 1971, it generally returned to the pursuit of immediate benefits, but without dropping calls for long-term and radical change. Although its membership has grown, it is clear that this membership does not necessarily share the more radical visions of some of its leaders.

The response of FO was distinctly confused, but in general it emerged even more 'moderate', anti-Communist and anti-*gauchiste* than before. Despite its animosity to the CGT and PCF, FO, under its General Secretary André Bergeron, was a crucial backer of the Grenelle agreements, thus helping to ensure that 'reform', mild at that, would be the outcome.

Promises and sounds of sweeping change were fairly rapidly diminished. The 'wilder' schemes of René Capitant (briefly Couve de Murville's Minister of Justice, charged with preparing a new labour code) died the death, stifled by the combined hostility of CGT and *patronat*. Although participation was severely limited, a number of changes were made. Profit sharing, introduced in very modest degree in 1967 and opposed by the unions, was given some boost; and the role of the *comités d'entreprise* was modestly strengthened. Most significant was the recognition, at long last, of union rights to organize and operate within the plant. There were more diffuse and less concrete changes, of attitude and mood. For a period (1969–72) the government (under Chaban-Delmas) talked of *politique contractuelle*, the involvement of representatives of labour in a fuller and more organized way at national level in economic decisions – a process of tripartite consultations which, if it fell far short of corporatism, yet seemed to move in that direction. Union membership rose, modestly; the number of *sections d'entreprise* grew much more rapidly, on the back of the 1968 law. There began a process which, with varying success, continued through the 1970s and early 1980s – of the more active involvement of workers in the organization of work-patterns and practices, and active consultation of them, much favoured by the FO. The glacial attitude of the *patronat*, too, showed signs of change, especially when François Ceyrac became its

President in 1973. Between them, Ceyrac and Edmond Maire may be taken as talismen of the new mood.

Union relationships

Relations with each other

Enough has been said to show that the main confederations differ among themselves not merely over economic strategy and issues, but over political issues also, and over the relationships between the political struggle and the pursuit of economic aims. The FO takes a basically non-political approach, in the sense of distancing itself from all the parties, and stressing the independence and separation of political action from the 'rightful' aims of trade unions. The CGT believes both in the political role of trade unions (or at any rate of itself as the largest, generally in support of the PCF though it occasionally maintains a tactical and tactful distance), and also in the 'Statist' tradition, placing main emphasis upon the role of the State in intervening, and of State ownership along traditional lines. The CFDT, although generally sympathetic to the PS, is by no means as close to it organizationally as CGT to the Communists, and tends to favour economic changes which rely far less exclusively upon the State. It is hardly surprising, therefore, that, even in terms of general policy and orientation, relationships between them are strained.

But there are at least three other sources of difficulty. The first concerns personalities and styles. The second is that, broadly, the three have rather different characteristic 'constituencies', different areas of strength and weakness both in terms of economic sectors and regions. Third, and notwithstanding this second factor, the three are ultimately in competition, not just to poach members from each other (which happens on a small scale) but rather to obtain the allegiance of some substantial part of the great majority of non-unionized French workers. To do this, they believe they need to maintain a degree of 'product-differentiation', to appear distinctive and different from the others.

Georges Séguy was for a long time General Secretary of CGT, until replaced in June 1982 by Henri Krasucki. Séguy was very much a tough, if on occasion genial, worker who saw the CGT through a number of important shifts of policy in the 1970s. In the days of the common programme of the Left after 1972, the CGT generally showed its 'liberal' face: later, it obediently followed the PCF in making a united Left victory in 1978 virtually impossible. There were those who, after that, hoped the CGT could be opened up, and its tight control by PCF activists and its role as recruiting sergeant for the party loosened. In the event exactly the opposite happened. Henri Krasucki is regarded by most as very much a Stalinist amongst the party faithful. By contrast, Edmond Maire, CFDT General Secretary since 1971, has proved an influential and reflective individual, his manner quiet and rather shy, combining realism about what is immediately achievable with longer-range idealism, or in some eyes utopianism. Though himself a PS member, he also proved one of the most influential critics of the 1981–6 governments, asserting too that it was a duty of trade unionists to speak truths which the parties did not dare, concerning the government's policies and the country's economic options. The CFDT had proved also ready to enter a 'real dialogue' earlier, with the Giscard-Barre government from about 1978 to 1981, and positioned itself to retain the ear of the Chirac government in 1986.

The CGT's great strengths lie in much of heavy industry, in public sector industrial activities, and in such areas as the automotive sector. The FO's has been in the lower and middling echelons of the public service, (including white-collar) and also frequently in establishments where the *patronat* made clear its disapproval of the other confederations. The CFDT's is spread more evenly throughout activities and industries, but without a heartland of support of the kind that both CGT and FO have. It has attempted to attack CGT strongholds, especially where the CGT's attitudes have alienated immigrant workers.

Competition for the allegiance of the non-unionized seems to fly in the face of what evidence there is about the preferences of most workers themselves. Surveys suggest that a majority believe the existence of several confederations damages workers' interests and weakens the movement. In general, relations between the main confederations have grown worse since the late 1970s, and, unlike the parties of government, few formal arrangements for co-operation bind them together.

Relations with the political parties

The trade union confederations are almost always at pains to assert their independence from all political parties. They are just as regularly accused by the bulk of French workers of having too close affiliations with one or other party. The CGT-FO goes farthest in avoiding partisan party allegiance, not surprisingly since a significant minority of its members are supporters of parties of the Right and Centre.

At the other end of the scale comes the CGT, practising the Leninist principle of overlapping membership, with party membership as the determinant of suitability for a union job. All secretaries of CGT *unions départementales* are said to be PCF members, as well as about 90 per cent of heads of the CGT's industrial federations. The CFDT rides a little uneasily between these two situations, and has felt it of great importance not to be seen to be the spokesman of the PS.

The closeness of the CGT-PCF link was apparent throughout the period of Left governments from 1981–6. The level and nature of its criticisms followed those of the Party throughout: muted at first; more strident once the 'U-turn' in economic policy became apparent in 1982–3 and until the PCF ministerial participation came to an end in 1984; moving to the 'day of action' in October 1985 in protest at the government's policies. The general verdict on this 'great day', as the CGT leadership called it, was that it had been a flop. *Le Monde* opined that most wage-earners had been 'spectators'; that even the heartland of the public sector had been far from fully in support. It was a good bench-mark of 'united action' and 'fraternal solidarity': André Bergeron spoke of the predictable failure' which had 'tarnished the image of the union movement': M. Viannet of the CGT accused FO, CFDT and CGC of being 'passive' and only acting 'against' the CGT's initiative.

As the 1986 legislatives approached, it was commented that seldom had the CGT been more tightly bound to the Party; and that, given the declining popular appeal of each, this was a risky strategy. To date, so it has proved for both.

Nor did CFDT find itself in a much easier position. Maire persuaded his colleagues in the leadership not to advocate officially support for the Left; but several grass-roots revolts occurred. Having established his credentials for constructive dialogue, Maire warned Chirac that if the government could not control its more extreme elements, then it was putting at risk the development of orderly and structured relations with the unions. He criticized in particular the government's proposals, enacted in June 1986, to make redundancies easier.

At FO, Bergeron was able to follow the 'traditional' line of 'no instructions' on voting; but knew that he could not let himself be outflanked by CFDT and CGT, or accused of inaction. His known excellent personal relationship with Chirac was in this respect something of a two-edged weapon, and it was clear that he would have to be careful not to be seen as the government's 'poodle'.

What of the link between union membership and political allegiance or preference for the ordinary rank-and-file union member? The trends which appear are hardly startling, and the direction of causation difficult to identify, but we may note two in particular. First is family background: it appears that workers from Left-voting backgrounds are considerably more likely to join the CGT than are others. Second, the question of level of political commitment: while fairly apathetic Right- or Centre-leaning workers may be prepared to join CGT, those more politically interested are much less likely to do so; also political interest among left-wing workers seems still to incline people strongly to joining the CGT.

Relations with government

From the unions' point of view, relations with government have not depended merely upon what particular governments were trying to do, important though this has been. A good deal has depended on how they have felt themselves to be received and regarded by the various organs of the State and the administration. Traditionally, they have not been held in high esteem most of the time. Initial attempts to involve them in the planning process were at best only a slight success. The CFDT showed itself the most willing to be involved for the longest time, but finally it too felt it should indicate displeasure at not being able to influence inputs and priorities in time to have much impact. The importance attributed to 'planning' has in any case been highly variable: the Left made somewhat hesitant attempts to restore it from 1981–6; the apparent commitment of much of the Right post-1986 to economic 'liberalism' and deregulation appeared to leave little room for it.

In general, the unions are aware that the administration, in framing legislation or in seeking advice or sounding out opinion, distinguishes rather sharply between what it sees as professional associations, who are carefully cultivated and listened to, and mere lobbies or interest groups, who are usually not thought able to contribute much (apart from requests or demands) to the process of policy-formulation or implementation. For most of the Fifth Republic, trade unions have been uncomfortably aware of being labelled as the latter. They have, indeed, an even longer history of regarding the doings of government with suspicion, and the tradition will be hard to overcome.

Under the Left governments from 1981, the unions saw several of their leading figures co-opted into governmental positions: for instance, André Henri of FEN was made Minister for Free Time; Michel Roland of CFDT was put in charge of the Energy Control Agency. Yet most trade unionists (especially the rank and file) remained suspicious of the 'intellectuals and technocrats' of the government. This was seen, for example, at the time of the 1982 wage-and-price freeze, whose introduction coincided with the CGT Congress at Lille. While union leaders gave a mixed response to the economic policy of a government containing PCF members, the grass-roots response was distinctly chilly.

If such was the pattern under the Left, there seemed little reason to expect greater 'incorporation' or co-optation under the Right after the 1986 legislatives. To be sure, such appointments as those of E. Balladur as Minister of Economy, Finance and Privatization, and of P. Séguin at Social Affairs, were widely interpreted as signalling Chirac's concern to avoid provoking labour unrest. Yet the Chirac government was speedily warned not to pursue policies 'without wage-earners, let alone against them'.

This raises a very central issue for government–trade union relations in any country: namely, how far do the unions wish, and does the government encourage them, to be 'incorporated' into the structures of decision-making? In the French case, the answer from most quarters most of the time has been – not very much. Communist ministers in the Mauroy government made plain that they felt trade unionists retained a right and freedom to attack policy which they themselves did not have. Yet non-Communists fretted that the PCF, in conjunction with the CGT, would operate through the nationalization programme and the Auroux reforms to establish a much wider bridgehead of 'workers' power', as they claimed had happened back in the 'cold war' days of 1947–8.

Perhaps one of the most telling episodes regarding the ability of unions to 'dictate' policy, even to a government of Left, occurred over the Savary education Bill. The 1981–6 period was, after all, dubbed '*la République des professeurs*'; the teaching professions were extraordinarily heavily represented amongst Deputies and Ministers. Yet it proved to be the case that the wide control enjoyed by unions over 'personnel' and 'internal' professional matters did not extend to an ability to dictate terms over national education policy at the level of 'high politics', the shaping of the system, even under the 'ideal' conditions of 1981–6. While the *issue* may not have been typical, the *outcome* was very much so: the unions were not able to dictate policy, and their internal fragmentation and divisions were an important part of that weakness.

Relations of union leaderships with the rank and file

It is well known that French workers express greater resentment and a general sense of grievance and social injustice than, for example, similarly placed British workers. Why this is so is a more difficult issue. It is sometimes suggested that the unions themselves are the most important agents shaping the attitudes of the working class. But in France, where union membership is so low, it appears that the direct effect of the unions may be limited. It seems, rather, that the unions have played a major part in reinforcing a climate of antagonism and division inside French factories; but that this may be as much the result of their sense of weakness and inability to influence decisions as it is the result of conscious policy on their part. The resentment about their position, and about social inequality in general, seems much more the result of the actual climate of French industrial relations in most factories (at least until very recently) combined with the acknowledged high degree of inequality of income and wealth in France – higher than in almost all other west European countries.

Further, it appears that there is not any very strong correlation between the opinions of leaders of any particular union organization, and the opinions of that organization's rank and file. For example, on *autogestion*, a main hallmark of the CFTD leadership in recent years, the rank and file were less in favour of it than rank-and-file FO or CGT members. Further, it has not seemed to matter a great deal whether individuals were unionized or not: *all* French workers, unionized or not, appear to have a greater sense of resentment and grievance than comparable groups in several other countries.

The legitimacy accorded to the union organizations by most workers appears low. A SOFRES (*Société française d'enquêtes par sondage*) survey in October 1979 indicated that while in general terms it was thought to be useful to be a union member, there was much more scepticism about unions' efficiency in defending their members' interests. Low membership figures are only one indicator of low legitimacy. The CGT in particular has recently seemed out of step: it suffered substantial loss of membership between 1978 and 1985. In addition, in 1979, CGT members in the steel industry accepted redundancy terms which the confederation negotiating for them had rejected.

Relations with management

French management has been characterized as 'at best paternalistic and at worst thoroughly autocratic'. This situation has been to a large degree sustained by both union and management attitudes and circumstances. Many major milestones of union rights and recognition have either been very late in being reached, or have yet to be reached. Yet in certain respects the opposite has been true: labour practice is quite evolved, and legislation is strong on the protection of workers – over dismissal and compensation, retraining, maternity and other leave. Alongside this, however, has been a situation where, in many plants, the idea of regular bargaining and consultation is a real novelty. The unions have often found that they were only consulted in times of crisis – be it the 'global' one of the Events of 1968, or an acute sectoral crisis such as that in steel from 1979.

A main purpose of the proposals which Jean Auroux, as Minister of Labour, introduced in 1982, was to achieve a massive update of the labour code by revising about a third of it. The proposals showed that much that was already supposed to be in operation – notably in the field of *délégués du personnel* and *comités d'entreprise* – had simply not up to that time been applied. For the large employers of the *Confédération nationale du patronat français* (CNPF), Yves Gattaz appeared ready to enter into a dialogue with the government. In many respects, however, it was in smaller firms that basic workers' rights seemed farthest from realization; and here it was not the writ of CNPF which ran, but that of the increasingly militant SNPMI (*Syndicat national de la petite et moyenne industrie*), whose 'neo-Poujadist' guerrilla warfare, under its leader Georges Deuil, seemed intended to sabotage the Auroux reforms. Nor was SNPMI any longer a tiny and insignificant minority. From the unions' point of view, the future direction of management attitudes under the Chirac government appeared highly uncertain: within the CNPF leadership, disagreements that had been apparent for some time led to the resignation of Vice-President Chotard; but it was not clear how far these really indicated disagreement over policy. The CNPF and government appeared to have moved swiftly to make dismissals easier, thus getting relations between them and the unions off to a tense start.

Conclusion

The present position and prospects

In 1986, both the political context and the economic context appeared very unfavourable from the point of view of trade unions in France. Government and the parliamentary majority appeared more wedded to 'liberal' economic policies, including privatization and the reduction of the role of the State, than any French government for a long time. The speed with which this programme would be carried out, and its extent, would be clearly influenced by electoral considerations and the demands of '*cohabitation*' for as long as it lasted.

The response of the unions, after a period of *morosité*, was to promise a hot autumn of strikes and disruption. While the policies of the Chirac government might seem to give their militancy some edge, their numerical strength and morale have been sapped considerably in recent years and seem unlikely to recover swiftly.

Any estimation of the position has to take account of the relations between the leading confederations. While in several respects relations between the CFDT and CGT have improved over the last twenty or so years, ambiguities remain. The CGT still appears to be hitching itself firmly to a star which has been falling rather than rising: that of the PCF. The CGT still finds certain truths hard to face: not until after the 1986 election, so disastrous for the PCF, did CGT Secretary Warcholak admit that the membership losses suffered had been worse than those presented to the 42nd Congress only the previous November. The CGT and CFDT still represent almost what have been described as two 'separate sub-cultures' within French working-class life.

For the unions in general, the picture appears to be of considerable continuity with their past attitudes and traditions. They have become numerically weaker, and the likely economic evolution on France does not encourage belief that this trend is about to be rapidly reversed. 'United action' appears in most fields as elusive as ever. They were not sucked very far into a 'corporatist' dialogue with the Left government of 1981–6; and it appears that this is a temptation which will hardly be on offer under their successors.

At the time of the 1986 elections, there was a good deal of slightly airy talk about an 'emerging consensus' in French political life. One quite good indicator of how true such prognostications are will be found in those areas of life which touch trade unions most closely; but there must be doubts as to how deep the roots of this 'consensus' are. So far, there is little indication that government is prepared to have dealings with the unions of a more consensual kind; nor that they are in a position to attract it with any new initiatives they might propose.

Bibliography

Adam, P., Bon, F., Capdevielle, J. and Mouriaux, R., *L'Ouvrier français en 1970*. Paris, Colin, 1970. An opinion and attitude survey of over 1000 workers.

Andrieux, A. and Lignon, J., *Le Militant syndicaliste d'aujourd'hui*. Paris, Denoël, 1973. A survey of the motivations and attitudes of trade union militants.

Ardagh, J., *France in the 1980s*. London, Penguin, 1982. See in particular Part 2: 'The economy, modernized but menaced'.

Johnson, R.W., *The Long March of the French Left*. London, Macmillan, 1981.

Lefranc, G., *Le mouvement syndical de la libération aux événements de mai-juin 1968*. Paris, Payot, 1969. An excellent history of the trade union movement in this period.

Nugent, N. and Lowe, D., *The Left in France*. London, Macmillan, 1982.

Reynaud, J.D., *Les Syndicats en France*, 2 vols. Paris, Colin, 2nd edn, 1975. A comprehensive introduction with documents and bibliography.

Ross, G., *Workers and Communists in France*. Berkeley, University of California Press, 1982.

Sudreau Report. *Rapport du comité d'étude pour la réforme de l'entreprise* (Présidé par Pierre Sudreau.) Paris, La Documentation Française, 1975.

West European Politics. (journal), 3 (1) Jan. 1980. Special issue on trade unions and politics in western Europe, ed. J. Hayward. See in particular the section on France by D. Gallie.

Four

Immigrants

Brian Fitzpatrick

Introduction

There are currently some 4.5 million foreign nationals (out of a total population of just over 54 million) living in France. The precise number is impossible to establish, partly because of the continual arrival and departure of foreigners and their dependents, and also because of the undetermined but apparently considerable number of *clandestins*, illegal immigrants who have decided to stay beyond the validity of their residence permits, who have entered France on tourist visas and have then 'disappeared' into the immigrant community, or who have simply crossed a land frontier illicitly. Thus, while officially registered foreigners make up 6.8 per cent of the population, it is estimated that the total size of the immigrant community may amount to as much as 8 or 8.5 per cent.

It is important to set these figures in a context. First, France has a long tradition of accepting immigrants for both political and economic reasons. In the nineteenth century Poles, Italians and east European Jews fled westwards to avoid political persecution. In the twentieth century White Russians, Spanish Republicans and Latin Americans have figured prominently among the political exiles, who now number some 142,000. Belgium, Italy and Spain also have long-standing traditions of seasonal migration to France and have, in some cases, well established permanent communities on French soil – the Belgian, Polish and Piedmontese mining communities, for example. Thus, by the 1930s, the immigrant community was proportionally almost as large as it is today.

Second, the foreign population of France should be seen in relation to that of other developed European countries. Immigration is now a phenomenon which affects almost all the world's developed nations as the citizens of poor countries seek a share of the wealth they see generated in the rich. At present foreign nationals constitute about 3 per cent of the population of the United Kingdom, 7 per cent of that of West Germany, 9 per cent of that of Belgium, 16 per cent of that of Switzerland and as much as 26 per cent of the population of Luxembourg. These countries and others like the Netherlands and Sweden have accepted immigrants for both political and economic reasons, but only France and the United Kingdom illustrate plainly the particular problems of immigration linked to a colonial past. Both countries have been trying to come to terms with people who, by their language, religion and general cultural outlook, are outsiders, but who are in many cases citizens of the mother country or are attached to it by colonial links only recently weakened. In the case of France the problem affects people born in Algeria before 1962 and who have not abjured their French citizenship, and citizens of those African states which, at the end of the Second World War, became members of the *Union française*, a kind of French Commonwealth. To a lesser extent popular prejudices affect the 120,000 natives of the *Départements d'outre mer* (Guadeloupe, Guyane, Martinique, La Réunion) and the *Territoires d'outre mer* (New Caledonia, French Polynesia, Mayotte and Wallis and Futuna) who live in France. We shall see that French attitudes to citizenship and the weight of past decisions combine with the present climate of unemployment and heightened social tensions to make life difficult for the children of immigrants.

A brief survey of the salient features of France's foreign population reveals the reason why immigrants have come to France and why the present economic climate has brought tensions to the fore. It remains clear that the principal reason was the prospect of work. In spite of a recent influx of dependants (*le regroupement familial*), males still predominate in the foreign community: 57 per cent against 48 per cent of the 'French' population. Fifty per cent of immigrants as opposed to 40 per cent of the 'French' population fall within the 25 to 55 age group. But now, while unemployment is affecting French and immigrant workers, the latter are experiencing higher levels. Almost 15 per cent of immigrants are unemployed while the level among the French is about 8.4 per cent; unemployment has tripled among immigrants in the last decade while increasing roughly 2.5 times among French workers. At the same time immigrants have larger families than the French, and are increasingly accused of being an unnecessary burden on the state. French women have 1.8 children on average; immigrant women an average of 3.16. In 1975 immigrant births accounted for 5.6 per cent of all births in France; in 1985 the figure was nearly 11 per cent. Within these broad figures lies a fact that is unpalatable to many French people: the biggest population increase is among Moslem North Africans of whom 45 per cent of Algerian couples and 49 per cent of Moroccan couples have more than three children.

Such facts have had a direct bearing on the way in which the conduct of immigration and the rights immigrants should enjoy has been debated over the last decade. In conjunction with the overall economic climate, *le problème des immigrés* has undoubtedly encouraged the resurgence of the extreme right in French politics. In the March 1986 general election, the *Front national* led by Jean-Marie Le Pen, who has made immigration a major plank in his political platform, took 9.8 per cent of the vote (as much as the Communist Party) and had 35 *députés* elected to the National Assembly. The campaign itself was littered with allegations of attacks on and by immigrants, so burning had the issue become. But it is not simply a question of unemployment ('2 millions de chômeurs, c'est 2 millions d'immigrés de trop' was Le Pen's slogan in the early 1980s). The current Islamic revival and the extension to France and to other European countries of various Middle Eastern disputes in the form of terrorism have focused further attention on the Moslems who now make up nearly 5 per cent of the population.

Sources of immigration

Since the end of the Second World War the national and racial composition of France's foreign population has undergone

profound changes. Before 1940 immigrants were almost exclusively European and Catholic – Belgians, Poles, Italians,
Spaniards and Russians. Now just over half of the foreigners are
from Moslem, Black African and Asian countries. This marked
shift has been brought about by changing political and
economic circumstances rather than by any conscious change
in immigration policy. In the aftermath of the war distant
lands like the Americas, Canada, Australia and South Africa
seemed to offer better prospects for those seeking to leave
behind the psychological scars of war and the shattered
economies of victor and vanquished alike. Moreover, the
reconstruction of the European economies provided fresh opportunities in more countries for workers who preferred to remain in Europe. Thus France, a traditional importer of labour
now dedicated to economic recovery based on the importation
of labour on a large scale, found herself in competition with
reconstruction in Italy and, most notably, West Germany
whose *Wirtschaftswunder* was due in no small part to immigrant labour. Consequently France resorted increasingly to
immigrants from the south-eastern fringes of Europe, from
North and Black Africa and from Turkey.

Immigrants from European countries now account for no
more than 48 per cent of the foreign population as compared
with 60 per cent in 1975 or 81 per cent in 1954. Moreover the
profile of the European immigrant community has changed
considerably. The number of Belgians has declined steadily,
from 349,000 in 1921 to its present level of 50,000; Poles have
declined from 507,000 in 1931 to the present level of just over
64,000; and Italians, who numbered 808,000 in 1931, are now
reduced to 333,000. If fewer immigrants are coming from these
countries, those who have been in France for a number of years
have integrated well: Italians and Spaniards together make up
almost half of the immigrant population aged 65 and above. If
figures were available for the number of French men and
women who are the children and grandchildren of immigrants,
the impact of immigration from countries like Italy, Spain and
Poland would be seen very clearly. Spaniards have, however,
displayed a slightly different tendency from the Italians and
Poles. The peak of Spanish immigration to France was reached
in 1975, and then fell dramatically, possibly a reflection of at-

titudes to the demise of the Franco regime and to industrial development in Spain.

In marked contrast to those national groups which have declined within the European immigrant community, the Portuguese have grown considerably in numbers, from 20,000 in 1954 to about 760,000 at present, and now constitute 20 per cent of the foreign population. This immigration accelerated dramatically in the 1960s as a result of French economic expansion and the closure of Brazil to unskilled labour. In spite of intergovernmental agreements and quotas, the demand from Portugal for jobs in France was such that Portuguese immigration became synonymous with illegal immigration. Subsequently French policy has enabled dependents to join the wage earner, and the Portuguese are showing clear signs of establishing themselves as a permanent community with their children making up almost a quarter of the foreign children below the age of fifteen.

For a time Yugoslavs represented a small but steady influx of immigrants. In 1954 they numbered only 17,000 but reached, in 1975, some 70,000. Again, Yugoslav immigration was the consequence of stated French manpower requirements in the 1960s and was the subject of an intergovernmental agreement in 1965. Since 1975 the Yugoslav community has declined to 64,000, and it has not shown signs of establishing itself on a significant scale in France in the manner of other immigrant groups.

The most striking feature of post-war immigration is the presence of a large Moslem population – Algerians, Moroccans, Tunisians in the main, but Turks as well. North Africans, *Maghrebins*, were barely 2 per cent of immigrants in 1946. They now constitute almost 40 per cent of the officially registered immigrant population. Algerians, of whom there are more than 800,000 in France, are by far the most numerous. They have constituted a special case in the history of French immigration and enjoyed between 1947 and 1962 the same freedom of movement in France as the French themselves. After Algerian independence in 1962 the French and Algerian governments collaborated to regulate population movements between the two countries. An agreement made in 1968 recognized the special status of Algerians in France by granting them a ten-year residence permit instead of the three-year permits normally delivered to immigrants. At the same time, the French authorities reserved the right to impose a quota each year and to repatriate Algerians who failed to find work within nine months of their arrival. This arrangement broke down in 1973 when the Algerians, concerned at the rise in anti-Arab feeling in France, suspended the issue of visas for France. A subsequent agreement, reached in 1980, is primarily concerned with improving the rights of Algerians already resident in France.

The volume of Algerian migration has been enormous, with 4.5 million entries to France recorded for workers alone between 1947 and 1973. But the size of the Algerian community in France and, above all, its rate of growth, has fluctuated considerably, almost on a year-to-year basis. The most extreme examples of the fluctuation were seen in 1951 on the one hand, when a massive crop failure in Algeria provoked an entry of 55,000 Algerians to France, and in 1958 on the other hand when, at the height of Franco-Algerian hostilities, the Algerian population of France decreased by 14,000. Over the past decade the Algerian community has increased less by immigration than by births, and Algerians currently make up just over 21 per cent of the foreign population of France.

The early 1960s witnessed a significant increase in immigration from Morocco and Tunisia as well. Both countries had been within the French sphere of influence since the mid-nineteenth century, and were happy to enter into an agreement with France in 1963 which sought to promote immigration. The impact was immediate. Twelve thousand Moroccans entered France in 1963 and by 1973 that figure had risen to 39,000. In the same decade the Tunisian rate of entry rose from 4000 to 25,000. Moroccans now number 421,000, Tunisians 189,000. Together they account for 16 per cent of the entire foreign population and display clear signs of becoming established in France, accounting for 23 per cent of the immigrant population under the age of fourteen, a higher percentage than any of the other immigrant groups.

The most recent source of Moslem immigration is Turkey. In the 1950s, Turks were as few as Tunisians – about 5000. Then, with the economic expansion of the 1960s, Turkish labour was sought by firms in France and in West Germany. Only 500 Turks entered France in 1965, but a decade later 17,000 entered the country in one year, by which time the Turkish community had grown to 48,000. In spite of the slump of the mid-1970s and attendant immigration controls, the Turkish community has not ceased to grow and at its present 124,000 represents some 3.3 per cent of the total immigrant population. The growth has come largely from the arrival of workers' dependents and Turkish births in France.

Black Africans constitute just 4 per cent of the foreign population. Like the Portuguese, Africans were involved in the massive illegal immigration of the 1960s and 1970s, and their true numbers are undoubtedly higher than the 138,000 indicated in official statistics. The principal nationalities present in France are the Senegalese (27–28,000), Maliens (18,000), Cameroonians (12,000) and Ivoiriens (11,000). Immigration from Black Africa has come essentially from former French possessions and has followed three broad phases. The first Africans to settle in any numbers were former colonial troops who chose to stay after their demobilization following the First and Second World Wars. These were followed in the late 1950s by Africans who had lived and studied or worked in French Africa's Europeanized towns – Abidjan, Dakar, Libreville, Douala and Yaoundé. After the demise of the post-war French Union and the creation of a much looser association of former French possessions, the Community, many Africans took advantage of co-operation and immigration agreements between France and the member states. The majority of these immigrants who began to flood in during the 1960s came directly from the interior of their countries and had little experience of city life.

Finally one should not overlook the 170,000 Asians in France. These, mainly Vietnamese, Cambodians and Laotians, make up some 4.6 per cent of the total foreign population. Their presence is a strong reflection of France's former role in the Far East as a colonial power, certainly, but also of the upheavals that region has experienced since decolonization in the 1950s. Between 1954 (partition of French Indo-China into North and South Vietnam) and 1975, the Asian population in France rose from just over 35,000 to more than 103,000. Since

1975 (collapse of South Vietnam; victory of the Communist *Khmer rouge* in Cambodia; establishment of a People's Democratic Republic in Laos), the figure has risen to just over 170,000.

French immigration policy since 1945

Immigration to France has been essentially a response to the country's economic development. As such it has been promoted and controlled by the State, frequently, but not always, in conjunction with the governments of countries willing or eager to export their surplus labour. At the end of the Second World War France embarked on a policy of reconstruction and growth based on a planned economy. The task the planners faced in 1945 was enormous. The material effects of war and occupation had reduced her productive capacity to 38 per cent of that of 1938. More important in the long term was the cumulative effect of two world wars on the size and character of the population. The First World War left 1,350,000 dead and 2,500,000 invalids and widows. It also left the legacy of *les classes creuses*, the severely depleted age groups caused by a dramatic shortage of births in the post-war years, so that on the eve of the Second World War deaths were exceeding live births in the annual statistics. The 600,000 dead and 98,000 badly wounded left by the Second World War compounded France's demographic problems. The *Commissariat au Plan*, the body responsible for drawing up the national plan, advised the government in 1945 that the target for the First Plan (*Plan Monnet*, 1945–51), to attain 125 per cent of the 1929 output, could not be reached unless 1.5 million workers could be induced to move to France. Sustained growth, it was argued, could be facilitated if immigrants settled in France and raised families, thereby contributing to population growth and stimulating demand on the domestic market. Consequently the French government formulated an immigration policy based on four principles: immigration would be massive; it would be carefully organized; the State would have a monopoly in the sphere of recruitment; immigrants would be encouraged to integrate into French society. This last point is crucial. It represented the government's intention to extend to immigrants the principle of assimilation which had pervaded French colonial thought, the ideal of enabling people of different races to become children of France, and it distinguished French immigration policy from that of the other main continental labour-importing countries, Switzerland and West Germany, where a rigid distinction has been maintained between nationals and immigrant workers. Without doubt the idealism of the November 1945 ordinance on immigration reflects the heady atmosphere of the Liberation. It was drafted by men and women who solemnly reaffirmed the Declaration of the Rights of Man and of the Citizen in the preamble to the Constitution of the Fourth Republic and who, condemning colonialism, sought to replace the French Empire with a Union in which there would be no juridical distinction between the French and the 'overseas peoples'. Contradictions inherent in many of the measures drawn up quickly combined with trends beyond the control of the French to distort an immigration policy which was intended to be both generous and efficient.

The government agencies established to oversee immigration (*Ministère de la Population et de la Santé publique*; *Office national de l'Immigration* or ONI) set out to attract immigrants from traditional sources. Immigrants were to be recruited from European countries with which France enjoyed long-standing good relations and whose people had already shown that they could integrate easily into French society: French-speaking Belgians, Basques and Swiss, for example, or Piedmontese. Immigrants from North Africa were to be discouraged, including Algerians, the majority of whom were second-class citizens at the time, even though Algeria was technically part of France.

Two things upset this approach to immigration from the start. First, those immigrants the French considered most desirable did not come to France in sufficient numbers. Paradoxically, the French authorities were trying to attract immigrants to a relatively penurious and inflationary economy. The United States, Canada and, in Europe itself, Switzerland and West Germany proved to be more attractive rivals. Second, in 1947 the National Assembly voted the Algerian Statute which admitted Moslem Algerians to full civil rights, including the right to move freely between France and Algeria.

As a result, hundreds of thousands of Algerians could and did seek work in France without having to go through the controls of the ONI. Thus, between 1947 and 1949, just over half of the immigrants who settled in France were Algerians, while Europeans (mainly Italians) and stateless persons made up just 48 per cent of immigrants. This pattern continued into the 1950s so that, by 1955, 155,000 Algerians had moved to France against 111,000 immigrants sponsored by ONI. Subsequently, France accepted that her labour force would have to be recruited increasingly from areas which the original planners had sought to avoid, or to which they had assigned only a marginal role, if planning targets were to be met. Thus, the Fifth Plan (1966–70) assumed an annual net immigration of 135,000 workers, while the Sixth Plan (1971–5) included a net annual immigration of 75,000, until the energy crisis of 1973 and subsequent increased costs forced the government to alter its perspectives.

France was faced with the problem of seeking to maintain levels of immigration while retaining some degree of control: it is thought that nearly half the immigrants entering the country in the 1960s did so illegally. The most significant step taken involved bilateral agreements with the labour-supplying countries. Quotas were agreed and some of the responsibility for vetting prospective immigrants was delegated to the countries of emigration. The first such agreement was made with Algeria shortly after she gained her independence in 1962, and an *Office national algérien de la main d'oeuvre* (ONAMO) processed intending emigrants, issuing health certificates and exit visas. This became the model for subsequent agreements with Morocco, Tunisia, Mauretania, Mali and Portugal in 1963; with Senegal in 1964; and with Yugoslavia and Turkey in 1965. In 1968 the agreements were revised in a manner which enabled France to determine unilaterally the annual quota of immigrants and to repatriate those who failed to find work within nine months of their arrival. By 1971, Black Africans, notorious illegal immigrants, were required to have a written offer of employment before they were admitted.

The curbing of illegal immigration was the other main way in which France adapted her policy. Until 1968 illegal immigrants were encouraged to regularize their status if they found steady employment. It was less troublesome to recognize successfully employed workers than to embark upon expulsion or imprisonment procedures, and according to official estimates many immigrants took advantage of the procedure: it is reckoned that as many as 82 per cent were legally registered in 1968 against 77 per cent in 1966. Critics of the procedure pointed out that this was a loophole: why should an immigrant bother to apply formally (and run the risk of being refused) when he could enter the country illegally, find a job and then register with little fuss? In the event, expulsion became systematic for anyone entering the country illegally after 1968, but subsequent governments have offered amnesties from time to time, evidence that the threat of expulsion has not deterred illegal immigration.

The slump of the mid-1970s and consequent increases in unemployment put pressure on governments to take more stringent action. The most striking of these was the suspension of immigration (with the exception of authorized dependents) in 1974. Then, in 1980, it was proposed that only three-year work permits be issued, subject to review in the light of local employment conditions when their validity expired. This proposal would have drastically altered the conditions in which immigrants lived, breaking with the principle of security of residence on which immigration policy had been founded in 1945. However, events overtook the government of Giscard d'Estaing in May and June 1981, when the Socialists came to power. Already other draconian proposals directed at weakening the position of immigrants had been tried but overruled by the *Conseil d'Etat*, most notably the Bonnet and Stoléru proposals of 1980 which aimed at expelling without appeal the estimated 30,000 illegal immigrants still in France and any foreigner charged with conduct contrary to public order – a measure many felt would be used to remove or to muzzle even long-established legal immigrants active in civil rights movements. In addition to these restrictive proposals, immigrants were encouraged to return home with financial inducements. The *aide au retour* was first introduced in 1975 under the Chirac government, but was substantially revised by the Barre government in 1977, when any immigrant who had been in France for five years or more, or who was unemployed, was offered 10,000 francs to go home and not to seek readmission to France. It has been estimated that 100,000 workers and dependants took advantage of this offer between 1977 and 1981, but critics of the scheme say that the wrong immigrants left – qualified Spaniards and Italians rather than unskilled North Africans.

The coming to power of the Socialists in 1981 eased the pressures on immigrants somewhat, but did not reassure them fully. Illegal immigrants were offered the opportunity to regularize their position (more than 132,000 did so); and the expulsion process was removed from the administrative domain and placed in the hands of the ordinary courts of the land (certain categories, minors, for example, were granted immunity against expulsion). At the same time, the issue of work permits remained restricted and related directly to employment opportunities in any given sector of the economy; and the *aide au retour* has been retained in a modified form which actively assists unemployed immigrants to find a job in their country of origin with the aid of that country's government. Some 50,000 took advantage of this process in the twelve months following its implementation in 1984. In the domain of civil rights, the Socialists passed a law which limited the right of police and gendarmes to demand people's identity papers on a random basis. Immigrants and their friends had long complained about police harassment based on what they considered to be nothing more than racial prejudice.

The election of a conservative coalition under Jacques Chirac in March 1986 will probably lead to further attempts to stamp out illegal immigration and to repatriate unemployed immigrants, although the RPR and UDF spokesmen emphasized that those with jobs and the required legal status would not be threatened in any way, provided they respected the law of the land. There is a clear move by the new government to distinguish between certain immigrant rights (education, social security, medical treatment) and those linked to the possession of French nationality – the right to vote, for example. The Socialist government had begun to examine the possibility of giving the vote to immigrants in local elections, and immigrants themselves had begun to seek that right. It seems certain that those who do not take out French nationality will not be allowed to take part in politics; there may well also be a move to end both the automatic acquisition of French citizenship which the children of immigrants enjoy unless they specifically reject it, and the automatic acquisition of French citizenship by marriage to a French citizen. Such moves imply a wish to create a distinction between 'authentic' immigrants, who choose to identify with France fully, and those whose only bond with the country is through employment, frequently for a period which suits them, and without any clear idea of settling in France and accepting French norms.

Immigrants and the French economy

Since 1945, French economic growth has counted on immigration to provide manpower and, to a lesser degree, consumption. Immigrants have traditionally undertaken unskilled and manual work, and the higher one goes up the social ladder, the fewer immigrants one finds. Thus, 64 per cent of the immigrant working population are labourers or factory workers against 29 per cent of the 'French' working population; 10 per cent are in service jobs like cleaning, refuse disposal and the domestic side of hotel and catering, in comparison with some 4 per cent of the French labour force. As soon as little or manual work is involved in a job, the proportions change significantly: if 18 per cent of immigrants are *employés* (office workers, shop assistants, caretakers, etc.), just over 26 per cent of the French workforce is employed in this rather general category; and immigrants number only 3.6 per cent of the artisans, *commerçants* and *chefs d'entreprise* category against 8 per cent of the French, and less than 5 per cent of executives and members of the professions which include 9 per cent of the French working population. Put another way, immigrants make up almost 14 per cent of the manual categories, less than 5 per cent of *employés* and less than 4 per cent of both executive and professional categories.

Certain types of employment have, over the past twenty-five years, become almost completely dependent on immigrant labour: building and public works, and the motor industry, for example. Undoubtedly the high concentration of immigrant labour in these areas has helped to keep costs down, but recently critics of the State's (and the employers') reliance on immigration have begun to suggest that the availability of cheap and docile labour may have made the *patronat* both lazy and greedy, and that, in the long term, French industry may have made itself less competitive. A case in point is the motor industry. When, in 1974, immigration was suspended, two of the largest car manufacturers made a special plea to the government on the grounds that production would be seriously affected if the supply of cheap labour was cut off suddenly. At the time, 80 per cent of the workers on the assembly line in car factories in the Paris region were foreigners. There are documented cases of industrialists relying on a plentiful supply of immigrant labour as an alternative to modernization which would have required a considerable capital investment beyond their means. In this respect, illegal immigration also had a role to play. However weak the bargaining position of recently arrived immigrants may have been even though they were unionized, the illegal immigrant was in an infinitely worse position and completely at the mercy of his or her employer with no recourse to law or to union representation. Labour-intensive industries with small units of production, like garments, were able to exploit illegal immigrants in the traditional 'sweatshop' manner, paying a pittance to workers who frequently slept on the premises and lived in terror of expulsion.

In the climate of expansion which prevailed in the 1960s, immigrants were deemed to be an economic asset to France. The Sixth Plan (1971–5) calculated that their contribution to the economy amounted to some 90,000,000 francs after the cost of wages, medical attention and public housing for them had been taken into account. Indeed, at that time, the majority of immigrants were young, single and healthy, making few demands on the State's resources. Since the mid-1970s, however, France has begun to look upon the immigrants as a financial burden. Unemployment has hit them much more severely than it has affected the French: immigrants now constitute 15 per cent of those who have had a job, and unemployment among young immigrants or the children of immigrants has reached 34 per cent. Also, the bulk of the immigration which has occurred since 1974 has concerned dependants: wives and children who, far from contributing to the economy, are taking from it in family allowances, medical costs and other aspects of the Welfare State. This is a dramatic reversal of the pattern in the 1960s, and one which few French people appear willing to accept as reasonable at a time when there is so much unemployment among the 'French' themselves. However, as one expert, Georges Tapinos, has pointed out (*L'Express*, 21 February 1986), any serious estimate of the benefits and costs of immigrants to the French economy should take account of the last thirty years rather than the last decade. Such objectivity is hard to achieve among the general public or among politicians, for whom the short-term effects of immigration are paramount.

Immigrants and French society

The lowly occupations of most immigrants reflect their place in French society. They are, broadly speaking, at the bottom of the pile with few prospects of rising beyond the ownership of a grocery shop or café in an immigrant *quartier* of Paris or an industrial centre in the provinces. As recent events have shown, they have minimal contacts with the French, and the two communities live in mutual incomprehension which can quickly turn to fear or hatred. There are many reasons for their marginal socio-economic position, some inherent in the immigrants themselves, others the result of the way in which their community was allowed to develop.

Many immigrants arrived in France with few or no skills and with very little education. Manual work was all they could do, and was all they intended to do. Emigration represented a chance of earning more money or of avoiding unemployment in their own country. Their lack of French was a handicap as much as their lack of skill. In the case of North Africans, their religious practices set them apart from the French as well. Even if many Moslems ceased to practise their religion strictly, they carried with them deep-rooted aspects of a general Islamic culture as well as local or tribal peculiarities which pushed them together in a sort of ghetto. Positive action would have been required to ensure integration and such action was simply not taken. First, ONI was utterly unprepared for the influx of Moslems, having expected Italians, Spaniards and Belgians; then, the bulk of the North Africans were Algerians over whom ONI had no jurisdiction. Consequently large numbers of immigrants were left to their own devices and to the goodwill of the French population, 63 per cent of whom had expressed their opposition to large-scale immigration in an IFOP (*Institut français d'opinion publique*) poll in 1948. Inevitably, national groups clung together, and began to take over the less salubrious parts of the towns to which they gravitated in search of work. The authorities took little interest in the phenomenon of immigration apart from its purely economic aspect until the massive illegal immigration of the 1960s produced the *bidonvilles*, the shanty towns which sprang up on the outskirts of most French industrial centres. In 1968 some 75,000 immigrants were believed to be *bidonville* dwellers. Such funds as were available for them – the *Fonds d'action sociale* (FAS) for example, were woefully inadequate in the face of the extensive immigration of the 1960s, and intergovernmental agreements on quotas and welfare came too late to relieve the problem of poor living conditions and cultural isolation which affected many. North Africans also had to contend with the hostility generated by the Algerian war between 1956 and 1962.

Indeed it was not until the 1970s and the saturation of the labour market that the authorities began to take a serious interest in the situation of the immigrants as part of an overall policy. Under Valéry Giscard d'Estaing, a Secretary of State for immigrants was appointed in 1974 and more funds were made available for housing. Plans were also announced to promote integration (*l'insertion*) by dispersing the inhabitants of dilapidated ghettos among HLM (*habitations à loyer modéré* or public housing) estates and by providing specialized education programmes. As far as dispersing immigrants was concerned, the plan failed because of a process of 'natural selection': certain housing estates were gradually turned into new ghettos because the French residents moved away as the immigrants moved in, bringing their own customs with them. The gulf which separated them from the French was too wide to be bridged overnight.

The slump which began in the mid-1970s also brought new pressures to bear as competition for jobs increased. Less equipped to compete, young immigrants and the children of immigrant parents began to figure more and more prominently in France's crime statistics. They were responsible for roughly 17 per cent of crimes committed in 1985, for example, while North Africans make up 15 per cent of the prison population of France. Such figures are taken up by sections of the population who are already frightened by the sea of dark faces they encounter every day in the street, on buses and in the underground, who fear unemployment and who seek security. Immigrants are the obvious target or scapegoat, and politicians on the Right have not been slow to play on these fears. Indeed, even the PCF found that attacking them won support from its traditional French electorate, and in one notorious incident a Communist mayor requisitioned a bulldozer and flattened a hostel intended for immigrant workers. Champions of the immigrants' cause argue that the level of delinquency and criminality among immigrants is a reflection of their isolation and despair, and that integration must necessarily be a long process and one in which the greatest effort must come from the French.

But how much integration do the immigrants want? This question is particularly important in the context of the Islamic revival. Islam specifically rejects integration into non-Islamic societies, and, even though most Moslem immigrants come from 'secular' states like Algeria, Morocco and Tunisia, the size and cohesion of the Moslem minority in Paris, Marseille and Lyon gives rise to fears of the development, if not of a 'state within the State', of a threatening cultural monolith capable of a fanaticism which Europe has not experienced for centuries. It is estimated that there are now about 1000 mosques and Moslem prayer houses in France, with plans to build many more. For many French men and women, the mosque is more than the place of worship of a foreign minority; it is a symbol of an alien culture which is perceived as increasingly threatening. The now banal photographs of a muezzin summoning the faithful to prayer from the heights overlooking Givors (Rhône), or of entire streets on their knees for daily prayer in parts of Marseille do nothing to play down the 'mass movement' aspect of Moslem France. Reactions can be brutal:

the indiscriminate murder of a young Moroccan in Menton by a Frenchman whose personal misfortunes had nothing to do with foreigners, but who obviously considered them to be somehow responsible for his plight; the white resident of a HLM complex who, driven to his limit by the noise made by immigrants, shot dead a small African boy who was in a group playing noisily near his window; the residents of Belle-Ile (Morbihan) who felt sufficiently provoked by a minor clash with the members of a Paris-organized summer camp for adolescents (90 per cent of whom were of North African parentage), to march on the camp one night shouting racist slogans in order to intimidate the campers; the Breton café proprietor for whom a nearby Turkish-owned café became such an obsession that he finally fired both barrels of a shotgun through the window, seriously injuring a number of the Turkish customers.

As the French press regularly records, such extreme cases of racial loathing are by no means uncommon. And it is by no means clear that such strength of feeling pervades only the less educated or lower classes, or what Yves Boisset, in the title of his film made in 1975, called the *Dupont Lajoie* of contemporary France. In a recent debate organized by the radio station RTL and the magazine *Paris Match*, the former Justice Minister, Alain Peyrefitte, stated that, although scientists may not be able to define the notion of race, 'les bonnes gens, eux, sont tout à fait capables de la sentir'. He went on to allege that General de Gaulle said to him in 1959 on the subject of North African immigration: 'Si on fait l'intégration, dans vingt ans mon village ne s'appellera pas Colombey-les-deux-Eglises mais Colombey-les-deux-Mosquées' (*Paris Match*, 22 November 1985).

In the same debate, an immigrants' rights spokesman, Harlem Desiré, made the point that conflict was no longer really about immigration, but about race. At present, there are about 950,000 children with foreign parents living in France, almost 26 per cent of the foreign population and 8.5 per cent of the total population of France. Given the higher birth rate among foreigners, this proportion can only increase. The law at present states that unless these minors opt for the nationality of their parents, they are automatically classed as French citizens at the age of eighteen and enjoy full civil and political rights as a result. In fact, the majority of immigrants' children are French in their experience of education, health and welfare, leisure activities, radio and television. Many have never visited their parents' homeland, and a considerable number of those who do return for a holiday find it impossible to relate to a world they have never known and to values which seem strange. They are French in many important ways, and yet they are very often marginal, partly because of handicaps inherent in their upbringing, partly because of widespread hostile social attitudes.

The second generation, or *beurs*, as they have become known, begin life with many handicaps. French is rarely the language spoken in the home, and their parents are rarely attuned to the way things are done in France. Nor are they generally wealthy enough to provide their children with material and cultural aids to integration and advancement. The language barrier causes immigrant children to fall behind at school, and a 'natural selection' occurs as many parents conclude that the presence in the classroom of a number of these children will hold back their own, French, children: 'Je fais 32 kilomètres par jour', avoue un commerçant, père de deux enfants, 'alors qu'on a une école à 200 mètres. Je ne suis pas raciste, mais je ne veux pas sacrifier l'avenir de mes enfants' (*Le Monde*, 20 September 1983). In the main, immigrants' children leave school earlier than French children and with fewer qualifications. Thus they are doomed to repeat their parents' experience of working in the lowest paid jobs. In the present economic climate, this also leaves them with a very high level of unemployment. Once they enter their teens, they frequently become painfully aware of their ambiguous position, having to relate to French norms outside the home but to 'foreign' norms within it. Tensions between society and the family can build up easily, putting considerable pressure on the adolescent, particularly if his or her parents are from an authoritarian culture and are unable or unwilling to recognize that behaviour which they consider intolerable – staying out late, frequenting discos, for example – is in fact normal in the society to which their children have become accustomed.

Such handicaps are then compounded by widespread and

crude social attitudes to the colour of their skin or other distinctive physical features. If immigrants have been made, collectively, a scapegoat for social and economic distress, individual immigrants can quickly become the scapegoat for their entire community and can experience personally the suspicion and animosity which is directed at it at large. Conversely, immigrants complain that they are all 'tarred with the same brush', and that the shortcomings and crimes of a minority are imputed to all without distinction: '*les* immigrés sont paresseux; *ils* font du bruit dans les HLM; *ils* vivent sur le dos des Français'. It is largely this undiscriminating attitude to 'les gens de couleur' that the *beurs* have been trying to challenge in recent years. Undoubtedly the Socialist government from 1981 to 1986 encouraged them to express their grievances and to raise their expectations by the creation of agencies like the *Conseil national des peuples immigrés* and by restricting the right of the police to check identity papers at will. The *beurs* undertook a spectacular 'tour de France' in the autumn of 1984 called *Convergences '84*, when hundreds toured the major towns of France on mopeds and motor scooters drawing attention to their grievances and seeking to increase support for and understanding of their cause. In the event, the exercise had little effect, preaching to the converted on the one hand, and hardening attitudes on the other: 'la revendication des 《droits》 de la citoyenneté est assortie du refus des 《obligations》 de la nationalité' noted the conservative *Spectacle du Monde* (February 1986).

Conclusion

For the first time since 1945, immigration has become a central political question in France. In the 1986 legislative election, all the main parties included policy statements in their manifestos. In practice, immigration has stopped, except for authorized dependants, and the focus of the debate has shifted to problems relating to the immigrants in France, problems of their numbers, their legal position, their rights and those of their children. It is clear that governments will pursue illegal immigrants and will maintain vigilance at French frontiers. It seems probable, too, that pressure will be put on immigrants to integrate more fully than they have done in the past, that is to accept French norms and the French way of life if they intend to stay. At the same time, a majority of the population wants to prevent them from affecting French laws and norms simply by weight of numbers. In a poll carried out immediately after the March 1986 election, 57 per cent of the voters expressed their desire to have the *Code de la nationalité* tightened so that immigrants' children no longer became French by default, without having to give any signs of commitment to the country (*Le Monde*, 25 March 1986). Such measures are bound to increase friction between immigrants and the authorities, and they are going to affect those from Black and North Africa in particular, now that Spain and Portugal are members of the EEC and their citizens have freedom of access to job vacancies in France. Increasingly, the problem of immigration is linked to racial attitudes and the limits of toleration in a society experiencing considerable economic and social hardship. There is little evidence at present that toleration will prevail: fear and insecurity are the emotions which dominate any discussion of the future of immigrants in France, and a large number of French men and women, including politicians, want the matter settled promptly and unequivocally.

Bibliography

In addition to the articles mentioned in the text, see:

Les Cahiers français, 219. (Jan – Feb. 1985); 'La population française de A à Z' for basic statistical data.

'*Dossiers et documents*', Paris, *Le Monde*, ten issues per year: 115 (October 1984), 'Les immigrés en France'; 122 (May 1985), 'L'Insécurité'; 130 (Feb. 1986), 'La Société française'.

Hargreaves, A., *Immigration in France*. London, Methuen, 1987.

Marangé, J. and Lebon, A. *L'insertion des jeunes d'origine étrangère dans la société française*. Paris, la Documentation française, 1982.

Le Nouvel Observateur, 1109 (7–13 Feb. 1986) contains an important article on Islam in France.

Oriol, P., *Les immigrés, métèques ou citoyens!* Paris, Syros, 1985.

Le Spectacle du Monde, 287 (Feb. 1986) contains a digest of recent and sometimes controversial studies of immigration.

Tapinos, G., *L'immigration étrangère en France de 1946 à 1973*. Paris, PUF, 1975.

Five

Foreign Policy

Alan Clark

The Gaullist heritage

The essential principles of de Gaulle's foreign policy in the 1960s were few and uncomplicated. The vital initial postulate was the paramount importance of national independence, the re-establishment of which would enable France to regain its traditional position of international eminence. In independence France would be free to enter into multiform co-operation with other nations and thus fulfil its historical 'vocation' of the promotion of peace and of certain civilized values. Without independence valid international co-operation would not be possible since it would inevitably involve the subordination of one of the co-operating partners. National indignity apart, such co-operation-in-subordination would in practice be bound to fail.

From 1958 French foreign policy quickly became *le domaine réservé* of the President of the Republic who accorded it prime importance, determining its major orientations and deciding particular, often crucial issues. De Gaulle conducted a personal policy in an individual fashion. For some it was a policy characterized more by its diplomatic style than by the solidity of its achievements. Yet, substantial or stylistic, important changes in French foreign policy did take place under de Gaulle. After the broadly successful and rapid decolonization of France's African possessions, and the settlement of the Algerian war, de Gaulle had worked to establish national independence on the only basis that, in his mind, was valid: French control of an effective national security system. This led him in 1966 to withdraw France from the integrated military command of a NATO dominated by the USA, and to develop a French nuclear strategy and strike capacity. As the converse of this disengagement from the American orbit, a policy of co-operation and *détente* with the USSR and the 'satellite' countries of eastern Europe was pursued with enthusiasm.

In European affairs, French intransigence concerning the establishment in the EEC of a common agricultural policy (CAP), effective though it proved to be, took second place in de Gaulle's estimation behind his political ambition to establish a confederal association of west European states, a 'Europe of nations' in which France would play a leading role. Between and distinct from the super-powers of East and West, de Gaulle's western Europe was to have become indispensable to world stability. In practice his political Europeanism was eventually reduced to an unshakeable opposition to any proposals which might lead to the emergence of a supranationalist Europe, more or less aligned with the USA.

The Gaullist gospel of the independence of nation states was appreciatively received in many parts of the Third World. France's international standing was enhanced by the vigorous co-operation and aid policies it pursued, particularly in the newly independent African francophone states. Nevertheless the function of arbiter in international conflicts which de Gaulle had on occasion loudly assigned to a 'neutral' France lost credibility at least with Israel as, in the Middle East, French sympathies increasingly lay with the Arab oil-supplying states.

For Couve de Murville (Minister of Foreign Affairs, 1958–68) de Gaulle was beyond doubt 'un homme d'une passion intransigeante et sa passion était la France'; his foreign policy pursued 'l'intérêt national au sens le plus élevé du terme'. Couve de Murville's assessment should not be accepted uncritically. Critics within and outside France have accused de Gaulle's foreign policy of being anachronistic, unrealistic and therefore dangerous, merely negative, or – most damning – of being the product of an old man's idiosyncrasies. But in principle the pursuit of national independence by de Gaulle was never a matter of ignoring harsh world realities; rather, he constantly affirmed the priority of the national reality as the vital precondition of international dealings. His basic position was not inevitably nationalist in the pejorative sense of the word to the extent that France's 'nationalness' sought peaceful rather than conflictual relations with other nations.

Foreign policy under Pompidou (1969–74)

At de Gaulle's resignation (April 1969) French prestige stood higher than at any time since 1940 and , arguably, since before the First World War. During the 1960s France had exerted a determining influence on the economic and political evolution of Europe and of a large portion of Africa. The voice of France had been heard – if not always listened to – in far wider fields, from Washington to Moscow and in many capitals of the Third World. Foreign reaction to the new French standing in the world was doubtless an unstable amalgam of resentment and respect, envy and affection. Apart from complaints at the cost of Gaullist co-operation and nuclear policies, domestic French feelings were still largely ones of sympathy with the needed restoration of national dignity. That the principles and personality of the President himself had been central to this restoration was also clear, in particular to those many Gaullists determined to ensure France's fidelity to the pattern laid down since 1958.

Georges Pompidou's foreign policy had its points of difference with this pattern, born of an acknowledgement that circumstances had changed. Yet, as in the 1960s, foreign policy remained firmly in the control of the new President of the Republic. Indeed, to the extent that it was informed by a greater awareness of France's internal economic needs and of the increasing integration of domestic and foreign interests, that control intensified under Pompidou. His Foreign Minister Michel Jobert made the distinction between *la vision* of de Gaulle's approach to foreign policy and *la gestion* of Pompidou's.

In defence policy Pompidou was faithful to his predecessor's line, maintaining the quiet modifications from the high rigidity of France's 1966 position that had been perceptible from 1968, but did not engage himself in any positive developments of that line. Criticism of the tiny size and doubtful efficacy of *la force de frappe* grew. Both financially and politically the cost of the nuclear effort weighed more heavily. Nevertheless France went ahead with its series of atmospheric nuclear tests in the Pacific with sufficient determination to resist the campaign of international protest led in 1973 by the governments of Australia and New Zealand.

A truly Gaullist President had no choice in the matter in any case: France had not signed the 1963 and 1968 international treaties on nuclear disarmament and arms control, and the agreement on the prevention of nuclear war signed between the USA and the USSR in June 1973 justified in Pompidou's eyes the earlier intransigence of de Gaulle. For France the June treaty was tantamount to the self-promotion of the two superpowers to the shared office of nuclear policeman for the rest of the world. It was, according to Jobert, a *condominium* which should not be confused with genuine progress towards international *détente*. The final twelve months of Pompidou's presidency amply underlined basic Gaullist principles and attitudes relating to national security. At the Helsinki conference on European security and defence (July 1973) and elsewhere France emphasized the need both for each nation, and for a united Europe, to exercise its defensive responsibilities: subjugation to the super-powers of East or West in so vital an area as defence was unacceptable.

Pompidou's relations with the super-powers were not always as difficult as they became in 1973 and were at no stage sharply marked by the temperamental anti-Americanism to which de Gaulle on occasion succumbed. However, relations deteriorated considerably in 1973 when, as well as the USA-USSR treaty on the prevention of nuclear war, further discord emerged. In an effort to ensure agreement with a Europe working more or less slowly towards economic and political union the USA proposed (June 1973) a 'new Atlantic charter' designed to promote an Atlanticist orientation of Europe. For the USA and for France's European partners the project had its merits: quite apart from its substantial economic interests in western Europe, the USA provided the lion's share of a NATO defensive system which sooner or later would be affected by the decisions of any politically united Europe of the future. But for France it was yet another attempt by the Americans at domination, and this time not only the sovereignty of France but also the autonomy of a possible union of Europe were threatened. By the end of Pompidou's presidency (he died in office, April 1973) France appeared again in the familiar Gaullist stance of isolated opposition to American intentions in several fields.

Pompidou continued to develop political links with the USSR in the context of Gaullist 'balanced' relations with the super-powers. Until 1973, exchanges were cordial and progress was made in Franco-Soviet commercial and technical exchanges. There was room for it: in 1970 just 2 per cent of French exports went to the USSR. But the treaty of June 1973 demonstrated that in matters of importance the USSR preferred to leave France out of account and treat directly with its American rival/partner. On his visit to Peking (September 1973), Pompidou found himself talking the same diplomatic language as the Chinese leaders: both disapproved of the 'collusion' between the USA and the USSR. For Pompidou their joint 'imperialism' was no less potentially dangerous than had been the conflict between the two blocs in the 1950s and 1960s.

Europe offered the greatest opportunity to Pompidou for creative departures in foreign policy. Innovation in this sphere was sorely needed. De Gaulle's intransigence had had much to do with the stagnant state in the late 1960s of both the EEC and the movement towards political union. Pompidou's desire to set Europe in motion again was evident at the European summit (The Hague, December 1969) which agreed to open negotiations with candidate countries, notably Britain. Following the Paris meeting between Pompidou and the British Prime Minister Heath (May 1971) it was decided in Luxembourg that Britain (and Ireland and Denmark) should enter the EEC on 1 January 1973.

From 1971 the bulk of Pompidou's activity was given to the promotion of greater European union, especially in the monetary and political spheres. His efforts suffered a political set-back from the relative failure of a referendum held in April 1972 on the enlargement of Europe: 40 per cent abstentions (the highest rate since Napoleon!) were recorded and only 36 per cent of the electorate voted 'Yes'. It was an attempt at the grand Gaullist gesture that did not come off: Pompidou had not received the clear popular mandate he had hoped for. Called at the French President's suggestion, the Paris meeting of the Nine (October 1972) drew up a calendar for a political union that was to be achieved by 1980. Pompidou did not depart from de Gaulle's insistence on a confederal union of states, although he was more sensitive to the isolation of France that was liable to result if that policy was promoted in too absolute a fashion. His temperamental preference was for progressive, concrete realizations. Only ineffectual goodwill was plentiful however, and 1973 ended with Europe struggling in the aftermath of the first oil crisis, still unable to agree on common monetary, energy and raw materials policies.

Pompidou remained firm in the pro-Arab stance adopted by de Gaulle in 1967, conducting his Middle East policy with a sure sense of national economic interests. The diplomatic position remained much as before (guarantees for both Israel and the Palestinian people and a negotiated settlement based on mutual concessions), but French energy supplies were also involved and had to be protected. Pompidou's pragmatism became glaringly evident when, while maintaining the embargo on arms to Israel, he agreed that France should supply Libya with 100 Mirages (January 1970). Gaullist claims to impartiality fell to pieces: Pompidou's France was no longer a peacemaker but was concerned rather to exert influence and cultivate interests. French diplomats covered the Middle Eastern states thoroughly in the context of a long-term policy intended to develop French industrial, commercial and cultural interests in the region.

Pompidou's action in the Middle East should be seen within his wider policy of expanding the French role in the Mediterranean. By emphasizing southern interests Pompidou thought France could re-balance the northern predominance that would result from the Europe of Nine, and regain some of its lost importance by occupying a prominent position in the 'new' Mediterranean that might emerge. Efforts made from 1969 met with moderate success. Diplomatic normality was soon restored with Morocco. By mid-1970 France had developed closer contacts with Lisbon and Madrid. Algeria posed a more important and more difficult problem. Relations were often delicate: the loss of French oil concessions in the Algerian nationalizations of 1971 was a heavy blow, the proportion of French aid going to Algeria declined steadily and, following racial tension in Marseille in 1973, Algeria suspended the heavy emigration of its workers to France. Pompidou nevertheless persisted in his efforts to cultivate good relations, looking to France's longer-term economic and strategic interests. His concept of an Arab-Latin Mediterranean was farsighted and perhaps feasible, but it was also not without its opportunism (at the expense of Israel) and somehow lacked the cachet of his predecessor's more loftily conceived diplomacy. It was a policy defensible as prudent manoeuvring, but one which also contained the implicit admission that France's role, after being played on the world stage, might in future be limited effectively to western Europe and the Mediterranean. And to a presence in Africa.

While President, Pompidou visited at least once most of the former French territories in Black Africa; after 1958 de Gaulle had not ventured further south than the countries of the Maghreb. The difference illustrates Pompidou's greater concern for a co-operation policy that was less paternalistic and more open to the evolving circumstances of the Third World. Wherever possible the privileged relations between France and its former colonies were maintained, although Pompidou agreed readily enough to African demands for liberalizing reforms of the 1960 co-operation agreements. Although it increased in volume, the proportion of the French budget given to co-operation declined to 1974; aid from the private sector (banks, industry, and so on) became almost as important as public aid – and less disinterested. Further, the French co-operation programme began to spread its funds and expertise beyond its traditional African spheres of influence: in 1970, 40 per cent of French aid went to developing countries outside *la zone franc*.

As the oil crisis deepened, Pompidou saw the problems of the Third World (the stability of prices received for raw materials, trade relations with the developed world) in global, long-term perspectives and, by 1974, the familiar Gaullist thesis of an international mediatory role for France had cropped up again. France's refusal to follow the American 'common front' strategy on oil prices (October 1973) and its stress on the necessity for developing countries to be fully involved in discussions related to international trade were welcomed by the many countries of the Third World dependent on prices received for their exports to the West.

Foreign policy under Giscard d'Estaing (1974–81)

Under Giscard d'Estaing the patterns of French foreign policy, while not breaking free from their Gaullist mould, in some areas underwent modification and in others became confused and difficult to decipher. At the outset Giscard indicated three principal points of foreign policy reorientation: an extension of French involvement in international (presumably other than bilateral) co-operation with developing countries and no less than a 'new era' of international relations based on 'le respect et l'estime mutuels, (et) un esprit de compréhension et de liberté' were promised. The form such change might adopt was not easy to imagine from the third point: while remaining independent in its commitments and decisions, '(la France) veut désormais consacrer ses forces, son imagination et son talent à forger son avenir'. A certain tone of imprecise idealism had been set.

A number of features of Giscard's reputation in the field of foreign policy were widely acknowledged at the start of his term of office. He was first and foremost a convinced European who looked to a politically united Europe having its own defence, currency and foreign policy. Although he always denied it, critics (many Gaullists, most Socialists and all the Communists) accused him of Atlanticist leanings, of working for greater French and European association with the USA, particularly with regard to economic and defence structures. By his own admission Giscard was more positively internationalist in his approach to foreign policy: problems now posed themselves on a world scale, state-to-state relations (*à la de Gaulle*) were no longer sufficient in many cases and what he termed *une politique mondiale* was vital, although national sovereignty was to be firmly preserved. Such a global perspective necessitated what Giscard regularly referred to as a policy of *concertation*, that is of dialogue and harmonious co-ordination rather than intimidation and conflict (*la confrontation*). To what extent an implied criticism of de Gaulle's resolute defence of (his version of) national interests was to be detected in these Giscardian emphases was a matter of political opinion.

But elsewhere change was undeniable, not least in Giscard's own political position. As leader of the *Républicains indépendants* (RI) he was the first non-Gaullist President of the Fifth Republic. While he chose an ambitious member of the UDR, Jacques Chirac, to be Prime Minister, it was clear from the start that the parliamentary Gaullists would see that departures, real or imagined, from their founder's principles (in particular with regard to defence and national independence within Europe) did not pass uncriticized. The narrowness of his electoral victory (less than 2 per cent more votes than François Mitterrand, the candidate of the combined Left in 1974) might have restricted Giscard's freedom to conduct his own foreign policy – after all he could not claim the solid majority support on which the confidence of de Gaulle and Pompidou (until the 1972 referendum) had largely rested. In fact Giscard's political base expanded significantly later in his term: gains were made by the Giscardian UDF both in the 1978 legislative elections and in the European elections of the following year. Presidential foreign policy in the three years to May 1981 often appeared in consequence more determinedly innovative and dynamic (or, as critics of both Left and Right put it, misguided and foolhardy), particularly concerning disarmament, Africa and Europe.

The parliamentary opposition on the other hand failed throughout the decade to make a decisive impact in foreign policy matters. In June 1972 the PCF, PS and left-wing Radicals signed their Common Programme of government; it remained formally valid until the March 1978 elections. Its scanty final section which outlined the foreign policy of a future French government of the Left was unimpressive: in the areas of defence and European policy, for example, it posed as many questions as it supplied answers. The disunity that re-emerged from the middle of 1977 between PCF and PS only exacerbated matters. The situation could have proved damaging: in the absence of effective challenge from a Left in impotent disarray and from a diminished Gaullist Right, the potential in 1980–1 for a neo-Gaullian abusive 'presidentialization' of French foreign policy appeared considerable.

Faced with political constraints at home, Giscard came to power at a time of serious and persistent international difficulties. The oil crisis of late 1973 promised to involve other raw materials and threatened shaky international financial systems. Europe was in conflict, immobile if not actually regressive. The USA was in the final throes of Watergate. The new French President's wide financial experience (Giscard had been a liberal Finance Minister under de Gaulle, 1962–6, and under Pompidou, 1969–74) was expected to produce in the conduct of foreign policy an intensification of Pompidolian sensitivity to French economic interests. Complex and rapid change on all sides also encouraged Giscard to develop his predecessor's pragmatism: in a world characterized more by chaos than by order, *le pilotage à vue* and *la gestion de l'imprévisible* (the phrases are Giscard's) became the only effective attitudes to adopt. Critics nostalgic for de Gaulle's loudly affirmed basic principles and long-term strategies were reluctant to admit Giscard's constant emphasis on change and on what he called '*le grand réaménagement des relations internationales*' in the late 1970s. The same critics could have been more sensitive to the sombre conflict that underlay Giscardian foreign policy: on the one hand, the advocacy of a humanitarian *mondialisme*, biased towards the indispensable implementation of greater international economic justice and the needs of the developing world; on the other, the no less necessary defence of national strategic and economic interests.

Even had he wanted to do otherwise Giscard would have been under pressure, for reasons at once political and technological, to adopt a defence policy acceptable to the Gaullists. Before election he promised to maintain and develop French nuclear weapons and guaranteed the absence of France from disarmament and non-proliferation talks which sought only to maintain the blocs of the super-powers. Between 1974 and 1977, however, perceived deviations from established defence policy occurred with disconcerting frequency. Nuclear tests at Mururoa were confined underground and their frequency restricted (three tests in 1975, two in 1976). Declarations made in 1976 by both Giscard and his Chief of Staff, General Méry, clearly implied an extension of the hitherto strictly national dissuasion policy (Méry's concept of *la sanctuarisation élargie*) and an increased degree of French involvement in NATO's military structures. Giscard's insistence on the need to modernize France's conventional forces and in particular to develop mobile, multi-purpose interventionist units was also seen as symptomatic of a relative departure from de Gaulle's priorities.

Deviation in defence policy was in fact more apparent than real. Following the relative pause of 1976–8, nuclear dissuasive policy was substantially redefined along Gaullist lines. Commissioned in 1979, France's sixth strategic nuclear submarine, *Inflexible*, was programmed to enter service in 1985 armed with the M4, a new generation of longer-range, multi-headed missiles. Existing FOST (*Force océanique stratégique*) submarines were to be renovated and similarly equipped from the later 1980s. As a result the megaton capacity of France's strategic forces was projected to quadruple in the seven years to 1985. More specifically Giscardian emphases on flexibility and innovation were discernible in longer-term projects announced in mid-1980: mobile, land-based strategic missiles for the 1990s, the technological development of enhanced radiation weapons (the so-called 'neutron bomb'). Consequences of Giscard's energetic reaffirmation of defence policy were soon evident. Underground nuclear testing in the Pacific accelerated again: eight tests were reported in both 1978 and 1979. Not surprisingly French defence costs rose significantly: by 30 per cent in real terms between 1977 and 1981, a rate of expenditure not achieved by most European NATO countries.

International interest was stimulated by Giscard's presentation to the UN (May 1978) of a number of disarmament proposals. His address, which marked France's return to the world disarmament scene after some twenty years' absence, was characterized by a typically subtle combination of Gaullist orthodoxy and Eurocentric innovation. His efforts to regionalize and in particular to Europeanize progress in international disarmament (Giscard proposed to the UN a pan-European conference on conventional disarmament) were as idealistic as they were necessary. Not only French but west European disquiet intensified as, in a context marked by increased Soviet military power in eastern Europe, the signing of SALT 2 (June 1979) brought into question the reliability of American nuclear commitment to European security. Subsequent deterioration of strategic tensions in Europe (Euromissiles, Poland) served to intensify fears in French circles, from the Gaullist RPR to the PCF, that the super-powers of East and West were effecively disposing between themselves of European security. It did not diminish the potential value of Giscard's Europeanist approach to security problems which in fact, in 1981, continued to underlie much of the work of the Madrid conference on disarmament in Europe.

Giscard's expected determination to effect a *rapprochement* with the USA became evident in the months following his election. Even before the considerable public success of the presidential visit to Washington in celebration of the American bicentenary (May 1976), a more positive tone in bilateral relations had been established. In the aftermath of Carter's visit to France (January 1978) relations between the two nations were, Giscard claimed, 'cordiaux, ouverts et respectueux des droits de l'autre' – that is, to a degree never previously equalled, the USA recognized France's right to pursue autonomous national policies.

Such formal assertions of the excellence of Franco-American relations became increasingly difficult to reconcile with multiplying points of conflict of a commercial or industrial nature: following 'illegitimate' tactics over replacement contracts for European NATO military aircraft (1974) and American landing-rights for Concorde (1977), interference by the USA in French civil nuclear sales to South Korea and Pakistan (1975–9) was resented by much French political opinion. Differences of position in the energy and security fields also became apparent. For several years Giscard pressed the USA, as an indispensable contribution to an internationally integrated resolution of the 1970s' energy crises, to import and use less oil, and to increase domestic American production. In vain. In mid-1979 France was prominent (for example, at the Tokyo summit of industrialized nations, June 1979) in voicing EEC resentment at the absence of a concerted American policy on oil imports. Carter's signing of SALT 2 was seen as a further indication of American indifference to European concerns.

As with the USA, France's relations with the USSR from 1974 were characterized by a change in tone, although in this case the evolution occurred more erratically, in the direction of uncertainty and, especially after 1977, prolonged ambivalence. At first France stressed its determination to develop still further the policy of *détente* and co-operation which, initiated by de Gaulle, had become established in the mid-1970s as a permanent feature of its foreign policy. Indeed the triple formula of *détente, entente et coopération* was still employed by France, at the end of the decade, to convey the essential of its formal relations with the USSR. Nor was this a mere diplomatic nicety, for Franco-Soviet co-operation had, by the later 1970s, become varied, substantial and, ultimately, expanding. In late 1974 important energy and industrial agreements were concluded, together with a general agreement on economic co-operation intended to triple bilateral trade to 1980. In 1976 the value of industrial contracts between the two countries was the highest ever. By mid-1979 all seemed set fair for the next decade: wide-ranging co-operation agreements – from marine research to gas technology contracts, from sales of electronic equipment and nuclear reactors to reciprocal language education arrangements – to 1990 were in place.

Subsequent diplomatic relations were decidedly less smooth. After almost three years of Soviet disquiet at both the confused evolution of French defence policy and Giscard's more conciliatory attitude towards the USA, 1977–8 was marked by a deterioration in relations so serious as temporarily to hamper commercial exchanges. Secondary areas of dispute were not lacking: Soviet rejection of the French disarmament proposals of May 1978, the Middle East, human rights, China. However, central to Franco-Soviet dissension were Moscow's virulent attacks on Giscard's African policy, and in particular its criticism of French 'imperialist' intervention against 'progressivist' forces in Zaire and Chad (see p.124). Then of some fourteen years' standing, Franco-Soviet *détente* may, as Giscard claimed, have made a significant contribution to peace and stability in Europe. But just as clearly no French impingement on the USSR's African strategies would be tolerated. So vulnerable a dichotomy between *entente* and *coopération*, diplomacy and trade, constituted at best an unpredictable basis on which to build Franco-Soviet relations in the future. Giscard himself discovered this when, in 1980, he attempted to maintain traditional *détente* with the USSR while at the same time condemning the Soviet invasion of Afghanistan (December 1979): the widespread political criticism this stand incurred in France may have contributed to Giscard's defeat in the 1981 presidential election.

The numerous uncertainties of relations with both the USA and the USSR reflected the recent shift in France's foreign policy perspectives away from the bipolar world of the super-powers towards an international scene conceived, where possible, in multipolar, regionalist terms. Complex, subject to constant redefinition, it was a movement compatible both with de Gaulle's criticism in the 1960s of the super-powers' hegemony and with his largely symbolic recognition of the importance of Third World nations. Pompidou's initiatives in Africa, the Mediterranean and the Arab world maintained the movement. In his turn Giscard attempted to co-ordinate French foreign policy more tightly than ever around the triple regional 'poles' of Europe, the Arab states and the Third World, especially Africa.

As Pompidou had done in 1969, Giscard set out with a high determination to relaunch Europe. Even more than his predecessor, Giscard had from the mid-1970s to pit his ideals against a Europe that was retrogressive and disunited. In particular, common monetary and energy policies were still lacking at a time when member countries were experiencing more or less acute economic difficulties. Analyses of the impotent condition of the Nine flourished and late in 1976 French observers even speculated sceptically on the survival of the EEC's fundamental customs union.

Particularly since 1977, however, Franco-German relations materially underpinned European development, providing much needed stability and stimulus. It was, for example, a text jointly presented by Chancellor Schmidt and Giscard to the European Council (July 1978) that supplied the basis for the European Monetary System (EMS) which came into operation in March 1979. If the birth was a difficult one (France suspended its participation for three months because of a disagreement with West Germany over Community agricultural subsidies), the EMS's early functioning was sound. A substantial advance in monetary co-operation had been achieved.

A European energy policy proved a more intractable problem. Progress had been reluctant, partial, and very possibly fragile since made only under the irresistible pressure of international circumstances. Under French presidency, the European Council called in 1979 for European dialogue with the OPEC states, announced its determination to restrict EEC oil imports, to co-ordinate the national energy policies of the Nine, and to develop their alternative energy sources (nuclear power especially, in the case of France). It also criticized the huge increases in American oil imports since 1973. The Council's energy front was impressive if less precisely quantified and far-reaching than France had wanted. The imprint of Giscardian Europeanism and of the ideal of *concertation* in international questions were evident.

Persistent French efforts were made from 1974 to promote a politically more united Europe. Giscard's early tactics in this field owed much to de Gaulle's European 'union of states': the new President suggested that the nine heads of government should meet regularly and informally in order to discuss current or longer-term matters of European concern. Prominent among Giscard's intentions in initiating this European Council was the idea of progressively accustoming the Nine to top-level political discussion from which co-ordination and perhaps, by accretion as it were, greater unity might emerge. At the same time such a process was to be supplemented by institutional change, in particular by a European Assembly elected by universal suffrage. After initial moves in 1975–6, smooth formal progress towards the realization of this major Giscardian ambition was made, culminating in the inauguration, in mid-1979, of the first democratically based European Parliament.

In at least the short term, and from the French point of view, the first European elections (June 1979) were seen as a political triumph for Giscard's European policy. The firmly Europeanist UDF received the largest proportion of votes cast of the four principal political groupings in France, and therefore sent the largest number of Euro-deputies to a broadly sympathetic Centre-Right Assembly's first session in Strasbourg. In contrast the two formations most fiercely critical of presidential enthusiasm for the institutionalization of Europe, the PCF and the RPR, came third and fourth respectively in the election. While the installation of the Assembly contributed significantly to European integration (after the elections Giscard justifiably stressed the importance of the existence in the 1980s of an acknowledged political expression of European opinion), it did so primarily on the abstract, institutional level. The Assembly's capacity for tackling persistent, immediate difficulties – unemployment; the budgetary dispute with Great Britain; industrial and agricultural policies within the EEC – remained to be demonstrated.

In the 1979 Euro-elections almost 40 per cent of the French electorate abstained from voting. With economic interests more pressingly at stake the next stage in the construction of Europe – the expansion of the EEC to twelve members by the inclusion of Greece (from January 1981), Spain and Portugal – was unlikely to benefit from such broadly sympathetic public disinterest. Giscard's unequivocal, if not unconditional, support for the Europe of Twelve was exceptional in 1978–9: to the PCF, parts of the PS, the RPR, to farmers' groups and some industrialists in the Midi, the entry of Spain in particular would threaten French social and economic interests. If to such hostility were added both left-wing and Gaullist charges that Giscard intended to establish an 'Atlanticized', supranationalist Europe (which, according to Chirac, would result in '*l'asservissement économique et l'effacement international de la France*'), and the necessity for sweeping institutional reform of an enlarged EEC, it seemed probable that the qualified success achieved to 1981 by Giscardian European policy would be difficult to equal, or even maintain.

For both economic and strategic reasons Giscard developed relations with the Arab world to a point far beyond that reached by Pompidou. The French diplomatic position with regard to Israel shifted in emphasis if not in fundamentals when, by late 1974, Giscard had already stressed the vital importance of arriving at a durable settlement of the Palestinian problem, a settlement which had to include the establishment of sure and recognized frontiers for all concerned, and in particular for Israel and the Palestinian people. By 1977 France maintained that Israel should withdraw to its territorial limits of 1967, while the Palestinians should have access to a homeland (*une patrie*). The need for a global settlement in the Middle East caused France to share the majority of the Arab world's anxiety and reserve about the Camp David agreements, seeing them (a further point of Franco-American dissension) as a fragmentary and potentially divisive response to a wider issue.

If relations with Israel were eventually normalized (in 1977) after France's effective recognition of the Palestine Liberation Organization (UN debate, October 1974), French identification and involvement with the Arab world expanded enormously throughout the 1970s. Such association ranged in later years from mercenary pro-Arab reactions (Abou Daoud affair, January 1977) to the promotion of dialogue between the EEC and the OPEC states, and to the elaboration in mid-1978 of an embryonic military and diplomatic axis with Saudi Arabia in an effort to respond to Soviet penetration in the Horn of Africa. But above all Franco-Arab relations were governed by economic necessity. Obliged since 1973 to pay escalating prices for its oil imports, France, as other industrialized countries, strove as never before to increase its industrial and technological sales to the Arab states. The inevitable identification of French policy towards the Arab world with the promotion of commercial and strategic interests was firmly underscored by Prime Minister Barre's productive visit to Iraq (July 1979). Iraq undertook to guarantee up to one-third of France's annual oil imports, thereby more than doubling its supply rate. In return France would sell Iraq a range of arms and military equipment, and a civil nuclear research centre. If in the wake of the Iranian revolution and the Gulf War France redefined some of its strategic relations in the Arab region, the perilous and fragile formula of 'oil for arms' had not outlived its usefulness, or its necessity.

Relations with the Third World were characterized by an unstable combination, not unknown in de Gaulle's day, of generous intentions and imperfect realizations of those intentions. Giscard consistently presented himself as a renovator of French co-operation policy. Long-established links with North and Black African countries were to be retained, but also revised. More importantly, the taint of imperialism was to be removed from co-operation in all its forms, technical, cultural or merely linguistic: *l'Afrique aux Africains* was the slogan Giscard brandished in talks with African leaders from 1975. In consequence the numbers of French medical, teaching and administrative personnel based in Africa diminished gradually as greater emphasis was placed on co-operation through investment and the establishment of self-sufficient structures within the developing countries: formation rather than assistance.

This revamped policy did not hinder the expansion and revival of French bilateral relations in Africa and elsewhere. Complementing significant *rapprochement* with previously critical 'progressivist' states such as Angola, Ethiopia and Madagascar, Giscard's historic visit to Guinea (December 1978) restored relations between Paris and Conakry which had been ruptured in 1985 at the start of de Gaulle's presidency, symbolized the more dynamic outgoing character of Giscardian co-operation – and promised to be profitable. Unprecedented French initiatives were subsequently undertaken in former British and Portuguese territories with a view to expanding and co-ordinating French co-operation on a broader regionalist basis throughout West Africa.

Of potentially equal importance was the long overdue revival of diplomatic, industrial and economic interest in South and Central America, as evidenced by presidential visits to Brazil (October 1978) and Mexico (February 1979), and by various ministerial tours of Argentina, Colombia and Panama (April 1979).

More controversial was Giscard's policy of military intervention in Africa. In western Sahara, Chad, and the Shaba province of Zaire in particular, French military personnel and equipment were repeatedly engaged in stabilizing chaotic internal situations. But at what point did stabilizing assistance end and 'neo-colonialist' interference begin? Reactions were divided and often extremist. The USSR and 'progressivist' African states (for example Tanzania, Madagascar) were unreservedly hostile. Among Arab nations, Libya denounced French policy in Chad as archaic colonialism, while Franco-Algerian diplomatic and economic relations went into serious decline from mid-1977 in the face of French assistance to Morocco and Mauritania and after the Algeria-backed Polisario Front held several French civilians hostage. On the other hand, numerous Black African states, not invariably francophone, expressed varying degrees of relieved approval of the French supportive actions. More discreetly, the EEC, the USA and even sections of the OAU associated themselves sympathetically with Giscard's initiatives.

By 1978 the risks inherent in such African interventionism were felt, not least by the French Left, to be acute: the prolongation and escalation of military involvement (in response to the civil war there, French troops in Chad were doubled to 2500 in March 1979), the detrimental identification of France with so-called 'moderate' regimes (Mobutu's Zaire, Bokassa's Central African Empire) and unenlightened policies (continued French interference in the Comores and presence in Réunion, ambiguous commercial relations with South Africa and so on). If in 1979–81 French interventionism in Africa appeared less militarily activist, diplomatically more balanced and reserved, the longer-term coherence of what Giscard termed *la fidélité africaine de la France* was still not evident. Many in France feared that the need to protect French economic and western strategic interests, as well as African security, could give rise to further piecemeal responses.

More durably innovatory was the importance Giscard repeatedly attached to the need to adopt international regionalist perspectives when responding to the situation of the Third World. While France still had a useful role to play in Africa and elsewhere, often limitedly national, bilateral action was insufficient: economic, political and strategic problems posed themselves on so complex a scale that only a multilateral approach, involving effective negotiations between industrialized and developing nations, was appropriate. Unfortunately Giscard's various proposals in this vein too often remained at the level of prestigious diplomatic initiatives, with little or no practical application. The North-South conference on international economic co-operation was launched in 1974 at the joint suggestion of France and Saudi Arabia. It ended (June 1977) with the participating Third World countries disillusioned by the industrialized world's reluctance to agree to extensive structural reform of international financial and trade systems. It may have been true, as Giscard was prompt to claim, that a spirit of dialogue had at least been born, but fundamental problems – energy supplies, prices for raw materials, Third World indebtedness – remained virtually unchanged. Two years later Giscardian assertions of *concertation* and *interdépendance* as the keys to a more just and workable international economic order were still more numerous than effective. Even the Lomé Convention (between the EEC and African, Caribbean and Pacific countries) was renewed only with difficulty and in confusion (June 1979).

Giscard's major address to the sixth Franco-African Conference (Kigali, Rwanda, May 1979) indicated the three principal interest areas of contemporary French policy, and encapsulated the undoubted farsightedness, the high ambition but also the disconcerting ambiguity of that policy. Fusing ideas of Euro-Arab and Euro-African association regularly mooted since 1974, Giscard proposed a Euro-African-Arab *trilogue*, the elaboration by carefully prepared stages of a triangular charter of solidarity. No fewer than seventy-eight states were, potentially, to be involved. Such a vast project in multilateral political and economic co-operation (technology/raw materials/oil) would not, however, supplant Franco-African bilateral relations, nor reduce French commitment to African security. Having recently cancelled the debts of eight African states, France announced at Kigali an increase of almost 50 per cent in its co-operation budget from 1980, as well as substantial additional contributions to African development bodies. Yet a few months later the decisive role played by the French Army in the overthrow of Bokassa's tyrannical régime (September 1979), while it stabilized a deteriorating situation, exposed Giscard to charges of metropolitan manipulation of the internal affairs of former colonial territories.

The editor of *Le Monde* came persuasively close to the truth when, in the early days of 1981, he summed up France's foreign policy since 1974 as the work of 'un diplomate ingénieux dans l'inspiration à défaut de l'être toujours dans l'action'.

Foreign policy under Mitterrand (1981–6)

The election in May 1981 of a Socialist President of the Republic roused more extreme hopes and fears for French foreign policy than had the arrival of his liberal conservative predecessor seven years earlier.

Within France rather than abroad, on the Left rather than on the Right, the hopes sprang from Mitterrand's and the PS's long recognized concern for European and international disarmament, for the economic and humanitarian development of the Third World and, more diffusely, for an approach to international relations that would be more firmly principled than for example that which, it was claimed, Giscard had exhibited in his hesitant, undignified responses in 1980–1 to the crises in Afghanistan and Poland.

The fears concerning Mitterrand's foreign policy were at once more numerous, more acute since more closely defined, and more widespread, being evident both abroad (in Washing-*and* Moscow, from Bonn to numerous Arab and francophone African capitals) and at home (among all Right of Centre opinion, but also in the PCF). After all, in the mid-1970s both PS and PCF had still favoured dismantling the national nuclear strike capacity: what would happen to defence strategy under Mitterrand? The consequences for NATO and European security at a time of increasing continental tensions were potentially critical. Surely French relations with the major powers of West and East would suffer disruption, especially following the introduction, in June 1981, of four Communist ministers into Prime Minister Pierre Mauroy's cabinet? Ideological common ground between Presidents Reagan (who took office in January 1981) and Mitterrand appeared minimal. Prospects for improving co-operation in a deeply recessive EEC were not enhanced by the new French government's anomalous reflationary economic policies (1981–2). Previous French policies towards Africa and the Arab world had been widely criticized as mercenary, opportunist and ineffective (according to Mitterrand, Giscard's sole diplomatic principle had been *épouser les circonstances*): what upheavals might be in store in those areas? And so on.

Most of such speculations have proved groundless. Certainly

the more excited fears – but also the more lofty hopes – have not been realized. Although for electoral reasons both Giscard and Mitterrand would resent the association, France's foreign policy under its two latest presidents has to a marked degree been characterized by incidental change coupled with essential continuity.

Since 1981 French commitment in security matters has been notably firm and clear. Having reaffirmed his government's adherence to the established Gaullist line of autonomous national membership of the Atlantic Alliance, Mitterrand went further than Giscard had ever done by supporting (July 1981) the USA's insistence on the need to respond to the build-up of Soviet military power by establishing NATO missiles in western Europe. Over the next five years his invariable argument was to say that worthwhile disarmament negotiations could proceed only once a position of equilibrium had in this way been re-established. 'Je crois, de toute ma conviction, que la paix tient à l'équilibre des forces dans le monde, à l'équilibre des forces en Europe', Mitterrand wrote in early 1986.

The apparently paradoxical *rapprochement* between French and Atlantic perspectives had little effect on the more specifically national dimensions of Mitterrand's defence policy. Underground nuclear testing programmes have continued at Mururoa, in the face of widespread opposition in the South Pacific. The political scandal which resulted from the bombing of the *Rainbow Warrior* in Auckland harbour by French secret service agents (July 1985) did not weaken French determination to continue testing. The nuclear dissuasive arsenal has been extended and modernized in ways that attempt to combine irreproachable Gaullist orthodoxy with the more flexible, Europeanist concerns of Giscard. Among numerous programmes, a seventh strategic nuclear missile-firing submarine is under construction, and a re-equipment programme will by 1991 increase six-fold the M4 missiles carried by the strategic submarine fleet. At the same time the 1982 defence budget proposed a trailer-mounted pre-strategic nuclear missile system (Hades), and by early 1986, Franco-German talks were grappling with the possible deployment of both French forces and pre-strategic arms on West German territory. Decisions are imminent regarding the evolution of dissuasive strategy beyond the end of the century. By the mid-1990s France's land-based Pluton missiles (sited on the Plateau d'Albion in Provence) and its modernized Mirage-IV P strategic bombers will have outlived their effectiveness. Current debate centres on the need to diversify French dissuasive capacities in order to respond to this situation, possibly in the direction of a new land-based strategic component. Unlike the situation in West Germany and some other European NATO countries, the implementation of French defence policy has barely been affected by popular neutralist pressures. However, problems concerned with the number, training and future role of France's conventional armed forces, and with total defence costs, continue to pose substantial challenges to the maintenance of national independence.

In June 1981 Claude Cheysson, France's Minister of External Relations, suggested that the USA would find in his country *un solide partenaire, sinon facile*. Broadly common Franco-American international responses (to the Euro-missiles question, to the Middle East imbroglio, to the Polish crisis) have since demonstrated their solidity. A year later, however, Cheysson referred openly to *le divorce progressif* which was dividing Washington not only from Paris, but from western Europe in general. Sharply divergent approaches to monetary and commercial policies, and the impact of these on East-West relations, underlay this erosion of Atlantic solidarity. Washington's calls for increased NATO defence spending caused resentment among European States which from 1980 had seen their recessions worsen as a consequence of persistently high American interest rates. Reagan's advocacy of unrestricted international trade did not extend to EEC steel exports to the USA, while active American opposition (1981–2) to the construction of a natural gas pipeline from Siberia to western Europe appeared to European eyes to be both incompatible with American cereal sales to the USSR and an infringement of European economic sovereignty. Subsequent Franco-American relations have continued to be mixed. His overriding commitment to Atlantic solidarity has not altered Mitterrand's disagreement with the USA's interpretation of and response to revolution in Central America, although effective French involvement in that region has greatly diminished since 1982. Unlike West Germany and Britain, France declined (May 1985) to participate at the national level in the Strategic Defensive Initiative (SDI) proposed by Reagan, Mitterrand seeing in it a threat to the hard-won strategic balance in Europe. Intermittently supported in his stand by other EEC nations such as West Germany and Britain, Mitterrand consistently distinguished between political and commercial relations with the USSR. While the former could not be regularized until, for example, Soviet troops withdrew from Afghanistan, the latter should continue (a massive contract for the supply of Soviet natural gas to France was signed (January 1982) just one month after martial law was imposed in Poland). De Gaulle, and Giscard, had thought along similar lines. From July 1984 the French cabinet no longer contained any Communist ministers. Released from this domestic political constraint, and with irreproachable Atlantic and defence policy records already behind him, Mitterrand moved to restore full diplomatic dialogue. The results were more symbolic than substantial. Soon after Gorbachev's official visit to France (October 1985), Mitterrand's controversial decision to receive the Polish leader General Jaruzelski at the Elysée Palace (December 1985) underscored his firm resumption of traditional Gaullist dialogue with the Eastern bloc states.

'Commençons par rendre son âme à l'Europe', Mitterrand urged (June 1981), while at the same time exhorting the European Council to develop the EEC's social legislation, what he called *l'espace social européen*. In a Community ravaged by high and increasing unemployment, Mitterrand's early Euro-Socialist idealism was lyrical, entirely appropriate – but unlikely to be realized; it has been largely neglected since. What co-ordinated action was accomplished by the EEC remained, perhaps inevitably, partial, defensive or circumstantial: common mobilization against Japanese exports, for example, or against the monetary policies and *(le) véritable protectionnisme déguisé* (the phrase is Mitterrand's) deployed by the USA, or the adoption in support of Britain of economic sanctions against Argentina during the Falklands War, or in 1986 of concerted measures to combat international terrorism. On the other hand the EMS (see p.120) functioned with increasing effectiveness, facilitating important currency adjustments (June 1982, April 1986). The EEC expanded to admit Spain and Portugal (January 1986). Otherwise European affairs too often remained dogged, as during the later years of Giscard's presidency, by politically linked disputes focusing on the size of, and (until 1984) British contributions to, the Community's budget, reform of the CAP, the running problem of agricultural surpluses and international trade policy disputes with the USA.

As for political relations, Mitterrand extended the high level of positive co-operation with West Germany that had been established by Giscard and Schmidt. He complemented this with wider, more diversified bilateral relations with Britain (Channel Tunnel agreement, January 1986), Italy and Denmark. Like Giscard, Mitterrand was convinced that political union (involving a recasting of the original Treaty of Rome) remained indispensable to the success of an expanded Europe. While working towards this longer-term institutional objective Mitterrand strove to extend European technological co-ordination by expanding French involvement in major European technological research and development programmes (JET, CERN, ESPRIT, RACE), and in major European industrial ventures such as Airbus and Ariane. Progress was not invariably smooth: Franco-German agreement regarding the Hermes space shuttle had not been reached by mid-1986. Mitterrand's Eureka project (launched in April 1985) offered a flexible range of market-oriented extensions of these ideas: a year later, some forty international high-technology projects had been proposed by the eighteen west European countries involved. 'J'estime complémentaires l'indépendance de la France et la construction de l'Europe', Mitterrand wrote early in 1986. In particular, the technological and political advance of Europe were interdependent. Their joint success would determine France's national future.

In the Middle East the pursuit of diplomatic equilibrium has been unremitting, delicate and, in multiple ways, costly. Known to be a long-standing friend of Israel, Mitterrand worked for what he saw as a more even-handed approach to the Palestinian conflict: guaranteed recognition of all sides, including a Palestinian state; a negotiated settlement within the Camp David framework. The effort gave rise to considerable

Arab apprehension as for the first time since 1967 France voiced active concern for Israel's interests. Humanitarian, non-partisan diplomacy was courageous but perceived as provocative as from 1982 inter-Arab, anti-French and anti-Zionist terrorism flared spasmodically in Paris. Arab criticism reached heights unknown throughout the 1970s when, in spite of Israel's annexation of the Golan Heights (December 1981), Mitterrand paid an unprecedented presidential visit to Jerusalem (March 1982). From mid-1982, however, Franco-Israeli relations deteriorated in their turn following French condemnation of the Israeli invasion of Lebanon (June 1982). In consultation with the USA, in close concert with Egypt, Paris's diplomatic involvement persisted at a high pitch, culminating in the repeated participation of French troops in UN multinational peace-keeping forces in Beirut. Arab, especially PLO, appreciation of French positions was progressively restored following Cheysson's meeting with Yasser Arafat in October 1982. Yet, in the context of the Gulf War, continued French arms and nuclear sales to the Arab world (to Saudi Arabia and Iraq, in particular) provoked Iranian hostility towards France. The old contradiction in French Middle Eastern policy between an interventionist role and a (commercially and therefore politically) partisan position exacted a high price in terms of soldiers' lives and (from March 1985) French civilian hostages held by Islamic extremists in Lebanon. In April 1986 a contingent of French observers was withdrawn from Beirut while moves began to normalize relations with Iran.

The distance between intention and performance was, unavoidably, widest in policies relating to the Third World. The Socialist government multiplied assertions of the pressing need for what Cheysson called un *'new deal' planétaire* and what, more sonorously, Mitterrand referred to as un *co-développement généralisé* or une *restructuration d'ensemble* of economic relations between developed and developing worlds. North-South relations had to be co-ordinated globally, enveloping monetary, energy, industrial and commercial strategies with more orthdox development aid. Not that this last was to be neglected: Mitterrand (September 1981) undertook to double French public aid – to the UN target figure of 0.7 per cent of GDP – to the Third World during his seven-year term of office.

France's solidarity with the Third World was repeatedly affirmed: it was to be structured progressively on the triple basis of exemplary relations with Algeria, Mexico and India. A substantial contract for the supply to France of natural gas on terms generous to Algeria (February 1982) was presented by Paris as an example for other industrialized nations to follow. Was it a legitimate example? Or was it, as conservative critics alarmed at France's record trade deficit in late 1982 alleged, simply bad business? And what of the fact, disturbing even to some PS parliamentarians, that Mitterrand's redefinition of Third World policies did not impede substantial sales, *à la* Giscard, of Mirage 2000s to India, or of (defensive) arms to Nicaragua? Or that Socialist trade embargoes imposed on South Africa excluded strategically important exports to France of uranium?

Global reorganization was not in any case to be pursued to the exclusion of France's established bilateral ties with many African, especially francophone, states. Without exception, treaty obligations with such countries have been respected and in some cases (Zaire, for example) French financial commitment has been increased. In the light of Giscard's experiences in western Sahara and Central Africa, interventionism has been minimized, *la non-ingérence* observed and *le développement autocentré* promoted. Nevertheless in Chad French military and logistical forces continued to support the established Habré government against the incursions of insurgents backed by Libya, although they did so in a more coherently organized, restrained and (to mid-1986) effective fashion than in the late 1970s. Annual Franco-African summits indicated that under Mitterrand relations with Africa were restored to high levels of mutual understanding. It will be interesting to see if they remain there in spite of both deepening Third World indebtedness and a struggling metropolitan economy.

A Note on 'Cohabitation' (March 1986–   )

La politique extérieure de la France s'ordonne autour de quelques idées simples: l'indépendance nationale, l'équilibre des blocs militaires dans le monde, la construction de l'Europe, le droit des peuples à disposer d'eux-mêmes, le développement des pays pauvres, (...et) l'ouverture de notre pays vers la Méditerranée et l'Afrique.

There words might have been written by de Gaulle in 1960. They were in fact written a quarter of a century later, in 1986, by Mitterrand (in *Réflexions sur la politique extérieure de la France*). The thrust towards continuity in the fundamentals of French foreign policy remains a powerful one. The outcome of the legislative elections (March 1986) – defeat for the PS, an RPR-UDF liberal majority in the National Assembly, and the appointment as Prime Minister of the RPR leader Jacques Chirac – has not to date deflected that thrust.

Where prior to the elections foreign policy differences had existed between Mitterrand and the Centre-Right parties they had usually been related to specific or secondary issues. Most seriously, the RPR and UDF had denounced as inadequate the Socialist government's spending on defence since 1981. The RPR criticized Mitterrand's rejection of French State participation in SDI (see p.130), and talked of renegotiating the entry into the EEC of Spain and Portugal. In the heat of the election campaign Chirac derisively dismissed as '(du) tiersmondisme échevelé' Mitterrand's high-principled efforts on behalf of 'tous ces pays – Nicaragua, Ethiopie – qui nous injurient'. 'Qu'avons-nous à faire de ces gens-là?' Chirac asked, before concluding: 'Il faudra revenir sur tout cela.'

After the legislative elections such differences were largely forgotten or at least minimized. Whether concerning the Maghreb or the EEC, relations with West Germany or in the Middle East, the basic continuity of French foreign policy reasserted itself. Between the Socialist President and the liberal Prime Minister and government a practical, consensual cohabitation became the rule. Working relations between Mitterrand and Chirac (and Foreign Affairs Minister Jean-Bernard Raimond, and Defence Minister André Giraud) were characterized by attitudes of reasonableness and mutual adjustment. Joint policy stands were efficiently adopted on the co-ordination of western economic policies and on international terrorism (Tokyo industrial nations summit, May 1986), on continued intervention in Chad, on Lebanon and

Iran. 'Sur tous les grands sujets évoqués jusqu' à présent (. . .)
MM Mitterrand et Chirac partagent les mêmes orientations',
Raimond commented after the Tokyo summit.

More potential than actual, policy differences do exist between Mitterrand and the Chirac government: defence spending, French involvement in Central America, Third World
indebtedness, and co-operation policy in general. Conflict
over the content of French foreign policy is, however, likely to
prove less significant than the struggle for the political control
over that policy. Presidential elections are due in France in
1988; they may be called before that date. Chirac will certainly
stand; Mitterrand may do. Established by de Gaulle, the
tradition of presidential dominance over foreign policy in
France obliges the present Prime Minister to assert his capacity
in this area in order to enhance his standing as a presidential
candidate. Accordingly, after the 1986 legislative elections,
Chirac took every opportunity to maximize his contribution to
French foreign affairs. His presence with Mitterrand at the
Tokyo summit countered the habitual presidential monopoly
of such events. Since April 1986 the prime ministerial cabinet
has contained a team of advisors which co-ordinates the
foreign policy activity of all ministries of the Chirac
government – a development unknown under de Gaulle or
Giscard.

Chirac's efforts to relativize, constrain and discredit
Mitterrand's authority over foreign policy are intended both to
promote the RPR-UDF government's policy and to further his
own electoral ambition. To the extent that his efforts also
erode the traditional presidential *domaine réservé* (see p.107)
they may, ultimately, bring into question an important
dimension in the continuity of French foreign policy.

Bibliography

Colombani, J.M., *Portrait du Président*. Gallimard, Paris,
1985. See pp. 132–3, 208–16 for a vivid impression of
Mitterrand's ideas and attitudes in the foreign policy area.
Colombani is a senior political editor on *Le Monde*.
Frears, J.R., *France in the Giscard Presidency*. London, George

Allen & Unwin, 1981. Chapters 5 and 6 on foreign policy and defence under Giscard.

Giscard d'Estaing, V., *Démocratie française. Préface inédite*. London, Methuen, 1983. Chapter XII reviews the principal areas of Giscard's foreign policy.

Grosser, A., *Affaires extérieures. La Politique de la France, 1944–1984*. Paris, Flammarion, 1984. A recent general survey by a French authority.

Mitterrand, F., *Ici et maintenant*. Paris, Livres de Poche, 1981. Chapters VI and VII: a lively *tour d'horizon* of major international questions, conducted a few months before Mitterrand was elected President.

——, *Réflexions sur la politique extérieure de la France*.Paris, Fayard, 1986. The Introduction (pp. 7–135) contains an extended account of French defence, European and Third World policies.

Pickles, D., *The Government and Politics of France*, Vol. II: *Politics*. London, Methuen, 1973. Part II offers a full and stimulating account of foreign policy under de Gaulle and Pompidou. A list of related French and English titles is included (pp. 481–3).

——, *Problems of Contemporary French Politics*. London, Methuen, 1982. Chapter 5: 'The decline of Gaullist foreign policy'; Chapters 6 and 7 discuss Giscardian European and defence problems.

Six

Education

Margaret S. Archer

Introduction

An understanding of any element in the French system of
education implies a knowledge of its history, precisely because
a system existed in France a century before its development in
England. The endurance of a structure designed to fit the needs
of pre-industrial society in the early nineteenth century leads
to problems of adjustment to modern politics, economy and
society. Even an understanding of the Events of May 1968 re-
quires that they should be seen not only as an attack on
modern educational institutions but also on the traditional
structure of the educational system as a whole.

The historical background

The dual tradition in French education

From the French Revolution onwards, two main traditions of
educational thought and practice can be traced, whose conflict
occupied the whole of the nineteenth century and has
not been settled in the twentieth. On the one hand, the revolutionary emphasis on individual rights to instruction is most
clearly expressed in the blueprints for educational reform put
forward in the Assemblies of the First Republic. On the other,
Napoleon's policy subordinated the amount and content of
education received by individuals to the needs of the State efficiency.

Condorcet's blueprint, the most influential on future

educationists, summarizes the basic tenets of Republican thought on education. Instruction should be given because the individual has a right to it: it should therefore be universal and for both sexes, and ought to be common to all at primary level. By contrast, Napoleon's purpose in organizing a new educational system was pragmatic. Unlike the series of revolutionary blueprints which remained largely theoretical, his reforms were immediately implemented. Napoleon's two overriding aims of bringing about efficiency in the State and stability in society could not be served by treating unequals equally. Abandoning an educational philosophy based on individual rights for one which he framed in relation to State needs, he relegated primary education to the lowest priority in his policy. As the inculcation of useful skills was to be the supreme end of instruction, and as the State required only small numbers of trained individuals, any extension of training to the masses would be economically wasteful and socially dangerous. The minimal amount of knowledge the people required could be imparted in fee-paying or charitable schools, run by the Church. Therefore the State need not create primary establishments, but could content intself with controlling the loyalty of its teachers, who were mainly members of Catholic orders. Napoleon did not want the masses to be instructed beyond a minimum level of literacy, sufficient for the needs of a mainly agricultural economy, and did not object to their being religious, since the Church encouraged social conformity by preaching the acceptance of a preordained station in life.

Unlike primary schools, secondary and higher establishments were vital to the State, since they were to provide the skilled administrators, professionals and officers who were to serve it. As a corollary, State control over the education they gave and the degrees they granted would ensure that the best available talent would be channelled into useful occupations. In this way Napoleon justified the State monopoly over education embodied in the Imperial University of 1808 – the name given to the centralized system of State education. This prevented any other secondary school from functioning without direct authorization by the university authorities and submitted all State establishments to the control of a rigidly hierarchical administration, whose head was directly responsible to the Emperor. Not only did this centralization remain a permanent characteristic of French education, but many component institutions of the Imperial University have survived until now. Thus the *lycées* (State secondary schools), the *baccalauréat* (degree awarded for secondary studies and permitting university entry) and the *Ecole Normale* (training establishment for teachers who become civil servants upon admission to it) are still features of the contemporary system. Not only have such specific institutions endured, but the overall educational philosophy of the Imperial University is not yet extinct. Its fundamental principle, that if the State has no need of education, the people have no right to instruction, led to the development of a bifurcated system. On the one hand, highly specialized institutions at the secondary and higher level provided skilled servants of the State; on the other limited instruction in primary schools sufficed to provide loyal citizens. The absence of a ladder between the two levels limited educational mobility and reflected the major social division between the bourgeoisie and the people.

The development of primary education under the July Monarchy

While Napoleon designed the educational system mainly to supply civil and military administrators, in connection with his policy of reconstruction in France and expansion abroad, subsequent regimes, without changing the basic structure of the Imperial University, modified some of its component parts. These reforms were largely prompted by the increasing pace of industrialization and the ensuing need for the propagation of some technical skills among the people. The July Monarchy (1830–48) was a predominantly bourgeois government, committed to industrial expansion and therefore disinclined to leave primary education to the Church, as under the Empire and the Restoration. The conservative bourgeois fear of elementary education as a source of social unrest – which had prevailed since the final phase of the Revolution – gradually gave way before the entrepreneurial awareness that industry required trained operatives. Hence the diffusion of primary schooling appeared to be a precondition of economic development and a prerequisite of the July Monarchy's motto: *Enrichissez-vous*. However, the educational structure inherited from Napoleon was ill adapted both in its form and its content to the inculcation of the skills required. The main inadequacy was the gap between an exceedingly elementary primary schooling and an exceedingly classical secondary one. The nature of secondary and higher education made it irrelevant to industry, while that of primary schooling made it insufficient. Thus the creation of *écoles primaires supérieures* as an extension of primary schooling by the law of 1833 introduced the degree of expansion in popular education which the evolution of the economy demanded and a stable society could accommodate. Considerations of economic utility rather than individual rights to instruction prompted this reform. These higher grade schools created in 1833, to which the best pupils passed after completing primary studies, were predominantly vocational. They trained workers for commerce and industry, without attempting to lead into secondary establishments. Thus the basic bifurcation was unchanged. The educational system had altered to meet economic needs, but had remained socially conservative. The sons of manual workers could gain more instruction than previously but without competing with the children of the bourgeoisie, who still monopolized secondary and higher education.

The survival of the Napoleonic structure under the Third Republic

After the fall of the July Monarchy in 1848, the Second Republic did not reform the educational system, but reorganized the division of responsibilities between secular and clerical teachers within the State system. This issue had remained contentious since the Empire, as the Church sought to retain its control over primary instruction and claimed a greater share of secondary. The *loi Falloux* of 1850 satisfied these demands by reducing the educational qualifications required from clerics and by giving the clergy seats on the educational councils of the *Université*. Such concessions were prompted by the fear of popular unrest, exemplified by the excesses of June 1848, and by the reliance of the bourgeoisie on religious instruction to restrain radicalism.

While the Second Empire (1852–70) was a period of religious reassertion in education, the Third Republic gradually secularized the State system and the separation of Church and State in 1905 was the culminating point in this process. As a result, the Church retained only 14 per cent of existing primary schools (in 1906–7) and all its establishments, primary and secondary alike, had to be fee-paying. Apart from the religious issue, the main concern of educational policy under the Third Republic was for numerical growth and institutional adaptation within the Napoleonic framework.

Primary education

Throughout the century there had been evidence of a growing desire for instruction, witnessed by the spectacular development of adult education. The increase in school attendance predated the institution of compulsory and free primary education under the legislation introduced by Jules Ferry as Minister of Public Instruction in 1880. In a country that was still predominantly agrarian, this provision was particularly important for the rural areas, which had lagged behind the towns with regard to schooling. While it was gradually made universal, primary education remained detached from secondary but became more complex to meet the dual demands of increasing industrialization and growing parental aspirations. Thus it collected a series of additional courses, largely vocational in content, each regarded as terminal and leading to gainful employment rather than formal study. Simultaneously the higher-grade schools broadened their curricula to include more modern subjects, in sharp contrast with the classicism of secondary establishments. While these remained terminal for most pupils, they came to supply some candidates for primary teacher training institutions. It is indicative of the isolation of primary instruction that its teachers should have been recruited from those who had no secondary education themselves. While additional courses and higher-grade shools offered a modern and popular alternative to the classicism of the bourgeois *lycées*, the development of technical schools and centres of apprenticeship provided training facilities for future foremen, skilled workers and craftsmen. By 1919 it had become compulsory for primary school-leavers to receive some form of vocational training until the age of eighteen. This growing differentiation within primary education mirrored the differentiation of the working class resulting from a more complex division of labour in industrial society. It did not, and was not intended to promote mobility from class to class, it merely diversified employment prospects for the working class.

Secondary education

Secondary curricula were intended to offer a preparation for higher education and the professions, and were therefore predominantly classical in content. Demands for the incorporation of modern subjects, the sciences and European languages, were in direct contradiction to the traditional structure of the *baccalauréat*. They met with considerable resistance from the supporters of a purely classical definition of culture. The addition of modern subjects was construed as a move away from the cultural role of education towards vocationalism. In this debate culture was seen as totally opposed to specialization: it was in fact defined residually as 'that which remains when all else has been forgotten'. This traditional approach was symbolized by the concentration on classical languages in the *baccalauréat* which was not modernized until 1902. From that date onwards, and as a result of parental pressures for a more practical curriculum, an alternative curriculum was introduced alongside the classical. Pupils could opt for either the classical or the modern section, each of them leading up to a different *baccalauréat*. However, classicism retained its prestige and the best pupils were systematically channelled into the classical stream. Thus the direct connection established under Napoleon between classical studies and administrative or professional careers remained unbroken. The new modern stream reflected the growing demands of industry and commerce, which had grown in economic importance rather than in social prestige.

Higher education

Higher education within the Imperial University was designed to staff the two major professions of the time – the medical and the legal. The appropriate training was dispensed by Faculties of Medicine and of Law, which were self-contained establishments. On the other hand, the Faculties of Letters and of Sciences were mainly degree-granting bodies, which organized examinations, but did not have any permanent students. The main occupation of the professors was the organization and adjudication of the *baccalauréat*. Since future lawyers and physicians were trainees rather than students, the concept of student was unknown in France until 1877 and the few lectures given were addressed to the general public. The reform of 1877 was intended to turn the faculties into teaching bodies by increasing their staff and by creating State studentships. As a result, higher education experienced an enormous expansion, doubling its intake between 1875 (9963 students) and 1891 (19,281) and doubling yet again between 1891 and 1908 (38,890). However, this numerical increase tended to be concentrated in Paris (52 per cent of students in 1888). To offset this excessive centralization, which favoured Paris residents and was detrimental to provincial interests, a policy of founding regional universities was put forward in the 1880s. This aimed at the creation of true universities, teaching a wide range of subjects and grouping many students, rather than mere collections of isolated faculties. In other words, there was a protest against the Napoleonic structure with its rigid centralization and its narrow definition of higher education. The policy proposed was to extend the range of subjects in order to include the new sciences and to incorporate the neglected specialisms, such as archaeology or modern history. All disciplines were to be taught under the same roof. These pleas for reform failed, as the law of 1896 merely conferred the title of 'university' upon groups of faculties existing in the same town, but did not amalgamate them into unitary bodies. Even if there were only two faculties in any one town, they were officially turned into a university, though neither their intake nor their courses changed. As a result, fifteen universities came into being, but their component faculties remained unaltered under this new name. Thus the law of 1896, generally considered as founding universities in France, actually destroyed the hopes of breaking away from the Napoleonic tradition.

The twentieth century

Plans for reform

Twentieth-century France inherited the Napoleonic educational system, virtually unchanged and characterized by the strict separation of primary and secondary schooling. This dichotomy firmly distinguished the bourgeoisie from the working class and the peasantry. As universal primary education threatened this distinction, the bourgeoisie strove to protect their privileged access to the *lycée* by sending their children to junior forms within the *lycée* (*classes élémentaires*), which were fee-paying when primary education had become free. The efficacy of this practice as a guarantee of admission to secondary education is illustrated by the numerical growth in the number of *lycée* junior pupils: from 16,000 boys in 1881 to 55,000 in 1940. Additional obstacles debarred working-class children from entry into secondary education – the length of the course that led up to the *baccalauréat* after seven years' study, the fees payable during this period which were not completely covered by the grants available, the small number of these scholarships and the preference given to children of minor civil servants in their distribution (in 1911, 51 per cent of grants were awarded to children of civil servants and only 20 per cent to children of peasants, artisans and workers). The increase in popular demand for education was not met by an expansion of existing facilities at secondary level nor by a widening of recruitment. Therefore, it was the higher grade schools that absorbed the mass of pupils from primary school. This is evidenced by the fact that their intake in 1914 exceeded that of secondary establishments.

While in the nineteenth century it could be argued that the division into primary and secondary reflected the social structure of a predominantly agricultural country, the growth of the middle classes made this argument invalid in the twentieth. Nor could it be maintained that the adjustments whereby the primary system had developed its upper forms and the secondary its lower forms had made education more democratic. They had merely resulted in heightening class distinctions by inculcating two different cultures – excessive classicism among secondary pupils and extreme vocationalism among primary pupils. It is on these grounds that a reform movement advocating the integration of primary and secondary into an *école unique* was formed at the end of the First World War. Throughout the period between the two wars the debate about this reform was interrupted and largely unsuccessful. Indeed, while secondary establishments became free in 1928, they retained their traditional curricula and their social bias.

The main blueprint for the *école unique* was produced by Jean Zay as Minister of Education in 1937. With its stress on equalizing educational opportunities and its acceptance of a universal right to secondary education, it is reminiscent of the revolutionary philosophy and stands in sharp distinction to the Napoleonic tradition. Zay advocated the creation of a middle school (*tronc commun*), which all pupils would attend between receiving primary instruction (common to all) and entering secondary schooling. The former courses of the *lycées* and of the higher grade schools would be integrated into a new secondary, divided into three branches of study: classical, modern and technical. The middle school would be concerned with guiding pupils to the appropriate stream of secondary studies according to their ability and interests. This proposal met with strong resistance, particularly from the unions of *lycée* teachers, and was only introduced in some establishments on an experimental basis. The war in 1939 and the collapse of the Third Republic prevented further debate on educational reform. After the interlude of the Vichy regime (which was strongly conservative in educational matters) the Fourth Republic was again faced with the issues that the Third had failed to solve. In 1947 the Langevin-Wallon plan, differing only in details from Zay's blueprint, was successfully resisted by the educationists' lobby. A similar fate was suffered by the Billères plan in 1957. Thus at the beginning of the Fifth Republic the dichotomy between primary and secondary remained almost intact.

The problem of democratization had not been solved: the main reason for this is instructive as it also accounts for failure to deal with the equally pressing issues of modernization and secularization during the same period. The answer lies in the fragmented nature of the political parties, and underlying this the cleavages dividing French society. In the first half of the twentieth century the political arithmetic of the multi-party system added up to Centre government – the alternation of power between Centre-Right and Centre-Left coalitions. Because of this, political policy was reduced to the minimum programme which the governing coalition could agree to endorse, and legislation was restricted to the even more limited measures for which parliamentary support could be marshalled. This situation, commonly described as political *immobilisme*, largely explains the long-drawn-out war of projects over the *école unique*, which remained unresolved at the end of the Fourth Republic. In addition, however, the failure of the Left to hold together as a political force and to steer through the legislation sought by those it represented must also be held partly responsible.

The second aspect of the twentieth-century inheritance was the inability of educational institutions to satisfy demands for modern professional training, especially for the lower levels of industry, agriculture and commerce. 'Former le producteur, l'enseignement français y répugne. Son rationalisme tourne à l'intellectualisme.' This judgement of Prost's was particularly true in the field of technical and applied instruction at all levels. Certainly the *Loi Astier* of 1919 began to tackle the problem of producing a skilled workforce by founding part-time schools and making it obligatory for municipalities to run them, employers to release their apprentices, and working youths under eighteen to attend. Its provisions initially implied decentralization, for such schools were to be controlled by the Ministry of Commerce, organized by local commissions, and financed by a tax on employers. However, in the following years they were reintegrated with the Ministry of Education and its successive directors steadily developed their general educational content at the expense of vocational specialization. As irrelevance increased so did evasion by apprentices and employers, such that by the outbreak of war apprenticeship training was still grossly deficient in quantitative and qualitative terms.

This tendency for specialized and practical training to be displaced by general education was even more marked at higher levels of technical instruction. There the creation of a series of national technical qualifications, each conferring rights to further education, resulted in uniformity rather than the diversity of skills required to match the occupational market. In particular the establishment of a *baccalauréat technique* in 1946 exerted a powerful downward influence, standardizing curricula in the upper reaches of the primary schools, the appropriate sections of secondary establishments, and the *écoles nationales professionnelles*. In one way it might seem that this recognition signalled a breakthrough in modernization (for it meant a complete hierarchy of technical studies), but in the absence of decisive legislation establishing self-standing institutions free to develop their own approach, technical education was caught up in the traditional system and loss of specialization, diversity and practical relevance were the prices paid.

Thirdly, the anti-clerical policy in education, pursued at the beginning of the century, by no means spelt a general consensus on the secular nature of public instruction. Independent Catholic schools continued to attract a substantial number of pupils, although they were facing economic difficulties in their competition with the public sector. After the First World War this led protagonists of the confessional schools to launch a political campaign for governmental funding in proportion to their pupil intake. This particular formula was never successful, due to strong Republican opposition, but after the introduction of free public secondary instruction the economic plight of the confessional schools progressively worsened and with it grew a determination to wrest support from the State in one form or another. Obviously this depended on a government favourably disposed to the Catholic educational cause, and it was not until the early 1950s that the clerical issue could be politically reanimated. When, despite the vociferousness of its opponents, a law was passed in 1951 permitting State allocations towards teachers' salaries and buildings in the private sector, an MRP Deputy described this as the 'breach through which the flood will pass'. In other words the Catholic Parliamentary Association signalled its intention of achieving a much more far-reaching settlement than the politics of immobilism had allowed.

The Fifth Republic

While the powers of educational control remain concentrated at the centre, this is the source of change, whether such transformations are initiated by political negotiation or induced by political disruption. Both processes were important under the Fifth Republic and their causes and consequences are closely intertwined. The first major reforms dealing with the problems of desecularization, democratization and modernization were directed by the government in a spirit of educational pragmatism. The situations it faced were inherited from the immobilism of the Fourth Republic and the dissatisfaction which had accumulated around these three issues. The Debré, Berthoin and Fouchet measures can all be looked upon in the same light, as piecemeal changes and pragmatic concessions intended to take the edge off discontent – giving away a little in order to conserve a great deal. As such these reforms tinkered *à la marge* rather than indicating a willingness to engage in large-scale structural change or devolution of educational control. Public education remained, in the words of the then Education Minister, Christian Fouchet, 'the biggest enterprise in the world apart from the Red Army' and was just about as responsive to the expression of social interests and local demands. In turn this rigidity was partly responsible for the outbursts in May 1968.

Clericalism

The *Loi Debré* of 1959, giving State aid to private and mainly confessional schools, was justified by specific reference to the 'indispensable unity' of national education. This concession to Catholic supporters of government, which involved overriding the opinions of the vast majority of teachers' associations and trade unions, offered private schools one of four solutions to their financial difficulties: total integration with public education; a contract of association; a simpler contract; or the maintenance of the *status quo*. The first and last formulae were only used in a minority of cases, and by 1967–8 over 85 per cent of private primary and secondary schools were under one kind of contractual arrangement or the other. Both meant that the State aided such schools and paid teachers providing that whilst conserving their 'own character', each school taught 'with complete respect for liberty of conscience' and conformed to certain requirements about numbers of pupils, qualifications of teachers and standards of the physical environment. With the full contract all expenses were undertaken by the State at the cost of a serious loss of autonomy, for the school also became subject to the rules and programmes governing public education. The simple contract which provided for less aid, but less State control, was intended, however, only to be a temporary formula. Integration, loss of autonomy and standardization were all implicit in the *loi Debré*. Its implementation led one to wonder whether national education had not lost one of its few sources of diversity for it was difficult to see how such schools could preserve much of their 'own character' when forced to conform closely to public educational practices. De Gaulle had made the passing of this bill a matter of confidence (a sign that the new style of government was asserting itself in educational politics), and he secured his majority. What this Act did not do, however, was to solve the clerical question in education. For the Church had lost in freedom what it had gained in funding, while defenders of *l'école laïque* were outraged at this manipulation of constitutional and governmental powers and organized massive demonstrations in favour of a single secular system of instruction.

Democratization

The Berthoin reform of 1959 came as an anticlimax after forty years of struggle to establish an *école unique*, and was intended to defuse and diffuse the discontent which had build up over the repeated failures of this movement. It was imposed imperatively by decree while de Gaulle still possessed the special powers granted to him before the new National Assembly had met. This compromise measure thus stemmed directly from the presidency without there being opportunity for parliamentary intervention or modification.

A cycle of observation starting at the age of eleven and lasting for two years was introduced for all pupils. At the end of their elementary studies pupils could continue at primary school, attend a *collège d'enseignement général* (CEG was the new name for the old *cours complémentaires*), or enter a *lycée*. Officially this 'placement' (affected either by teachers' recommendations, parental preference, or simply by pupils staying where they were) was not viewed as decisive, for after two years of observation pupils would be orientated to the appropriate secondary course. In other words the observation cycle took place in different kinds of establishments, much to the satisfaction of the *professeurs* who had always opposed the idea of autonomous middle school for all. Moreover, the content of this cycle was not the same for all, for it was made up of the normal programmes followed in the sixth and fifth class in these different kinds of institutions. The notion of a lengthy *tronc commun*, followed by all pupils and used to establish the pattern of ability of individuals, was reduced to a single term during which syllabuses were 'harmonized' in different kinds of schools.

At the end of the cycle, the *conseil d'orientation* in each school advised parents on appropriate further studies. *Classes passerelles* situated in the fourth class provided conversion courses for those who had taken the wrong turning during the orientation phase. However, since assessments were made in establishments varying from the *lycée* to the primary school, and moreover were made on the basis of their respective curricula, it is not surprising that this resulted in very little individual mobility – only 1 per cent of pupils transferred from the latter to the former.

In respecting the vested interests of different groups of teachers, the compromise reform had left existing structures intact, but in doing so it had merely perpetuated these interests and the activities associated with their defence. Devices like the harmonization of curricula and the *classes passerelles* had certainly linked different parts of the system, but without providing the vast majority of pupils with more equality of educational opportunity. The dissatisfaction manifested by the primary and technical teachers, trade unions and political Left indicated that this decree was not the final solution to grievances which had rankled for half a century. Continued pressure from these quarters led the Minister to admit that the object of orientation was indeed defeated when it took place in different types of schools. Following this the *collèges d'enseignement secondaire* (CES) were founded in 1963. Theoretically they were to cater for the whole age group from 11 to 14, thus functioning as common or comprehensive middle schools. Some pupils would proceed from the CES to secondary establishments, others to full-time vocational training and yet others to apprenticeship schemes.

However, they were to be formed by converting the first cycle of *lycée* studies into independent units and by transforming existing CEGs, but this was opposed by *professeurs* and municipalities alike. Had the reform engaged in audacious structural change and created a multilateral institution of a self-standing type, it would have overridden vested interests: as it was it placed itself at their mercy. On the one hand conversion of schools was resisted (there were only 220 schools of this type in 1964 and 1500 in 1968 with many still refusing to transform themselves in the 1970s). On the other hand the CES was made up of a classical and a modern section from secondary, a *moderne court* section from the CET, and the old *classe de fin d'études* from the primary school, yet professional resistance prevented fusion from taking place between them. The hope was that flexibility would replace separateness, to the benefit of all pupils, but this was not discernible outside a few pilot schools that had overridden the traditional curricula – inherited from the courses making up the CES. In sum the conversion modifying the Berthoin solution drew off little of the discontent stimulated by inequality of educational opportunity.

Modernization

The Fouchet reforms at secondary and higher level were a package of changes whose contents were intended to alleviate some very different kinds of discontent – that of students with the 50 per cent failure rate at the end of the first year (likened by a subsequent Minister of Education to organizing a shipwreck to find who could swim), of large employers with an encyclopaedic culture irrelevant to occupational needs, of staff at both levels with rising numbers and falling standards, and of the Left in general with its marked social discrimination. The same mechanism was adopted at secondary and higher levels and involved the differentiation of cycles of studies within them, giving a greater opportunity for vocational specialization. Simultaneously this was intended to satisfy students (by giving greater choice, better orientation and thus a lower failure rate), to produce school-leavers and graduates better suited to occupational outlets, and to have a democratic appeal because it established shorter courses for those whose cultural or financial background had previously excluded them altogether. At university level the complementary reforms were mainly intended to obviate the disadvantages inherent in lack of pre-entry selection, for all holders of the *baccalauréat* had an automatic right of admission to higher education, without further test. Faculties of Letters and Science were reorganized by creating three cycles, the first one to provide the basic knowledge required to bring entrants up to university standard. This lasted two years and students chose a particular branch of study within each faculty, which led to a diploma. Specialization became more intense in the second cycle, where after one year (that is, three years of undergraduate study in all) the *licence* could be gained, or after two years (four in all), students could obtain the master's degree. The third cycle represented the beginning of postgraduate study.

In accordance with the philosophy of 'short' alternatives, a two year course for the training of *cadres* (at supervisory and lower managerial level) was given at new institutions, *instituts universitaires de technologie*, created alongside the university faculties. Staff were to be recruited partly from university teachers and partly from among specialists working in nationalized industries or private enterprises. The subjects taught were to be selected for their vocational value, assessed in the light of current economic needs, and teaching methods were to concentrate on practical projects in fields such as civil engineering, electronics, information processing and statistics.

These reforms were applied identically in all institutions, including the new universities created to cope with overcrowding. Even in broad technocratic terms they were less than successful, to judge from the divergence between the proportions intended to follow science and technology courses under the national plan and the much lower percentage of students enrolling in them. Not only did this spell manpower deficiencies *vis-à-vis* the economy, but also the continued growth of a body of pupils and students without clear vocational expectations or opportunities. In addition, the chaotic application of the laws (more than 2000 decrees were involved) placed many students in an anomalous position because of these constant changes and heightened the awareness of many staff to continuous ministerial interference. Finally the Left was not impressed by the democratic intentions of a reform which created an inferior opportunity structure for the non-privileged by consistently directing them towards the shorter alternatives, at all levels of instruction. Clearly many of the demands the reforms sought to assuage were mutually contradictory, but it is precisely because of this that any attempt to impose a uniform solution common to all schools and universities was bound to satisfy no one. Only a strategy which showed a willingness to sacrifice some control and allow some institutional autonomy, so that truly differentiated establishments would provide specialist services, could hope to satisfy conflicting demands simultaneously.

Groups inside and outside the system publicly registered their dissatisfaction with the educational policies of the Fifth Republic. The Caen colloquium of university teachers meeting in 1966 rejected the Napoleonic concept of a single national structure, with identical regional establishments, as more suitable for the post office or police than for education. Instead they sought the creation of diversified universities, autonomous in policy and administration, and for which the ministry would merely ensure adequate financing, equipment and staffing. Such universities would develop their own courses, curricula and examinations. The same demand for decentralization and the same condemnation of uniformity was voiced in connection with secondary education at the Amiens colloquium, only two months before the May Events. But confronted with the highly controlled system there was little teachers could do at any level to introduce changes internally and thus to alter the nature of instruction from within. Given this position of powerlessness, the reactions of the teaching profession took two different forms.

Cut off from playing a constructive role in educational administration, or being able to respond directly to pupil requests or community requirements, much of the profession turned in upon itself and pursued an academic traditionalism which was not politically contentious. The cumulative effect of this reaction was to increase the gap between the nature of education and the facts of active life. In particular many teachers at secondary and higher level worked at reproducing themselves in their pupils and at reinforcing a *subject*-based organization of knowledge. For students the effect was to separate their present studies from any future relevance: for employers it was to deprive them of school-leavers or graduates whose knowledge was organized on a *professional* basis. In his brilliant analysis, Pierre Bourdieu sums up the irrational situation which resulted as one where all were treated 'as apprentice professors and not as professional apprentices'.

At the same time, however, a different section of teachers turned to political action as a means of introducing change and pursued this end in conjunction with their professional associations, the trade unions and the left-wing parties. In 1967 the Communist Party published an issue of *l'Ecole et la Nation*, condemning Gaullist reforms as mere shunting operations, the *instituteurs'* syndicate passed a motion at its September congress condemning government policy, and in November students went on strike at Nanterre over application of the Fouchet reforms. This signalled the growth of frustration shared by certain parties, students and sections of the profession. However, it did not indicate the emergence of united action. Although teachers themselves had some unity within their professional federations, many teachers in turn were also members of the broader unions, the CGT and the CFDT, which were not themselves on good terms. Furthermore many university teachers and students looked to the parties and factions of the extreme Left which were viewed with the utmost suspicion by both the CGT and the Communist Party. Given that none of these groups, organizations or parties was in a strong enough political position peacefully to negotiate educational changes with the Gaullist majority government, the steady accumulation of grievances finally exploded into direct action – the May Events. However, their internal divisions prevented them from forming other than temporary alliances, cemented by the euphoria of revolt, but never holding together for long enough to consolidate real educational gains.

The Events of May 1968 and their aftermath

A vast amount has been written about the course of the Events and the explanations advanced have been almost as numerous. These range from various kinds of conspiracy theory, through the official chain-reaction account (endorsed by government and Communist Party alike) which interpreted the revolt as a fortuitous series of episodes tenuously linked by accident and opportunism, to explanations couched in terms of a new form of class conflict. There is not the space to assess such theories here, but the most tenable general explanation is that the events were the explosion of a number of grievances which had accumulated over the decade, as political closure replaced political immobility. More specifically, as an educational revolt, the Events appear to have represented a massive condemnation of the mania for centralization and a movement for educational autonomy and localized diversity, contrary to the revolutionary, monarchical and Republican traditions alike. It now remains to be seen how far the reforms introduced in 1968 and after reflected a willingness to concede to these demands in order to solve the crisis.

What was significant about the 1968 reform was that it set a new pattern which was consistently repeated throughout the remaining Gaullist and Giscardian periods. In the first Gaullist decade the policy had been to take the edge off discontent by scattering a few crumbs to the most persistent clamourers: the second decade opened with the realization that much greater concessions were essential to stem the rising tide of grievances. The new formula basically consisted in conceding various types of educational democratization in order to conserve the instrumentality of education to the polity. As such it represented a revised version of the Napoleonic credo, namely, 'let the people's rights to instruction not infringe upon State educational needs'. This was embodied in the *loi d'orientation de l'enseignement supérieur* and in subsequent measures dealing with lower levels. The new principle was also to be accompanied by a distinctive method of policy implementation; generous reformism in the initial legislation followed by administrative reneging on the more radical clauses.

Higher education

The *loi d'orientation de l'enseignement supériéur* was a typical piece of panic legislation, adopted in the National Assembly by 441 votes to none, the Communists and six Gaullists abstaining. The major political parties had restricted themselves to textual criticism and minor amendments, the whole tenor of the debate being summed up by one *député* who commended Edgar Faure's text for having the merit of existing. The parties of the Left no less than those of the Right had an interest in defusing the educational problem. In the face of virtual parliamentary unanimity on the bill, the teachers' associations and student groups were all hopelessly divided. Thus no concerted extra-parliamentary opposition impeded either the passing or the implementation of the Act.

It was adopted in November 1968 and appeared to break away from the Napoleonic *Université* in each of the three main principles it endorsed: multi-disciplinary study, participation and autonomy. The break, however, was more moderate than it appeared since pluri-disciplinarity concealed an official concern for increased vocationalism, while the extent of participation and autonomy which were granted did not seriously undermine central control.

Officially autonomy was substantially increased. The basic unit on which the whole system of higher education was to be founded was the university and not the *Université*. Each university was to become an autonomous establishment from the financial point of view and to be free to draw up its own statutes. In the past the major limitation on academic freedom derived from the existence of national degrees and diplomas which meant that the corresponding courses were based on ministerial regulations. The new universities were now free to issue their own certificates, but even the most extreme opponents of centralization have been unwilling to relinquish the State-guaranteed qualifications which future employers still seek. Experiments with specialist subjects and approaches were largely confined to the second and third cycles and to certain isolated institutions. Furthermore the experimental excesses taking place in one or two establishments, which exploited their formal rights to the full, were counter-productive in convincing many that the only defence of academic standards lay in clinging to traditionalism. In addition a later provision that funding should be allocated according to the types and quality of courses offered was a major central infringement of institutional autonomy and the capacity for pedagogic innovation.

As far as *participation* was concerned the parity between staff and students, promised after the May Events, was in fact reduced to a maximum of one-third for students. Moreover the limitations imposed on participation were broad and excluded such areas as curricula and course design, the allocation of credits, the testing of aptitude and knowledge, the recruitment and promotion of staff and all matters of selection. Thus this legal hedging contrasted sharply with the initial statements about equal shares in university management. In consequence the French Union of Students advised UNEF members against voting in the first university elections and student voting rates have since dropped lower still. Limited participation was not perceived as genuine power-sharing and the students accordingly resented their assigned role of *électeurs mineurs*.

The first responsibility of the council elected in the 630 teaching and research units, set up to replace the former faculties, was to meet with those of other units with which the creation of a university was contemplated. Through this cumbersome procedure, which appeared to bow to the spirit of May – the initiation of reforms from the grass roots in contrast to the centralized tradition of making decisions at the top and transmitting them downwards – *multi-disciplinarity* was to emerge. As a radical principle of reorganization, a break with the antiquated faculty structure which no longer matched the diversified occupational structure, its implicit vocational drive was diluted and distorted from the start by academic traditionalism.

To begin with a number of faculties survived in disguise by constituting themselves into the new units for teaching and research. In larger towns, greater student numbers forced a split into several units per faculty, but few original regroupings of subject matter within each unit were actually adopted. Almost everywhere, after less conventional proposals were put forward and then rejected by a majority, it was the solution most akin to traditional habits which was re-endorsed, the sub-division by subjects. For example, Faculties of Science turned themselves into units of physics, chemistry, maths and natural science. In other words a vertical division along the lines of the major courses taught in the past was the dominant pattern to emerge, rather than any radical reorganization of different knowledge systems in relation to one another.

When the units then had to engage in recombination, most played safe by avoiding co-operation with those which were unfamiliar, competitive or politically uncongenial. Thus 'compromising' entanglements were shunned and in the process few experimental combinations emerged. Most pure scientists found the social sciences too politicized for comfort, as did lawyers, and the former association between letters and social science within the old Faculties of Letters tended to endure in the new universities. The Faculties of Science and Medicine, well endowed with research facilities, did not like to merge with poorer specialisms for fear of having to share resources. Add to this the fact that partnerships were often based on shared political attitudes rather than intellectual complementarity (for example, the 'marriage of reason' between medicine and law) and we can see the types of motives which gave shape to multi-disciplinarity in practice.

The resulting mishmash of some seventy universities was a far cry from both the academic flexibility overtly demanded by the students during the May Events and the vocational orientation covertly sought by the government. The failure of the May Events to introduce radical educational change through direct action caused the membership of many participant organizations to shrink. This was particularly true of the Students' Union (UNEF), which collapsed into a number of factions, and meant that just as the legal influence of students in university administration was recognized, their disorganization made them completely ineffectual. Equally their factionalism and extremism cut the students' links with other educational interest groups, including the trade unions, and thus the possibility of aggregating educational grievances and pressurizing government was lost. To this extent the aftermath of the Events defused extra-parliamentary opposition. On the other hand, although the reform gave the government an interval of relative peace it brought it no closer to its goal of a modernized higher education, harnessed to the mixed economy.

In sum the reform had generated institutional variegation rather than functional diversification. At the same time it had introduced changes in the decision-making processes within the universities without entailing a fundamental redistribution of authority between central government and higher education. In the next decade the official aim was to increase the functionality of education through the continued use of these central powers. Policy in the 1970s represented an increasingly conservative interpretation of the reform. The aims were to reduce the threat of autonomy associated with differentiation, by controlling politically sensitive aspects of university development and to make servicing the economy the prime aim of academic specialization.

Given the saturation of the public sector labour market (plus its preference for the products of the *grandes ećoles* rather than the universities) and the endurance of non-selective entry to university (the traditional rights of the *bacheliers* had been protected during the reform), it was clear to the government that more graduates would have to be absorbed by the private sector. Yet it was equally obvious to the central authority that private enterprise was unenthusiastic about graduate employment: while the private sector employed three-quarters of the active population in 1970, it recruited less than a quarter of that year's graduates, preferring those with non-university diplomas. If opposition to selection for university entry prevailed then the projection was that private industry would have to absorb two-thirds of graduates. Attempts were thus made to articulate university outputs with occupational outlets.

The vehicle for the professionalization of the universities was the violently contested reform of 1976 which sought to transform the *licence* and *maîtrise* degrees into self-contained, one-year vocational programmes. Universities were instructed to evaluate their existing courses, eliminating those without occupational outlets and redeploying their resources to create new vocationally relevant courses. Proposed programmes would then be reviewed by 'technical study groups', with representatives from the appropriate vocational area, to estimate market demand for them before final authorization was given by the new Secretariat for Higher Education. This authorization process represented increased power for the central authority and a further clawing-back of autonomy from the universities. Official approval meant that a university could offer a course as a national degree for five years, after which renewed authorization was needed; unapproved degrees, whilst permissible, would lack national recognition.

The response was the largest protest since 1968 – most universities were closed for several months. On the one hand the students objected to their studies being limited to vocational and terminal courses as well as to 'handing over the university to the service of capitalism.' On the other hand the faculty abhorred this new infringement of academic freedom in which curricula assessment was in terms of marketability, and their unions tenaciously defended existing courses. Thus academic traditionalism and student radicalism joined forces to repulse this renewed central incursion and hostilities intensified between the Secretariat and the universities.

Although these reforms became law in 1977, the concessions wrested from the (now) Minister for Universities by internal opposition effectively nullified the professionalization of the universities. In particular, the centrally organized unions of teachers and students, which counterbalance ministerial control, precluded the direct manipulation of individual universities by the central authority. These oppositional forces extracted the crucial concession that automatic authorization would be granted to such existing programmes as gave fundamental training in a discipline. In turn this killed vocational reorganization for it left no redeployable funds for the development of new practical courses. Equally importantly it compelled the Minister to re-endorse the principle of disinterested cultural study for the majority of students, which was precisely what the government had sought to make a minority affair.

Thus central attempts to rationalize the diversification conceded in 1968 have been wholly frustrated through internal counterpressures against vocationalism – by the traditional vested interests of academics and the radical political opposition of students. But this stalemate has benefited neither side. Rationalization from the centre having failed, some believe that the government then started to abandon the universities –witness a 20 per cent financial reduction in real terms since 1973; the reliance for its own recruitment on the *grandes écoles*; and changes like selection for medical degrees and the reform of teacher training when the polity did seek specific university outputs. Talk of abandonment is too strong – at the end of the Giscardian period the government was still supporting a vast enterprise which in its view was instrumental to neither the public nor the private sector. Yet the universities themselves had not benefited from their opposition: the devaluation of degrees continued through over-production in relation to job opportunities, the divorce between studies and active life was perpetuated, and the social advancement of university students was enfeebled as the élite *grandes écoles* reinforced their superior standing.

Primary and secondary education

In broad terms the same pattern of legislative reform followed by administrative retreat also characterized lower levels of education. The trade-off between concessions towards democratization, to pacify the Left, and vocationally-orientated diversification, to satisfy the Right, was even more striking. The course of reform can be divided into three main phases – first a series of Gaullist changes in which technocratic concerns outweighed democratic concessions; second the official recognition, contained in the Haby reform, that these priorities had to be reversed in the face of parental, pedagogic and political pressures; and finally the Giscardian implementation of these new provisions during which vocational relevance regained priority over equality of opportunity.

(i) In the aftermath of the May Events de Gaulle had also contemplated a *loi d'orientation de l'enseignement secondaire* to introduce selective university entry among holders of the *baccalauréat*. To the Right, the termination of the historic open-door policy would have reduced the numbers in higher education, increased the standards of those graduating in the new specialisms, and improved the employability of those for whom the *baccalauréat* was terminal. At the time organized public opinion was so hostile to the un-democratic implication of selection that this policy was dropped in favour of reforming the examination itself – on vocational lines.

Consequently, in 1969, the last years of the *lycée* were transformed into specialized sections leading to different kinds of *baccalauréats*, defined with reference to the modernizing economy. Thus sixteen technical examinations (for example in electronics, biochemistry, administration, management, or computer programming) were differentiated from twelve general ones and accorded parity with the latter. But parity involved the same automatic right of entry to university for its holders, so although the new technical options were attracting over a quarter of all candidates by 1976, this became an additional avenue to further education rather than a preparation for active life.

By 1973 the failure of this reform to attain its technocratic aims was accepted and Joseph Fontanet, then Minister of Education, attempted a further trade-off, this time within secondary education itself. In basic terms his plan entailed grading the *baccalauréat* into a 'good' pass (giving university entry) and a 'straight' pass (giving admission to vocational training centres): to propitiate left-wing opinion the Minister proposed stepping-up democratization at the *start* of secondary studies. Here the three parallel tracks, which had largely confirmed pupils' social origins, would be replaced by ability grouping, supplementary teaching for the disadvantaged, and mixed-ability work in some subjects to reinforce the democratic principle. However, what the government had seen as a concession to left-wing and pedagogic egalitarianism was received as precisely the opposite – instead, ability-grouping would merely accentuate differences in social background. The intensity of criticism meant that these proposals were never implemented, but the fact that a reform of the lower levels had officially been mooted then fuelled demand for their complete transformation on egalitarian lines. Thus not only had the policy of intensifying vocationalism in the *lycée* failed, it had backfired by stimulating pressures for a genuine democratic reform of the secondary level in its entirety – to which the government had to bow.

(ii) In this context, the Act of 1975, initiated by the new Minister René Haby (a former *recteur*) did not represent an official conversion to educational equality but rather the political realization that further democratization was the price of national unity – essential for the development of the technocratic society.

Haby's own proposals sought to cut through the tangle of past compromises which, without significantly improving the equality of educational opportunity, had merely cluttered the interface between the primary and secondary levels. His major reform was to install a common middle school (*collège unique*) which, as an independent institution for all pupils, would place the 'same opportunities in every satchel'. Nor, initially, were the proposals to be limited to streamlining the secondary level, but also included reforms of nursery, primary, technical and 'long' *lycée* instruction.

Passage into the *collège unique* would be monitored by teachers, parents, doctors and psychologists and based on an assessment of the mental age of each child. The middle school itself would have a common curriculum for its first two years, plus compensatory tuition designed to bring all up to roughly the same standard, even if this involved abridging the syllabus. Then in the last two years options would be selected in relation to individual aptitudes. Although some could leave early to receive special vocational training, most would gain the leaving certificate after the four years, or then proceed to an apprenticeship scheme or a *lycée*, guidance again being given by an advisory panel with parents having the right of appeal against its decision.

(iii) On the one hand the *collège unique* was not far removed from what the egalitarian *compagnons* had sought fifty years earlier, for the new plan embodied a *tronc commun*, *observation* and *orientation*. The new Act however, was not an unmitigated victory for the reformist tradition. For, on the other hand, these proposals which aimed at a full-scale transformation of the system suffered from the eternal bane of centralization — truncation in order to fit in with existing provisions or priorities, and standardization such that one universal 'model school' was centrally imposed throughout the nation. Truncation of scope affected both 'ends' of the proposals. The nursery provisions and the earlier start (at five years not six) remained unimplemented, undermining the notion of getting pupils off on a more even footing; so did reform of the *lycées* (now giving only the 'long' general or technical course) and of the *baccalauréat*. In practice the Haby reform was topped and tailed during implementation. The *collège unique* was inserted between the upper and lower levels and the fact that the *lycées* remained virtually unchanged meant that the spirit of the secondary school reform petered out carefully short of the universities. Once again, instead of the reform of the whole system, a reform had been fitted into the existing system.

The effects of the centralized introduction of the *collège unique* (which involved 11 decrees, 19 *arrêtés* and 20 circulars in the first two years) were immediately apparent in its uniformity. Indeed the very concession of a whole 10 per cent of the timetable, to be used at the teachers' discretion, highlighted this enduring feature of the French educational system. From the start the justification for imposing a standardized plan was, as ever, the goal of national unity, a theme which could always harmonize with egalitarianism if emphasis was placed on 'the same provisions for all citizens'. Gradually, however, the tune changed and more stress began to be laid on the Giscardian notion of citizenship for an advanced industrial society – witness the introduction of 'manual and technical training' as a new compulsory subject.

Moreover, the orchestration of change from the centre meant that the new Minister appointed in 1978, Christian Beullac, had the means to manoeuvre the reform into closer alignment with the economy while professing that he was simply continuing with its implementation. Consequently the innovation of *éducation concertée* in 1979 placed pupils taking the shorter secondary courses in industrial firms for probationary periods. This redirection not only tightened the links with industry but also served to conceal the failure of the existing reform to redistribute educational opportunities. By that time it was already known that after two years of post-primary instruction 30 per cent of pupils did not proceed along the common course but received pre-occupational tuition or were channelled into apprenticeship schemes. As such they nullified the notion of a common school, let alone equality of outcome. What *éducation concertée* did was to give a positive face to this failure in democratization by presenting the scheme as an opportunity for all rather than a device which served to confirm the restricted opportunities of the socially disadvantaged. The fact that educational change had been centrally engineered, rather than change spelling decentralized powers of control, meant once again that a new governing élite could make it reverberate to its current political philosophy.

The advent of Socialism

Throughout the twentieth century those seeking greater equality in education (the unions, primary teachers, students and political parties of the Left) recognized that its attainment depended upon a change of government, away from the Right or the Centre-Right. During their long sojourns in the political wilderness the tenuous left-wing coalitions shared a common educational cause and elaborated detailed programmes of reform. However, their brief periods of office (in the 1920s and 1930s) were taken up with economic disputes which prevented the delivery of educational promises. Throughout the *longue durée* of Gaullism, these groups still pinned their educational hopes on an electoral victory for the Left. Given the centralized nature of the educational system and the failure of direct action in May 1968, there was no other means through which they could introduce significant changes in education. When the Socialists assumed office in 1981 the new government became the focus of half a century's frustrated aspirations for educational reform. Since half of its newly elected *députés* were ex-teachers or academics there seemed no danger this time that educational reform would be elbowed-out by more pressing concerns.

Mitterrand immediately stated that his aim was for 'national education as a great secular and unified public service', but one which should be developed by persuasion not coercion and involve 'ni spoliation ni monopole'. This method was adhered to by the Minister of Education, Alain Savary, who spent the first two years listening rather than legislating. Basically the task was to find Socialist solutions for the three problems which had dogged the educational system through the century – secularization, modernization and democratization. Yet since this was to be done via consultation and conciliation rather than by immediate and thorough-going legislation, reform was placed at the mercy of two factors which were its undoing – the centralized structure of the system and the vested interests surrounding it. The attempt to accomplish these reforms without any radical structural change meant that they all had to be accommodated within the same standardized framework and to confront the interest groups which were deeply entrenched there.

Indeed it was significant that the first reform, designed to integrate the private (and predominately Catholic) sector more closely with State schooling, thus sought to extend rather than to eliminate centralization. There had been a firm electoral pledge to restore the position of State secular schools whose primacy had suffered due to concessions made to confessional education under the Fifth Republic. (The *écoles libres* now enrolled 16 per cent of all schoolchildren, received substantial financial subsidies and had been able to retain more of their 'own character' than earlier expected because they won increased denominational control over staffing and teacher training in 1977.)

Since the primary and *collège* teachers were still wedded to militant secularism their union, the SNI, sought complete *laïcité*, now that 'their' party was in power, through immediate nationalization of religious schools. More broadly, the popularity of the *écoles libres* was seen as an explicit rejection of the State middle school because private enrolment peaked (22 per cent of the age group) at the onset of secondary schooling. Parents thus seemed to be avoiding the egalitarian pedagogy of the *collège*, condemned by many as holding back the gifted child without helping-on the disadvantaged pupil, if not for treating all children with too much progressive laxity.

However, Mitterrand was unwilling to declare war on the *écoles libres*, perhaps because the Socialists had benefited from increased Catholic support in the 1981 elections. The reform bill put forward by the government was thus a compromise measure which proved totally counter-productive. Simul taneously it disgusted the SNI and led a million right-wing opponents to protest on the Paris streets in 1984. The bill was promptly withdrawn despite the fact that it had already been adopted in the National Assembly and within weeks Alain Savary, the 'over-cautious and over-scrupulous' Minister, had departed too. But perhaps the main things that were gone were high hopes for sweeping reforms and any prospect of a new supportive relationship between government and teachers.

The second victim of the consultative process was the reform of higher education, intended to democratize methods of entry and move away from the three-tier system consolidated under the Fifth Republic, with prestige *grandes écoles* at one extreme, utilitarian university institutes of technology at the other, and the mass of students sandwiched between them in what became known as '*universités-parkings*'. During the lengthiest consultative process, the concessions made to each of the interest groups in turn robbed the reform of any rationale – democratic or otherwise.

To begin with the success of pressures from the Right gained exemption for both the *grandes écoles* and the IUTs, which were placed outside the scope of the reform. Instead of democratizing access to higher education as a whole, the policy was now concerned merely with rationalizing university entry. Next, student strikes and demonstrations against university admission becoming more selective persuaded Savary to retain the historic privilege of open access for all those holding the *baccalauréat* and even to widen the doorway to include others with equivalent qualifications or indeed experience. (This was a somewhat dubious privilege given that only half of those taking arts and social sciences survived the examination at the end of the first year.) Similarly the proposal to set quotas for disciplines in the second cycle, which was intended to align university outputs with occupational outlets, attracted Socialist condemnation for perpetuating Giscardian vocationalism. Consequently this policy became diluted and, with the exception of medical and allied options, meant little more than optional student guidance at the point of registration. Finally various provisions which spelt reduced professional control in university administration completed the alienation of the academics.

The statutes which became law in 1983, after the most bitter debate in the National Assembly, allowed Edgar Faure to compare this reform unfavourably with his own *loi d'orientation*, fifteen years before, as an unwarranted imposition on universities and thus a 'centralizing, bureaucratic and, in short, a Napoleonic law'. As is typical in a centralized system, the only response open to professional educators who are hostile to official policy is the negative manoeuvre of blocking its implementation: by 1986 almost half of the universities were still refusing to adopt the statutes.

The assault on the problem of modernization fell to the new Minister, Chevènement, the flamboyant successor to the 'over-scrupulous' Savary, and his message to mainstream schooling seemed to be 'back to business'. In the primary schools this meant the end of progressive self-expression (*activités d'éveil*) and a return to 'basic' subjects, according to the programmes introduced in 1985–6. French was restored to the central place on a curriculum which also accentuated maths and technology (earmarking 50 hours specifically for computer science) and defined a new subject, *éducation civique*, to familiarize pupils with republican symbols and the workings of civic institutions. The same themes were pursued at secondary level where the revision of the curriculum was designed to incorporate scientific advance and to further technological development. Simultaneously the tightening-up of academic standards meant that Haby's concern for child-centredness was displaced by a national drive to emulate Japanese efficiency.

Pedagogic traditionalism, vocational relevance and tougher standards might seem an odd amalgam for a Socialist philosophy of education and indeed was often condemned as such. Nevertheless Chevènement countered that this 'republican élitism' embodied a concern for quality, 'work, merit and talent' which would benefit the working class. At that time only one-quarter of working-class children entered the *lycée* (compared with 85 per cent of those from professional and upper-managerial backgrounds) while only one-third of all children reached its last *baccalauréat* form. Thus the democratic aspect of the reform was the determination to turn the *collèges* into institutions which actually taught the academic skills necessary for academic advancement, rather than rewarding pupils for culture acquired at home, and in this way make the *collège* feed directly into the *lycée*. Indeed the Socialist aim was for 80 per cent of all children to attain *baccalauréat* level by the year 2000.

Wholly in line with these changes at lower levels were reforms to modernize, upgrade and extend technical instruction and to shift the balance away from short-cycle studies by stimulating the growth of technical *lycées* – through large cash injections for the in-service training of teachers who would then provide updated, attractive courses leading to the *baccalauréat*. Their relevance would be ensured by twinning schools with firms. Similarly, the reform of the *lycées* as a whole, planned immediately before the 1986 elections, repeated the same themes. The new vocational *baccalauréats* (four of the eight new ones were to be in maths and science, pure and applied) again reflected the belief that the mastery of technology was the answer to economic recession, while the stress placed on French and History in the remaining literary sections emphasized the importance of creating a republican national identity through the socialization of pupils.

Conclusion

In 1981 the new Socialist government confronted three enduring problems in French education – those of secularization, democratization and modernization. Retrospectively it appears to have got nowhere with the first two (religious schooling became no more integrated and higher education became no more egalitarian), while most of the plans for modernization remained incomplete and unimplemented when the government lost its majority.

Before the Socialists had gained office they had seemed determined to resist the eternal temptation of maintaining the centralized structure of education in order to make it serve its own goals. Historically this has always been politically irresistible, but equally it has always proved socially defeating: education as an instrument which is responsive to the polity is simultaneously a lumbering over-standardized machine, insensitive to regional, sectional or internal interests. If Socialism was to have broken with the Napoleonic structure it could only have been through decentralization: without this, the new policies introduced in the traditional uniform manner simply generated the time-honoured effect – a swelling reservoir of educational grievances threatening to break its political banks.

The new Chirac government gives high priority to reversing many of the steps and half-steps taken in the 1980s. Plans are afoot to give autonomy to the universities (repealing the *loi Savary*) ceding them control over entrance requirements, degrees and diplomas. Since this would mean that the universities would become more selective, the top forms of the *lycées* are to change (withdrawing the Chevènement reform) in preparation for the expected decline in the status of the *baccalauréat*. There is also discussion of increased autonomy for secondary establishments to allow them flexibility of response to diversification in higher and technical education.

However, talk of decentralization is now standard electoral rhetoric. The blunt fact remains that no government yet has brought itself to a voluntary renunciation of the centralized Napoleonic system. Once in power each succumbs to the belief that this politically responsive structure will promote the speedy achievement of its political aims – despite the experiences of every predecessor in government.

Bibliography

The books recommended below refer to the two parts of this chapter.

The historical background

Anderson, R.D., *Education in France 1848-1870*. Oxford, Clarendon Press, 1975. A detailed historical account with an extensive biliography.

Prost, A., *L'Enseignement en France: 1800–1967*. Paris, Colin, 1968. Perhaps the best account existing to date of the historical changes in the French educational system; contains extracts from major reform bills and influential authors.

Vaughan, M. and Archer, M., *Social Conflict and Educational*

Change in England and France. 1789-1848. Cambridge University Press, 1971. A comparative sociological approach to educational development in the two countries.

The twentieth century

Archer, M.S. (ed.), *Students, University and Society.* London, Heinemann, 1972. Chapter 6 presents an analysis of the May Events.

Archer, M.S. *Social Origins of Educational Systems.* London, Sage, 1979. See in particular pp. 306–81 and pp. 639–69.

Bourdieu, P. and Passeron, J.-C., *Les Héritiers, les étudiants et la culture.* Paris, Minuit, 1964. An extremely good summary of the influences of pupils' social origins on school and university entry, followed by an analysis of the student condition in the 1960s.

Fournier, J., *Politique de l'education.* Paris, Seuil, 1971. An excellent review of contemporary educational problems and their relationship to the political structure.

Fraser, W.R., *Reform and Restraint in French Education.* London, Routledge & Kegan Paul, 1971. An examination of the difficulties of introducing educational change in a highly centralized system.

Talbott, J.E., *The Politics of Educational Reform in France 1918–40.* Princeton University Press, 1969. The best account available in English of the *école unique* movement before the Second World War.

Vaughan, M., 'French education in the eighties: cultural persistance and institutional change', in P.McCarthy (ed.) *The French Socialists (1981–6).* Westport C.T., Greenwood Press, 1987. The best and most up-to-date discussion of Socialist government and educational policy.

Seven

The Church

J.E. Flower

Introduction

Few periods in the history of the French Church since the Second Vatican Council have been more disturbed than the mid -1980s. In many ways the anticipation of the twenty-fifth anniversary of the Council itself prompted a number of activities and, by implication, invited the Catholic hierarchy in particular to take stock of its position and achievements. But the reverberations of other political and social events and debates were felt as well. On a world scale was the bitter issue of the nuclear arms race which caused churchmen in countries such as America or Germany to express their opposition in a vigorous and much publicized manner. At home the new Socialist government's proposals for a total review of the secondary school system provoked an outcry and a series of demonstrations certainly without precedent since 1968. Indeed, according to the historian René Rémond, the gathering in Paris on 24 June 1984 protesting against the proposed reforms was probably the biggest manifestation of its kind in France's entire history. Ecumenicalism too remained a central topic for debate, enlivened by the presence of increasingly vocal Moslem and Jewish groups, and by the Protestants who in 1985 commemorated the three hundredth anniversary of the Edict of Nantes. And the papal visit of Jean-Paul II to Lourdes in August 1983, the second in three years, was a welcome affirmation, for some Catholics at least, of their Church's authority and presence.

Much, if not all, of this activity suggests that religion or at least an awareness of the importance of its role and influence has been growing. In some ways this is undoubtedly true. In 1983 the review *Prier* claimed that a resurgence of 'spiritualité populaire' was to be seen everywhere as people – and especially the young – turned away from an increasingly materialistic society to embrace 'faiths' as divergent as eastern religions, astrology, scientology, and even Freemasonry. Almost as proof, a pilgrimage organized by the ecumenical Taizé group at the very end of the same year attracted around 25,000 people to Notre-Dame, Saint-Sulpice and Saint-Germain in Paris.

The effect of this move towards a broader view of faith upon the Catholic Church may be reflected in the fact that while the number of baptisms, at about 80 per cent of the population, remains much as it was ten years ago, regular practice appears, from various polls which have been conducted, to be falling. Many consider the religious part of the marriage ceremony to be less necessary than it was only a few years ago and there has been a reduction in the number of children being instructed in the catechism in preparation for confirmation. Even the numbers at Lourdes for the Pope's visit in 1983 (150,000 per day) were lower than anticipated.

Accompanying this apparent shift of emphasis, the erosion to the structure and organization of the Catholic Church which has been quite pronounced during the last forty years, shows little sign of diminishing. While the numbers of new seminarists seem to have stabilized each year as do those for ordinations at approximately 100 (285 in 1970), demographic predictions suggest that with retirements the 29,000 priests active in the mid–1980s will be dramatically reduced to 16,000 by the turn of the century. Nowhere will such fundamental changes be more felt than in rural parishes. During the last few years over 1000 churches have fallen into disuse and many are threatened with demolition. The priests in such areas are also having to cope with an entirely new life-style. Statistics produced in June 1984 show that the priest of a rural parish may travel as many as 4000 km per month – yet on an average salary of less than 4000 francs for the same period, a car is a major financial burden. Security of employment, free accommodation and no family expenses are acknowledged by some to allow them to exist without too much hardship, but an increasing number have voiced their misgivings about the difficulties of their tasks and about the real threat of loneliness. One priest, not without some poignancy, spoke for many: 'la boîte de sardines mangée seul, un jour de Noël à midi, a un affreux goût de solitude'.

Yet whatever the apparent disaffection amongst Catholics and despite problems of organization and morale which remain to be faced, the Church still has a massive presence and influence within French society. Nowhere was there a more striking recognition of this fact than Mitterrand's electoral poster with its picture of a quiet village dominated by a church tower, with the caption 'la force tranquille'.

While it is inevitably in the Catholic Church that most changes have been noticed and debates most keenly felt and reflected, other religious communities have also made their voices heard. Yet ecumenical relations are now not as easy as they were a decade ago. In April 1983, for example, at the now triennial conference on ecumenicalism, Lukas Vischer, a Swiss professor of theology, remarked: 'Il ne faut pas nier que les relations officielles sont gelées et que nous entrons dans une phase nettement plus difficile que la première période euphorique.' In the same month the Catholic Episcopal Commission for Christian unity published a pamphlet entitled 'L'Hospitalité eucharistique avec les Chrétiens des Eglises issues de la Réforme en France' which, somewhat patronizingly, pointed to what it saw as fundamental differences between Catholics and Protestants: 'des points sérieux et contentieux dans la foi demeurent; en particulier certains aspects de la doctrine eucharistique [. . .] et des ministres [. . .] la place et le sens de la sacramentalité dans la vie chrétienne'. Not surprisingly the pamphlet was rejected by the Protestants who, as they see the Catholic Church trying to come to terms with issues which in the main they have for long accommodated – married and women priests, abortion and contraception or political activity, for example – regard Catholics as their 'frères séparés'.

The Protestant voice is increasing though only diffusely. It is claimed that there are now about 2.3 million Protestant '*sympathisants*' in France, though well under half of these formally belong to the Reform Church and nearly three-quarters admit never having listened to the radio broadcast of a service. For some of these, allegiance is often based on a vague, intangible sense that Protestantism is a more direct, meaningful and above all personal religion. For others it is a reaction against the hierarchy of the Catholic Church and what they see to be ambiguity in that Church's attitudes towards political issues or, more recently, education. This is not to say that the Protestant Church is without internal struggles of its own: its fundamentalists, the Lutherans, are much more rigid in their interpretations than most, for example. But, in general, for those fully and actively engaged in the Reform Church their immediate task is to attempt to establish a better dialogue with the Catholic Church, all the while remaining constructively critical of it.

In addition to the Protestants the three other major religious communities are the Jews (about 700,000, of whom 15 per cent practise regularly), members of the Orthodox Church (nearly 250,000) and the Moslems. Not only the most numerous, the last of these are also the most active and organized, so much so that historical reasons apart they may be considered to have overtaken the Protestants as the second most significant religious group in France. (It should be noted in passing that there are more Moslems in France than in any other European country except Turkey.) They number about 2.5 million of whom 1.5 million are practising; 700,000 are of French nationality and 30,000 converts, principally from Catholicism. In addition to the thousand or so places of worship they already have throughout the country, more mosques are anticipated and it is hoped to extend the *Grande Mosquée* in Paris so that it will accommodate up to 8000. A second is also planned. In addition to the capital, Lyon and Marseille in particular have a high incidence of Moslems; in Marseille they account for 10 per cent of the city's population and have their numbers temporarily swelled at regular intervals by new arrivals from North Africa; in Lyon there are 5000. As a national body they are extremely active, believing strongly in self-help, and despite feelings held by some that their leader Sheik Abbas allows his own country, Algeria, to be too influential, there is general harmony among them. Their undoubted problems come not from any fundamentalist element within their numbers – though

this exists – as from what is seen as French inability or unwill-
ingness to understand and accept their ways. Abbas himself
preaches peace and tolerance: 'Nous sommes là pour prêcher
un islam tolérant, ouvert et universel.' But their strict rules
concerning marriage, for example, (while men may marry a
Christian or a Jew, women may not) or the upbringing of their
children and their central place in the whole immigration
problem result in an *impasse*. In some places they have been
given disused churches for their places of worship, but right-
wing Catholics increasingly argue that this is a sign of weakness on the part of their Church and is a recipe for trouble.

More striking is the Moslems' own view that it would be
foolish to build another mosque in Marseille since it would
inevitably be blown up! On 14 June 1983 Michel Serain, who is
responsible for relations between the Catholic Church and the
Moslems, remarked with particular reference to the young: 'ils
se trouvent sans issue pour l'avenir et sans l'espoir d'une insertion dans une société où ils semblent condamnés à être des
marginaux'. Since then there has been no reason to suppose
that his analysis was wrong; nor does any change appear likely
in the immediate future. Indeed with the growth of the *Front
national* in places like Marseille, prospects for Moslems could
be even bleaker.

While the *Front national* remains at least for the immediate
present a minority phenomenon and one that is publicly condemned by the Catholic bishops, the more general swing back
to the Centre and Right in reaction to Mitterrand's successive
Socialist programmes has not been without echo in the
Church. Involvement with politics remains, inevitably, an
issue, but the episcopacy has produced a number of statements
in the last few years underlining its distance. Thus their
general secretary in May 1983: 'L'Eglise fait de la politique à sa
manière, mais elle n'accepte pas d'entrer dans le jeu politique,
nous ferons tout pour nous déprendre de cette espèce de filet
qui nous est continuellement jeté sur le dos.' Or later in the
same year after the papal visit:

Nous ne voulons absolument pas entrer dans les
mécanismes du pouvoir. Nous ne sommes ni un allié du
pouvoir ni un contre-pouvoir. Nous essayons de prendre une

distance par rapport aux forces politiques, ce qui nous rend plus libres pour intervenir sur les grands problèmes de la société.

Many would claim such a position to be the only appropriate one for a church to adopt. Lustiger as Archbishop of Paris has been seen as an ideal, 'neutral' figure, good at communicating and enjoying the open support of John-Paul II. But there have been objections. From the Right have come accusations of inadequate authority, lack of discipline and support for traditional Catholic values: from the Left those of aloofness and limited understanding, especially at a local diocesan level. Lay participation too remains an issue, and is planned to be central to the debates of the *Assemblée plénière de l'épiscopat français* in 1987.

When John-Paul II visited France in May–June 1980 his message and the positions he adopted towards various issues seemed at times less than consistent. He expressed approval of the worker-priests, was disapproving of extreme progressive and traditionalist groups alike and was authoritarian over a number of doctrinal matters. To have decided to return to Lourdes in August three years later may simply reflect his belief in the need to communicate directly with Catholics throughout the world: the Pope is one of the world's most widely travelled leaders. But the visit may have been prompted by a degree of anxiety at the state of the French Catholic Church and especially at the relative eclipse of certain fundamental spiritual and pastoral matters. Certainly on what he defined as 'un pèlerinage d'une journée' carefully planned to coincide with the *Fête de l'Assomption*, he aimed to set an example and to emphasize the value of confession and a need for a 'renouveau intérieur'. But he received two sharp reminders of the now inevitable wider, more public dimension that even the Church's activities attract: first, a bomb which partly destroyed the First Station of the Cross just before his arrival; and second, the wild reception he received from hordes of youthful members of right-wing political groups.

Whatever the Pope's wishes and whatever those of millions of his followers, the Catholic Church – and others too – is often fundamentally caught up in issues of a socio-political nature. The nuclear debate and education are but two and the history of involvement goes back long before the Second Vatican Council. There is no doubt, however, that the general encouragement given to the Church in the early 1960s to become more open and active has produced a series of responses both for and against that are often acute and always instructive.

The Church since the Second World War

From the experience of the Occupation and Resistance probably the most important direction the Church was to take was towards missionary work of one kind or another. In particular many lay Catholics assumed influential roles. For them involvement with politics did not present the problems it might to priests, and their Resistance record often served them in good stead. After the Liberation the first ministry of the provisional government contained five former members of the *Action catholique de la jeunesse française*, for example, and the MRP, in its early years at least, enjoyed the support of a number of bishops.

Catholic action in these years – the missionary work of various groups and movements of Catholic inspiration – in many ways picked up and developed that which had come into being from the late nineteenth century. Two organizations in particular merit attention: the *Mission de France* and the worker-priests.

The *Mission* was founded in 1941 by Cardinal Suhard in an attempt to produce an interdiocesan association providing specialized training for priests who would be sent to work in dechristianized parts of France. Unlike the worker-priests who worked individually, those of the *Mission* worked in teams initially in rural areas but subsequently in towns where their activities were most needed. Soon, however, they were criticized by the bishops with whom they were meant to work in close collaboration. In 1952 and 1953 the priests in turn complained (like the worker-priests) that the Vatican had very little idea of what was happening in the dechristianized areas of France. Also in 1953 rumours of Marxist literature being read by the seminarists prompted an investigation, and in August the *Mis-*

sion was closed to await a new statute to be promulgated by Rome. In the following year the new conditions of the *Mission*'s activities were published, and it was now noticeable that only those bishops who actually requested the assistance of priests from the *Mission* would receive them; an episcopal commission was also set up to be responsible for them and to give them their directives. Although such centralization and control may have disappointed some members of the *Mission*, an attempt was being made to create an organic unit linking missionary priests, other Catholic Action groups and the general clergy. Today there are over 300 priests from the *Mission* spread throughout France of whom more than two-thirds are in full employment. At its annual congress in September 1980 the *Mission* reaffirmed its basic aim which, in Suhard's original words, is to 'rendre au Christ les foules qui l'ont perdu'. Teamwork has always been considered essential and an emphasis is placed on a liberal (but not free) interpretation of Christian teaching as it is contained in the Gospels. But in more recent years the importance of the bishop's role in his diocese has been re-emphasized. At the Episcopal Assembly at Lourdes in November 1983, for example, the following directive was issued: 'chaque évêque jugera de quelle manière il convient d'assurer la continuité de l'effort d'évangélisation en monde ouvrier'. As it has already done in the case of many worker-priests, such refocusing may prove to be contentious.

Worker-priests

Although its roots may be traced back to pre-war years, the growth of the worker-priest movement owes its real impetus, like the *Mission de France*, to the years of Occupation. In 1943 two Paris chaplains, the abbés Daniel and Godin, produced a book, *France, pays de mission*, in which they argued that the continued association in the minds of working-class people of the Catholic Church with the bourgeoisie caused it to be cut off from those who most needed its ministerings. After the war a number of selected priests were sent into the working-class world but the move presented almost instant problems, particularly of an emotional and political nature. As one worker-priest remarked: 'Le fait formidable, c'est que lorsqu'on devient ouvrier, le monde bascule du côté ouvrier'. Although a number of them disagreed with Gilbert Cesbron's portrayal of the worker-priest's dilemma in his novel *Les Saints vont en enfer*, the fact remains that they were very much alone, regarded often with suspicion by more traditionally minded Catholics and by their bishops, who had little or no conception of working-class conditions. Such a situation could lead only to friction and discontent, and in 1951 uneasiness in Rome led to a suspension in recruitment. In 1952 two worker-priests were arrested in a Communist-inspired demonstration against General Ridgway when he arrived as Allied Commander in Europe, and in the following year the experiment was stopped altogether and the priests withdrawn. The majority of them obeyed Rome's decision without hesitation, and in January 1954 a number were linked with the teams trained by the *Mission de France* and known as 'prêtres de la mission ouvrière'. For some worker-priests, however, the Vatican's decision was little more than a betrayal, while, more embarrassingly still, the three French cardinals at the time (Feltin, Suhard and Gerlier) all approved of the experiment and yet were bound to enforce the ban. Outside the Church, militant lay Catholics, particularly those in movements like the *Jeunesse ouvrière catholique* (JOC) or the *Action catholique ouvrière* (ACO) were quick with their criticism: 'L'Eglise nous a trompés deux fois, une première fois en ne s'occupant pas de nous malgré ses promesses, une seconde fois en s'occupant de nous par les prêtres-ouvriers pour nous les retirer quand ils n'ont plus fait ce qu'elle voulait.'

Such criticism as this, together with considerable sympathy and pressure within the Church itself, was sufficient to ensure that the ban could only be short-lived, and in 1959 Cardinal Feltin made a specific request to Pope John XXIII for it to be lifted. John refused, but during the Second Vatican Council (1962) the question was re-opened with new enthusiasm. There were, now, a number of indications why the whole concept of the worker-priests should be more favourably received. Political contamination was for some reason less feared; Paul VI, John's papal successor, was more determined in the view that workers would not come to the priests if priests did not first go to the workers; and in addition the Curia in Rome was beginning to realize that bishops might well understand local problems better than someone several hundred kilometres away. As Henri Fesquet remarked in *Le Monde*, what did an Italian cardinal who had never been to France know about the mind of a Renault factory worker near Paris? Such a view is clearly a simplified one, but it does single out the crucial issue of the whole experiment and one that was largely met by the new conditions imposed on the worker-priests, or 'prêtres au travail' as they were now to be called.

In 1965 the second phase of the experiment was revived for a trial period of three years. In addition to the change in name which some argued was too fine a distinction to be generally recognized, there were five important modifications: no priest would be allowed to assume union or other responsibilities during his years of office (though he could become a member of a trade union); there should be a more thorough training before the position was actually taken; the priest should remember that he is and must remain 'un homme d'église'; he should not be isolated in his parish but remain in contact with other ecclesiastical bodies (an idea already practised by the *Mission de France* teams); and as a body the worker-priests should come under the direct jurisdiction of an episcopal committee headed by the Archbishop of Paris. The two major differences, therefore, were the attempts to limit the priests' political activities and also to create some kind of organic missionary unit, of which the worker-priest would be a single (albeit the most important) element.

For the most part these reforms were greeted with enthusiasm, though there was some criticism from certain quarters: traditional and conservative right-wing Catholics who remained in opposition to the whole action of missionary work expressed in these terms; the few worker-priests who had chosen to disobey their superiors in 1953–4; and those priests who had continued in 1954 as 'prêtres de la mission ouvrière', some of whom now considered that they and their efforts were being overlooked. In spite of such criticism, however, Paul VI saw fit in November 1968 to prolong this second phase of the worker-priest experiment (during which forty-eight priests had been used) for another three years. During this period further reforms were announced: numbers were no longer to be limited and priests could exercise union responsibilities – a directive which appeared to have been left sufficiently vague to enable Rome to intervene if it was felt that political commitment was becoming excessive. The immediate results were impressive; over 400 worker-priests were active throughout France by the end of 1971, a number which has swelled since to more than 1000. Increase in numbers has not been accompanied, however, by any noticeable increase in effectiveness. Certainly the elevation in May 1975 of Jean Rémond, a priest within the *Mission de France* since 1950, to the rank of bishop, was an acknowledgement of the movement's status, but it may also have been a sign that it was less of a revolutionary and critical force than it had been before. Certainly Rémond criticized the Church's attitude to society ('Elle vit dans un monde à elle, un monde qui n'est pas réel'), but other groups and movements have developed since the Second Vatican Council whose members are much more outspoken and active than the worker-priests. Furthermore, the fact that such a high percentage of them are now members of unions and overtly political groups does suggest, together with the relatively low attendances at the annual worker-priest assemblies, that even in its most recently constituted form the experiment is considered by many of those who take part in it to be relatively ineffective. Given other developments during the last fifteen or twenty years, the worker-priest movement must, whatever its original significance, be considered to be of little more than historical interest.

Revolution or reaction?
The aftermath of the Second Vatican Council

In broad terms the Second Vatican Council encouraged a variety of liberalizing attitudes within the French Catholic Church on a whole range of issues from missionary work to canon law, administrative reorganization and a new catechism, *Pierres vivantes*, written and illustrated in a way which, it was hoped, would make it more suitable for children. But within this general climate, initiated by John XXIII and encouraged by Paul VI (an 'artisan consciencieux' as *Témoignage chrétien* called him) more extreme tendencies were not slow to develop.

Towards a religious revolution

On the Left one of the earliest and most important groups to emerge was *Echanges et dialogue*. In November 1968 a letter signed by over a hundred priests and sympathizers was published. Like many progressive Catholics before them they argued for priests to become independent of the structure and constitution of the Church. Only by doing this would their position in society become easier. Priests should be able to act independently of their order, have the right to express themselves freely, participate in political affairs, marry and be allowed a voice in the nomination and deployment of new recruits.

By January 1969 over 400 priests had joined the movement. In the same month a further statement was issued in which the whole question of authority within the Church was challenged. What they sought, they maintained, was to introduce 'de nouvelles formes de relations entre évêques, prêtres, et laïcs, indispensables à l'annonce du Christ au monde d'aujourd'hui'. In the spring of 1969 the movement was partly responsible for interrupting a service held by Jean Daniélou, showering the congregation with pamphlets released from the roof questioning Daniélou's right to be a bishop: for whom and by whom had he been elected?

Not surprisingly *Echanges et dialogue* was received by many bishops with considerable hostility. Some attempts were made to counter the issues raised and in March 1969 the Episcopal Assembly issued in particular a statement arguing the case for celibacy. The movement continued to grow, however, and in December 1974 was formally replaced by *Camarades chrétiens critiques*, a movement which is openly more political and directly challenges the Church hierarchy:

Nous refusons une Eglise qui a choisi le savoir, l'avoir et l'ordre établi. Nous refusons un Credo, une théologie et une morale préfabriqués. Nous refusons une image de Dieu qui renforce la notion du pouvoir. L'important est d'appeler les chrétiens à prendre leur destin en main, à devenir eux-mêmes théologiens, à gérer eux-mêmes leur vie sexuelle. (June 1976)

Five years later another movement emerged, *Le Collectif pour une église du peuple*, supported by priests from the industrial north and east of the country in particular who are critical of the role they are obliged to fill: 'Dans le monde où nous vivons, nous ne pouvons pas être prisonniers d'un modèle de prêtre qui a sa valeur, mais qui ne correspond plus aujourd'hui aux exigences de l'annonce de l'Evangile.'

Such movements as these, coming from within the body of the Church itself, present special problems. The unrest and dissatisfaction which they express have also been reflected in the growth of a large number of smaller, often essentially lay groups whose criticism has been no less strong. In this period of 'pluralisme inconfortable', as the Episcopal Assembly defined it in 1975, we find, for example, *La Vie nouvelle*, *Témoignage chrétien*, *Chrétiens marxistes révolutionnaires*, the *Communion de Boquen* under its leader Bernard Besret, the *Commnauté chrétienne de Béthania* whose members share a simple but non-programmed faith, the *Communauté de Saint-Jean* or the *Frères de Bethléem*. Some are quite apolitical or only moderately so, preferring to work instead towards ecumenicalism; others, particularly lay groups, can be uncompromisingly militant. In July 1974, for example, Huguette Delanne, leader of the JOCF, remarked: 'Nous agissons d'abord parce que nous sommes de la classe ouvrière et non parce que nous sommes chrétiens.' In June 1977 the movement *Chrétiens pour le socialisme* (recognized by neither the ACO nor the JOC) maintained that for Christians and non-Christians alike there could be a 'cohérence entre les engagements pour le socialisme et les exigences de l'Evangile'. Within such a climate of liberalization, it is not surprising that the way to some form of compromise between the pastoral and the political should grow clearer. Indeed in June 1976 Marchais, in words which recalled Thorez' famous 'main tendue' forty years earlier, appealed to Catholics to join Communists in a struggle against all forms of oppression. And since the late 1970s theologians have propounded progressive ideas, drawing the Church more deeply into debates concerning, for example, divorce, abortion, homosexuality and the position of immigrants.

The episcopacy's position in the face of such rapid and at times turbulent developments was – and indeed still is – difficult. Total collective capitulation to such demands is always unlikely, of course, however progressive individual bishops may wish to be, and official statements have been cautious. In October 1972 in a critical speech of recent years entitled 'Pour une pratique chrétienne de la politique', Cardinal Marty, while still underlining the need for debate and discussion, also stressed the view that the Church should not allow itself to become a victim of political struggles; its pastoral mission should remain pre-eminent: 'le comportement des évêques et des prêtres en matière politique doit toujours être cohérent avec la mission de l'Eglise et leur mission spécifique dans l'Eglise'. In 1977, admittedly with Lefebvre and the resurgence of traditional Catholicism much in evidence, he observed that 'on ne peut pas être à la fois bon communiste et bon chrétien' and in October 1978: 'L'Eglise est aujourd'hui moins politique et administrative, elle est plus pastorale.' Etchegaray, Archbishop of Marseille and, since June 1979, a cardinal, also warned priests against excessive political involvement at the Episcopal Assembly in 1977. In May 1978 on the fiftieth anniversary of the JOC he pointed to what he called a no-man's-land between the world of the working class and the Church – an attitude for which he was quickly rebuked by *Témoignage chrétien*. Four years before his retirement Elchinger, Bishop of Strasbourg, in a message to his diocese in March 1980 accused a number of Catholic Action groups of 'ambiguïtés doctrinales' and of 'une confusion dans le rôle des laïcs et des prêtres', and he warned against those interpretations of the Gospels which made Christ into a political figure.

Such caution as this is not only the result of natural conservatism, however. Since his first Easter message in 1979 Pope John-Paul II has consistently reminded the French clerics that, after a period of dialogue and some liberalism, certain traditional positions should be recovered and even strengthened. In particular priests should remember that whatever their activities they are 'porteurs de la grâce de Christ' and that expectations of them are by definition greater than those of a lay member of the Church ('on attend de vous, prêtres, une sollicitude et un engagement bien supérieurs et différents d'un laïc'); celibacy too is essential. These are positions from which he has shown little sign of shifting and have been echoed on several occasions in the 1980s by individual French bishops. In September 1983, for example, François Favreau, Bishop of Nanterre, observed: 'sans minimiser l'importance du sacrement, il faut considérer les autres actes pénitentiels – célébrations, pèlerinages, témoignages – qui sont porteurs de grâce'. Lustiger, as Archbishop of Paris, has been able to rely on this new vocational emphasis in his handling of the Lefebvre affair. Nowhere is it more popularly in evidence perhaps than in the proposed revisions to *Pierres vivantes* which were finally approved in October 1984. The new 'national' catechism with its emphasis on moral teaching, Augustinian doctrine and original sin is without question a more severe and pessimistic document than its short-lived predecessor. Not surprisingly it has been opposed. Monique Chomel, the President of the *Fédération nationale des animateurs et parents pour l'éducation chrétienne* (FNAPEC) spoke in February 1983 for many: 'Comment transmettre la foi, aujourd'hui, hors d'un contexte de dialogue et de liberté? Nous sommes inquiets. Depuis vingt ans, il nous semblait avoir avancé: et nous redoutons d'assister à un retour en arrière.' But many Catholics see this as a sign of the beginning of a new and much needed reaffirmation of discipline, especially for the young, an answer to what Lustiger defined in July 1983 as 'un naufrage moral qui atteint déjà de larges couches de la société [. . .] facilité par le messianisme du progrès scientifique et le ''stress'' de la vie'. The extreme traditionalists have been even more enthusiastic and, not without some justification, argue that at long last the dangerous liberalizing tendencies of the 1960s and 1970s have been stemmed.

The traditionalist reaction

Left-wing progressive Catholics have not been alone in voicing their opinions and in some cases challenging the Vatican head-on. Since the early 1970s various traditionalist groups, which all to some degree or other chose to ignore the Second Vatican Council, have expressed concern at what they see to be a progressive erosion of the Church's authority and true role. The abbé Georges (*Centre réforme catholique*) in 1972 accused both the Second Vatican Council and Paul VI of revolutionary activity; the *Alliance Saint-Michel* whose members professsed themselves to be 'excédés par la situation révolutionnaire' interrupted Paris Masses chanting Latin; and late in 1980 the *Union pour la fidélité* called on French bishops to reject 'cette nouvelle église' and to assist all those 'qui se meurent dans les ténèbres de la secte conciliaire'.

No one, however, has undertaken such a sustained and vigorous defence of traditional Catholicism as the former Archbishop of Dakar and Bishop of Tulle, Marcel Lefebvre, who late in 1978 claimed to have established thirty centres throughout the world, especially in the USA and Europe. A man who admits to having been vitally influenced by the monarchist Charles Maurras and for whom Communism is 'la plus monstrueuse erreur jamais sortie de l'esprit de Satan', Lefebvre has, by his activities, clashed directly with Paul VI, the Archbishops of Paris and the French episcopacy in general. In 1974 his book *Un Evêque parle* expressed his feelings unambiguously. Having challenged social and political trends within the Catholic Church since the early 1960s (he had been part of a minority opposition group at the Second Vatican Council), in March 1972 he founded a seminary at Ecône in Switzerland for his movement *Fraternité sacerdotale de Saint-Pie-X* and for the training of priests along traditionalist lines. His refusal to accept the Pope's ruling led in 1976 to his being forbidden to ordain priests and on 12 July he was officially suspended from his priestly function – *a divinis* – a position in which in theory he remains today even though he has seen fit to continue to celebrate Mass and administer the sacraments. He has also maintained that papal directives may be misguided or wrongly inspired. Thus in New York in November 1977, for example, he recognized that he and his followers were ready to follow Paul VI but only when the Pope showed himself to belong to the true Catholic Church: 'Nous sommes prêts à suivre les instructions du pape. Mais lorsqu'il ne suit pas les instructions des deux cent soixante-deux papes qui l'ont précédé, nous ne pouvons pas suivre les siennes.' From the moment of his suspension, in fact, his Masses have been enthusiastically attended and the faithful have regularly heard the same message in his sermons – a warning against what he sees as neo-modernist and neo-Protestant developments in the Catholic Church, against the threat of Communism in particular and against all attempts to undermine authority and discipline in secular and religious society alike. In September 1979 at the celebration of an open-air Mass attended by about 15,000 people in Versailles he claimed in his sermon: 'La messe est essentiellement anticommuniste. Le communisme c'est: tout pour le parti, tout pour la révolution; la messe c'est: tout pour Dieu. Elle s'oppose au programme du parti, qui est un programme satanique.' Lefebvre has continued to defy the Vatican too over confirmation (in many cases by the *re*confirmation of children into what he considers the true Catholic faith) and by the ordination of traditionalist priests of whom there are now about forty each year.

The most direct clash with the established Church in France, however, occurred in Paris. Late in February 1977 Paul VI announced he would not grant Lefebvre an audience until he had satisfactorily responded to his requests of the previous year to modify his position. On 27 February, as an instant response, traditionalist Catholics, organized by one of Lefebvre's principal supporters, the late abbé Ducaud-Bourget, occupied the church of Saint-Nicolas du Chardonnet in the fifth *arrondissement*. In spite of various 'threats' by the Archbishop of Paris, Marty – notably of recourse to the civil authorities – the occupation continued. In May 1979 the parishioners of Saint-Nicolas wrote to Giscard d'Estaing as President of the Republic demanding action: not only was it a matter of civil liberty, they argued, but also of religious tolerance and political activity. Certainly this last point has been increasingly noticeable. The church of Saint-Nicolas is in the heart of Chirac country and in addition to a large proportion of elderly people at Mass are found younger members of extreme right-wing groups, often anti-Semitic and racist in attitude, and others who look somewhat nostalgically back to the period of collaboration during the Occupation and to the values of the

OAS during the Algerian crisis. Since the rise of the *Front national* the name of Le Pen has also been linked with a number of integrist groups and personalities such as *Chrétienté-Solidarité* and Bernard Antony, the founder of the right-wing daily paper, *Présent*. Le Pen himself has also had the traditional Mass celebrated at some of his principal political meetings and makes no secret of the value he places in it.

Faced with these kinds of developments Marty and later Lustiger found themselves in an impossible position even with their authority as archbishops. Marty tried to distinguish between '*tradition*' and '*fixisme*' or '*passéisme*', but to no avail. He allowed the parish to call in the civil authorities and offered the traditionalists another church, the rather aptly named Marie-Méditrice near the Porte des Lilas, but the problem refused to disappear. Lefebvre's representative Ducaud-Bourget was a formidable opponent, an intransigent interpreter of the traditionalists' policies who gathered around him a rapidly growing and admiring congregation. Before ill-health forced him to retire in September 1983, one of his last statements neatly and unambiguously summarized his position. His task – and that of his successors – was to maintain the struggle against 'la dérive protestante de l'Eglise, le dévoie-ment de la religion, les messes sans prêtre où l'on bat des mains comme les nègres'. And almost as if to ensure that his spirit should live on, his last sermon and his funeral service (he died in May 1985) were recorded. Available on cassette for fifty francs, the recording sells well.

Ducaud-Bourget was replaced by the 30-year-old Michel Laguerie who had been ordained at Ecône and was, before going to Paris, assistant head of a traditionalist school in Châteauroux. Since his arrival all the signs are that Ducaud-Bourget's wishes and moral authority, as Laguerie has called it, remain influential. Commenting on the move towards ecumenicalism, for example, he has said quite bluntly that his aim is 'la restauration de la civilisation chrétienne. Je n'ai rien contre les Arabes, mais notre Dieu n'est pas celui des musulmans.' In a parish bulletin issued in April 1986 he also dismissed ecumenicalism as 'cette dissolution de Jésus-Christ, qui est le propre de l'antéchrist'. He has acknowledged that the 1977 occupation of Saint-Nicolas was illegal, but nonetheless legitimate: 'Il s'agit de sauvegarder la norme absolue de la foi: la tradition.'

Such conviction compounded by a growing sense of security of position has meant that Laguerie and his followers present Lustiger with a problem every bit as difficult as the one faced by Marty. In December 1984, however, a significant development occurred. Authorization was given by Jean-Paul II for the Tridentine Mass to be celebrated once more. This reversal of his predecessor's ruling is said to have been prompted essentially by genuine public demand, but while this may be in part true, it does seem that it is further evidence of John-Paul II's reaction against excessive liberalism. Yet interestingly enough it has not met with complete satisfaction. In the same month a number of traditionalists complained that a mass at Saint-Etienne-du-Mont had been celebrated by the priest facing the congregation and that the supreme cry of humility, 'Domine non sum dignus' had only been spoken once. It is possible that such objections may be voiced by a minority group only, but there are other signs that the extreme Right wing of the traditionalist camp is becoming more outspoken and influential. In 1984 the *Fraternité johannite pour la résurgence templière* was founded, priding itself not only for upholding the traditionalist position, but also for its chivalrous (*chevaleresque*) qualities. The Church militant may not be far away. In January 1986 a priest belonging to another extreme body, the *Fraternité de la transfiguration*, was dismissed by the archbishop of Bourges, Pierre Plateau, but has defied the ban and has continued to celebrate Mass in public.

Whether such attitudes and behaviour are going to continue and if so to what extent is difficult to judge. Having appointed someone as young as Laguerie to Saint-Nicholas, Lefebvre has indicated at least his belief in stability and long-term planning. This had been suggested as well by his handing over responsibility for the Ecône seminary in September 1982 to the abbé Franz Schmidberger who was at that time still only 36 years of age and is presumably destined to become head of the movement as a whole. Even so Lefebvre himself, now well into his seventies, remains the source of much inspiration and guidance. The official re-instatement of the Tridentine Mass and the extent to which traditionalist Catholics have been influential in national debates concerning the catechism and education are clear indications of the support the movement can muster, albeit over specific, critical issues. Yet, at the same time, there are worrying and potentially dangerous political overtones. One reported remark from a supporter of Lefebvre is nicely illustrative: 'Pétain, de Gaulle et Monseigneur Lefebvre sont curieusement tous trois originaires du nord de la France. Je les crois tous les trois également utiles. Ce sont souvent les minoritaires qui ont raison et font avancer les choses.' Le Pen too is from the north and the *Front national* is a minority party. The French episcopal commission has warned Catholics against the philosophy of the *Front national* and when questioned about 'le phénomène le Pen' during a televized interview on Easter Monday 1984, Lustiger curtly dismissed it as 'pas bien'. There is also the simple but basic problem, however, that Le Pen and most of his followers *are* Catholics. The kinds of problems raised by their involvement in the political arena, for so long a dominant feature of developments within progressive Catholicism, look as though they may develop into a significant issue. Lefebvre and his senior assistants may well be concerned only with the spiritual well-being of their Church and with their country, but so condemnatory and challenging are some of their statements that it would be naive of them not to imagine how they might be exploited. Late in 1985 Lefebvre still blamed the Second Vatican Council for all current ecumenical and liberal tendencies. These, he said, constitute 'un grand danger pour l'Eglise (et sont) une nouvelle étape de la révolution provoquée par le dernier Concile, qui ne peut que conduire à l'autodestruction'. Such words do not fall on deaf ears.

The Church and the educational debate of the mid-1980s

However committed Catholics are to their own particular views of the Church's role and responsibility in debates such as those outlined above, no single issue during the last twenty years has provoked such a massive response on all fronts as the Socialist government's proposed changes to the secondary school system. That the response was so huge was due, of course, to the fact that social and political values were involved as well as religious ones. For many, token support for progressive ideas was abruptly challenged and, as several commentators pointed out, a not inconvenient confusion developed between 'école libre', 'école catholique' and 'école privée'. Paul Thibaud, writing in *Esprit* in June 1984 made the point succinctly: 'Des familles bourgeoises gagnées par l'indifférence religieuse craignent moins pour leurs enfants l'embrigadement par les bons pères que l'embrigadement marxiste des profs d'histoire et de philo.' Some, of course, were quite genuine in voicing their apprehension; the phasing out of Catholic schools was seen by them to be a direct attack on their right as parents to ensure that their children should receive an education infused by the Catholic faith. This view received important support from bodies such as the *Commission permanente du comité national de l'enseignement catholique* (CNEC). Others were concerned but nonetheless supportive of government action.

In the end public pressure against the government was in part successful; in July 1984 Savary resigned as Minister of Education and his replacement Chevènement proposed a series of compromises to which in substance only the PCF and the *Front national* objected when they were debated in the National Assembly the following autumn. Yet what is interesting is the role the Church hierarchy adopted from the early stages of the whole debate.

In an address to the massive anti-government demonstration at Versailles in March 1984, Lustiger called on the Declaration of the Rights of Man and urged: 'En revendiquant devant la nation la liberté d'un projet éducatif catholique, vous contribuez ainsi non seulement au bien de l'Eglise mais au bien de la nation tout entière.' A month later he again argued that 'un processus de fonctionnarisation mettrait en péril l'identité de l'école catholique'. And in June he joined with a number of influential bishops in issuing a supportive if slightly more reserved statement: 'Nous voulons que les parents gardent leur droit de choisir le genre d'éducation qu'ils désirent pour leurs enfants, leur droit de choisir une école qui propose l'Evangile au coeur même du projet éducatif.'

Not surprisingly traditionalist Catholics did nothing to hide their pleasure, but not all were quite so sanguine that the episcopal hierarchy should have allowed the Church to become embroiled in this way. In March 1984 *Témoignage chrétien* published a letter signed by over 13,000 Catholics in which, while freedom of choice was defended, an appeal was made to the bishops to distance themselves from events. In the same month they were accused more directly by FNAPEC of witting complicity: 'Ils ne sont pas innocents et, malgré leurs dénégations, savent bien à quelle récupération ils s'exposent. Ils font le jeu de la droite politique.' Criticism also came from the *Comité national d'action laïque* (CNAL) and from the Protestant Church. Michel Bouchareissas, general secretary of CNAL, remarked: 'L'Eglise doit respecter la non-croyance, abandonner toute supériorité et ne pas s'immiscer dans les affaires de la société civile. L'Eglise a le droit de donner des directives aux chrétiens, mais je perçois toujours une prétention à donner des directives plus universelles.' And on 25 April a counter-demonstration to the one held in Versailles was organized jointly in Paris by the CNAL and some Socialist politicians calling for the proposed revisions to be implemented. Meanwhile Jacques Maury, President of the *Fédération nationale des protestants* dismissed the Catholic bishops' actions as 'un mauvais calcul qui risque de les enfermer dans des situations politiques impossibles'.

With this view it is difficult not to agree. Certainly the Church has a responsibility to support what it believes to be in the interest of its faithful, even if it does so against the government of the day. They may not have compromised themselves to quite the extent that their opponents claimed, but there can be little doubt that the bishops, by their words and actions, moved the Church an important step away from the kind of dialogue that had characterized the previous decades.

Conclusion

While education may have been a passing issue and one not likely to reappear in this form at least with the change of government, the implications for the role and status of the Catholic Church in France towards the end of the twentieth century are important. Mitterrand was correct; however materialist modern society may be becoming, Catholicism remains a force capable of wielding very considerable influence. But that force does seem, guided by directives from the episcopacy, gradually to be moving back towards the Centre; we are witnessing what some commentators label a 'recentrage' or a 'retour aux valeurs'. In some respects this is not surprising. The history of the Catholic Church in France over the last hundred years especially shows an oscillation between liberalism and traditionalism with neither one ever holding sway for a prolonged period. At present, despite various claims of non-involvement in political matters, there does appear to be if not complicity, at least some sympathy between the Church and the political Right and Centre. (Both too are seen by a large percentage of the population to be potential corrective forces in a society showing signs of increasing moral disintegration.) How far this will be allowed to develop remains to be seen. Certainly in October 1984 the Episcopal Assembly warned against all 'idéologies élitistes', but the scale of the response to the education problem indicates the difficulty of control.

Bibliography

For the background to this period consult:

Dansette, A., *Destin du Catholicisme français*. Paris, Flammarion, 1957. Detailed survey of the period 1926–56.

Duquesne, J., *Les Catholiques français sous l'occupation*. Paris, Grasset, 1966. A fascinating, well-documented account.

Latreille, A. and Rémond, R. (eds), *Histoire du Catholicisme en France*. Vol. III, pp. 487–684, Paris, Spes, 1962.

Pierrard, P., *L'Eglise et les ouvriers en France (1840–1940)*. Paris, Hachette, 1984. A useful synthesis of earlier studies of this problem together with some interesting observations about the Church's role in an increasingly technological society.

Rémond, R., *L'Anticléricalisme en France de 1815 à nos jours*. Paris, Fayard, 1976. An introduction in which anticlericalism is discussed from a variety of angles – sociological, cultural, and so on – and is followed by a long historical account of the phenomenon in France. Particularly good on the period from the Second Vatican Council to the early 1970s.

Other books and articles focused on particular topics or problems include:

Casalis, Georges, *Les Idées justes ne tombent pas du ciel*. Paris, Cerf, 1972. A handbook of progressive Protestant ideas.

Hourdin, G. and Marchais, G., *Communistes et Chrétiens, Communistes ou Chrétiens*. Paris, Desclée, 1978. An interesting discussion of a key issue by sympathetic representatives of opposing sides.

Mehl, Roger, *Le Protestantisme français dans la société actuelle*. Eds Labor et Fides, Paris, 1982. A sympathetic, wide-ranging survey. Good on 'internal' disputes within Protestantism.

Solé, R., *Les Chrétiens en France*. Paris, PUF, 1972. In the main a collection of texts relating to all the central problems which confront both the Protestant and Catholic Churches. An interesting discussion in the last chapter on sexuality, love, celibacy, and so on.

A collection of documents concerning the worker-priests is *The Worker Priests: A Collective Documentation*, translated by J. Petrie. London, Routledge & Kegan Paul, 1956.

An interesting and amusing investigation of what it called 'le retour en force du sacré' was carried out by *Le Nouvel Observateur* No. 1017, 4 May 1984.

A very thorough summary of information about all religions and sects is 'Religions et Société en France' in *Problèmes politiques et sociaux*, La Documentation française (No. 518: 6 September 1985) Paris.

Eight

The press

W.D. Redfern

Introduction

As with the world's press, the crisis of the French press has become endemic. Falling sales, decrease in advertising revenue, huge increases in the cost of paper, highly paid yet often superfluous staffs, are some of the material causes. But there is no shortage of groups or individuals anxious to buy up or to launch newspapers.

France comes twenty-second in the world tables for the number of newspapers sold per 1000 people, and sixteenth in Europe; consumption is about half that of Britain. The obvious inference that French citizens are less thoroughly informed on public events than Anglo-Saxons is tempting but unproven. The French also read fewer books and go less often to the theatre or cinema; radio and television have developed there less rapidly. Proportionately fewer papers are read today in France than before 1939. Young readers are in short supply: one-third of the 14–34 age group never buy a paper or magazine. The Paris dailies are essentially a press for the Paris area, which has the lowest rate of readership of all France. Before the Second World War they sold twice as many copies as the provincial press, but now sell only half as many. This exchange of position started in 1945, when the metropolitan press was too poorly equipped to develop provincial editions. Nowadays the regional dailies can obtain news as quickly as those in the capital, and are physically and temperamentally nearer to their readers. They are also cheaper. In Rennes, for example, the Paris papers between them sell 6500 copies, while *Ouest-France* sells 80,000. The provincial press continues to expand its circulation but, rather surprisingly, more in the countryside than the towns. This situation stems from the multiplicity of editions, each specializing in local, even parochial, news. They are less threatened by television than Paris papers.

At the same time, they have experienced the same concentration of resources. There is an increasing tendency for regional papers to form *couplages* (partial mergers), especially in the fields of advertising, printing and distribution. The aim is to avoid mutually unprofitable competition, particularly on the boundaries of regions where some overlap occurs. Hence the reciprocal non-aggression pacts. One result is that *Ouest-France* (700,000 circulation) has become the largest daily in France. On the other hand *Le Progrès* and *Le Dauphiné libéré* split up in 1979, though both are now under the control of Robert Hersant, a financial manipulator of talent. In general, the strength and independence of the provincial press have impeded so far the creation of huge newspaper chains like those of Great Britain, the United States, Japan or Germany. The French press is the least concentrated in the west.

Of late, however, there have been long and loud protests from journalists and some politicians, as Hersant extended his empire by adding control of *France-Soir*, *L'Aurore* and *Le Parisien libéré* to that of *Le Figaro*. These acts defied the 1944 edict aimed at thwarting press monoplies. Despite some resistance from the journalists he employs and frequently sacks, Hersant is well on the way to deserving the title of 'the French Axel Springer'. He holds 38 per cent of the total circulation of national and 19 per cent of provincial dailies. The Socialists' press law of 1984, by which no proprietor can control more than 15 per cent of either national or regional dailies, has no retroactive force, and the Chirac government is likely to repeal it.

There are fewer French papers, national or provincial, than before the war, and those that survive are, in the main, examples of *la presse industrielle*. Though like all industries it has its victims, it remains big business, and figures between fifteenth and twentieth in the list of French economic giants. It employs nearly 100,000 people and ensures the livelihood of twice that number. The State helps it by indiscriminate aid of various kinds (after Italy, the highest in Europe) which amounts to a form of indirect subsidy: newspapers are wholly exempted from taxes on turnover and various local taxes; they can start tax-free funds to fit themselves out with new equipment or can obtain loans from the State; they enjoy preferential postal, telegraph and telephone rates; and overseas sales are subsidized, in keeping with the official policy of spreading French 'culture' the world over.

In France, unlike Germany, the United States or Britain, there are no appreciable differences in price between 'quality' and 'popular' papers. Until 1967, the selling price of French dailies was fixed by the government. The increase in price that year caused a big drop in sales from which most papers have not yet recovered. A chasm separates the cost price and the selling price, and it can be bridged only by actively encouraging advertisers to buy space. Three-quarters of the income of *Le Figaro* comes from advertisements. The pursuit of advertisers is even more fierce than that of readers. Between the two wars, a feudal consortium of five leading Paris dailies, together with the chief agency, conspired to keep the price of advertising space high and thus to shut out any rivals. This stranglehold was eventually broken, but today advertising continues to favour the more flourishing papers and to accelerate the downfall of the less successful. It is sometimes argued that a paper well off for advertisers eager to use its surface is freer from any pressure they might try to apply than is an economically weak paper. In addition, it is not really necessary for advertisers to pressurize newspapers, for the interests of both sides are identical: to sell as much as possible. Perhaps collusion is a more apt term. At the same time, advertisers' pressure positively promotes neutrality, as a paper or periodical appealing to the largest number (preferably well-heeled) is the obvious target. Advertisers would see little hope of benefit from a sectional, politicized press. Since advertising remains an under-developed industry in France, roughly the same amount of money is being spread over an ever wider network of media. The press suffers most.

The post-war press and the Algerian crisis

Just as the political militants engaged in Resistance work were
already manoeuvring for supremacy after the Liberation, so
newspapermen were determined after the war to make a clean
sweep. A great purge of the collaborationist press was carried
out. The avengers confiscated and shared out its equipment,
premises and capital; the former clandestine press benefited.
There were high hopes (still alive in some journalistic quarters) of setting up a completely reformed, 'decapitalized' press
– that is, one freed from the control of financial interests.
Polemics erupted as to whether the essential auxiliaries of the
press (the paper industries, distributing organizations and
news agencies) should be nationalized, or whether this step
would put the press at the mercy of arbitrary government. In
fact, because of such hesitation, a considerable part of the old
order was able to re-establish itself. The much needed statute
of the press was blocked in the National Assembly. In the confusion of post-war France, a large sector of the press pushed out
varying forms of propaganda, often anti-Communist. Much of
it was gutter-journalism. When the editor of *Le Monde* advocated neutralism as the only solution to the Indo-Chinese
dilemma, he was derided as a eunuch.

As well as the civil war waged at various points in history
between newspapers themselves, on occasion the French
government has laid its heavy hand on the press. There is a
long tradition in France of governmental confiscation or censorship of 'dangerous' publications, dating back to the suppres-
sion of anti-government pamphlets in the seventeenth and
eighteenth centuries. In fact, the care taken by authoritarian
regimes to muzzle the press indicates its importance, especially in those countries where, as in France, the expression of
ideas is valued highly (Karl Marx said, with a sting in the tail:
'La France est le seul pays de l'idée, c'est-à-dire de l'idée
qu'elle se fait d'elle-même'). During the Algerian crisis, the
government had many reasons for wishing to limit dissent in
the communications media. One reason was the hostility of
the army officers to what they considered a 'treason press',
which they had already blamed for helping to lose them the
Indo-Chinese war, by its critical and therefore 'demoralizing'

reports. In addition, the government wanted at first to represent the Algerian rebellion as the handiwork of mere terrorists, and later tried to make out that the end had come when it was nowhere in sight, and that peace could be obtained without negotiating with Algerian nationalists. A strong opposition press would obviously hinder such aims. During the Algerian war therefore, dissenting papers and periodicals were seized by the police on over 250 occasions in France. The irony was that few convictions followed these seizures, as open trials would have given too much publicity to the government's dubious right of confiscation. To show its 'impartiality', the government sometimes suppressed both right- and left-wing papers.

Its various actions did not in fact arrest the spread of information, at least to the educated reading public. A heavy responsibility lay on the French press, because of State control over television and radio. In addition, the sole French news agency, the *Agence française de presse*, often withheld cables containing items detrimental to the government or other vested interests. In many such ways, public opinion in the 1950s slowly lost contact with events. *Le Monde*, *L'Express*, *France-Observateur*, *Le Canard enchaîné*, *L'Humanité* and the Catholic monthly *Esprit* all made sustained protests, or simply printed factual statements that spoke for themselves, especially on the question of torture. The big-selling dailies told very little. Like the torturers themselves, who used jargon to shroud their doings, these papers tended to camouflage the whole issue in euphemisms.

The popular press

Randolph Churchill once said that the popular press provided a meal, in which murder was the hors-d'oeuvre, a juicy sex-story the dessert, and a Royal Family scandal the main course. The first 'yellow' journal in the world was French. *La Gazette burlesque* (Paris, 1650–65) abounded in reports of scandals, crime and society gossip. *France-Soir* continues and extends this tradition. It has a circulation of around 400,000 (which has slumped from nearly a million a few years ago), and is now a morning paper. It took up where the pre-war *Paris-Soir* (nicknamed *Pourri-Soir*, because of its unscrupulousness) left off. In eight years during the 1930s, *Paris-Soir* jumped from sales of 60,000 to 2 million by reason of its masses of photos (thus reducing eye strain and brain fag), an enormous staff of reporters everywhere (thus ensuring widest coverage and frequent scoops), and a calculated exploitation of sensationalism. The stress, now as then, falls on 'human interest' stories, strip cartoons and picture serials; on American-style gossip columns and belligerent opinionating (on non-political topics). *France-Soir* also uses the typically French trick of occasionally employing an academician to act as special envoy or commentator on big events. It is doubtful whether it has ever wielded much political influence (popular papers have been called 'leaders who bring up the rear') but, in its pandering to the lower instincts of its readers, it probably has a stultifying, or at least sedative, effect on their minds. The French popular press, like that of other countries, tends to melodramatize news by presenting politicians as actors in some exotic drama rather than as functionaries, to trivialize it by anecdotage, to warp it by innuendoes and suppositions. All this so that the reader may have the illusion of living, by proxy, more intensely. Such an escapist press offers collective psychotherapy. René Pucheu has said: 'Le journal est beaucoup moins un moyen d'information qu'un moyen d'incantation, il est à la société technicienne ce que le sorcier est à la religion primitive.'

Although *Le Monde*, *Le Figaro* and *Le Matin de Paris* have tried weekend supplements, a Sunday press on the Anglo-Saxon model does not yet exist in France. On the other hand, photo-journalism, now defunct in Britain, is represented by *Paris-Match*, with a weekly circulation of 750,000 and sometimes considered to be the best picture magazine in Europe. With its commando reporters and photographers always on standby to rush to any big event ('*Match* men move in on a story like locusts. After they're through, there's nothing left for anyone else to reap'), *Paris-Match* maintains an 'apolitical' but essentially anti-Communist line. Aiming to attract the greatest number possible, it tries to offend none of them, and consequently works hard at smoothing the rough angles of any item. But photos, its staple produce, can bias reporting more insidiously than words do: the camera can and does lie. Its sales have increased considerably since 1982.

Some leading papers

Le Figaro

Le Figaro is a rough equivalent to the *Daily Telegraph*, and is the traditional organ of the conservative and moderate bourgeoisie. It had the advantage of reappearing as early as August 1944, with the same title as before the war and with much the same staff. It is moreover the oldest Paris daily but, despite its circulation of around 370,000, it is heavily dependent for revenue on advertisements for the Paris property market. Its professed policy is eclecticism. It is proud of its long tradition of using as contributors established writers and academicians. *Le Figaro* was the paper that, in his cork-lined room, Proust relied on to keep in touch with the world outside, especially the affairs of high society. Readers of its pages are unlikely to be extremist, avant-garde or very intellectual. Since its takeover by Hersant in 1975, there have been many struggles between the owner and the editorial staff, some of whom have resigned in order to affirm a kind of independence. It has recently shown signs of moving more frankly to the Right. Its offshoot, *Figaro-Magazine* (650,000 circulation) is already there, and indeed provides a platform for the New Right. It offers also more leisure reading than the other serious weeklies. *L'Aurore*, long the journal for small businessmen, and now also under Hersant's control, has become virtually an identical paper to *Le Figaro*.

L'Humanité

At the other end of the social spectrum, *L'Humanité* has existed for eighty years and has been the official organ of the PCF for three-quarters of that period. In the 1920s, soon after it became specifically Communist, *L'Humanité* was subjected to harsh treatment by the government. Several seizures of whole issues were made and contributors imprisoned, for inciting the proletariat to strike for better wages and working conditions, and for denouncing French imperialist exploitation in the colonies. At various times it has supported the Viet-Cong, the Algerian *Front de libération national* and the rebels in Cuba.

But it wore Stalin-coloured spectacles when reporting on the Hungarian uprising in 1956. It suffers attacks from Socialists, moderates, extreme right-wingers and, increasingly, is out-flanked on the Left by more radical elements. As well as calls to direct action, it also plays more often nowadays the waiting game of political alliances. It has half the number of pages of its rivals and has always had to scratch along financially by means of appeal funds and unpaid assistance from readers. The present readership is oldish and the circulation drops steadily. For all its numerous faults, however, by its continued existence and its occasional campaigns, *L'Humanité* does remind the world that a large number of often militant Communists live in France, and that the French proletariat is probably more politically conscious than its British counterpart. Its Sunday edition, offering more culture and leisure features, outsells the daily. *L'Humanité* is only the most visible part of the largest press empire in France. The Communists own scores of newspapers and magazines, many printing-presses and several publishing firms.

La Croix

The only truly national daily is the Catholic paper *La Croix*, as, unlike the other Paris dailies, it sells its 120,000 copies mainly in the provinces. Starting in 1883 and up to 1914, it published two versions of the daily (one for the élite and one for the popular audience), in keeping with the Catholic convention of hierarchy. After the Second World War, it was regarded with some suspicion, despite de Gaulle's *Nihil obstat* and the support of the Christian democrat MRP, because it was rather late in 'scuttling itself' (June 1944). It fulfils a semi-official role as the vehicle of Church opinion. Far from being obsessed, however, with religious matters, *La Croix* devotes more space to foreign news than, for example, *Le Figaro*. Its crucifix symbol was dropped in 1956 with an ensuing increase in sales of several thousand, but, in the main, the Catholic press in France remains very much a closed-circuit organization, conceived principally for the faithful, though there are millions of such faithful. Its financial independence surpasses that of the commercial press, largely because its distribution system excludes costly middlemen. The pattern is: postal subscriptions (90 per cent of the sales), unpaid home delivery, or stands set up after Mass. On the other hand, *La Croix* wins little advertising revenue, for its readership, oldish and relatively well-educated, is socially too undifferentiated. Its losses are made up by other enterprises in its group, such as printing. Ecclesiastical advisers sit on the boards of all Catholic publications, but usually exercise their control only after the journal has been published. There is little need for overt interference by the Church hierarchy when self-censoring already prevails. Since 1968, a whole page in *La Croix* called 'Dialogue' has been devoted to readers' letters, which over the years seem to have improved in thoughtfulness and to avoid the wasteful jokiness often found in the correspondence columns of the British 'quality' press.

Le Monde

Le Monde is the major serious paper. In shape it resembles the *Daily Mirror*, but there the likeness ends. Instead of yelling headlines, the reader sees a rather forbidding mass of small print, broken only by the occasional map or graph. The paper's policy is: *faire dense*; and the density of the lay-out is counteracted by the intelligence of its content.

Its title reflects its readership, which is world-wide: one-tenth of its 350,000 readers are non-French. It is the paper of the urban élite: the magistrature, administrative grades, the whole *Université* (that is, *lycée* teachers, students and academics), and top men in industry and commerce. Nevertheless, *Le Monde* is widely respected by militant trade unionists for the thoroughness of its reporting. It has the youngest readership of any major French daily, which might explain what many see as its recent movement towards the Left.

It was born four months after the liberation of Paris and so was rather late on the scene. Most of the team that got it going belonged to the pre-war *Le Temps*. Its initial line was support for de Gaulle and a plea for overdue reforms to benefit the workers and young people of France. Clearly, *Le Monde* set out to be less conservative than *Le Temps*, but it placed the same emphasis on the arts and on international affairs. From the beginning, the guiding idea was to launch a paper free from all kinds of influence, such as big business and political parties. It was immediately attacked by left-wing journals, who thought that it would continue where *Le Temps* had left off, as a semi-official source of government news. But very quickly *Le Monde* differentiated itself from its forebear. Apart from combating external opponents, the staff at times disagreed among themselves, and *Le Monde* did not try to conceal its internal difficulties. With similar frankness, it decided to publish its accounts regularly, a practice unheard of in the French press, in order to prove that no financial lobbies were influencing its policies. In 1951, some former editorial staff attempted to return in order to change the paper's neutralist line on foreign affairs. The reigning editor, Beuve-Méry, offered his resignation, but received so much support from his staff and from readers that he agreed to remain. This was an important stage in the development of the French press, as it established a precedent whereby editorial staff were enabled to demand more participation in running the papers they work on. Above all, it was a notable victory against the widespread hatred of independence and fair play. It is said that the Communists are less afraid of their biased antithesis *Le Figaro* than of the more objective *Le Monde*. Beuve-Méry believed unashamedly in certain intellectual and moral values, and was always hostile to the lies, scandalmongering and muckraking of so much of the world's press. At the risk of boring his readers, he gave a full-spread treatment to all important documents.

Le Monde has naturally made mistakes. Over Suez, it urged that Nasser should be jumped on heavily. On the Algerian question, its policy shifted from one of supporting the spineless Guy Mollet to that of pleading for negotiation with the rebel nationalists. On the other hand, its apparent indecision on some issues is caused by its attempts to represent conflicting opinions. It acts often as a forum for discussion. Of all French journals, the non-kow-towing Catholic monthly *L'Esprit* is perhaps closest in outlook to *Le Monde*, whose staff sometimes publish articles there. Both stand for moderation, independence, liberalism of a realistic kind, 'révolution par la loi'.

Le Monde has no photos, horoscopes or gaudy advertisements. Precise and vivid reporting is the house rule. It has agreements with *The Guardian*, *La Stampa* and *Die Welt* to interchange articles. It diversifies continuously, with regular supplements on the arts, literature, leisure, science, education and economic affairs. It was run for a long time by a benevolent despot, in close co-operation with a disciplined team, who hold 49 per cent of the shares. Beuve-Méry was called the misanthrope of the French press, a cactus, a Cassandra-figure. He was hardly any wealthier than his assistants and had a profound scorn for money. He was not anaemic in his moderation and commanded a caustic and, if need be, crude style. His instructions to his staff were twofold: 'Pas de bourrage de crâne, pas de léchage de cul.' *Le Monde* is more reliable than *The Guardian*, less shifty than *The Times*, and far less conservative than the *Daily Telegraph*. Its comprehensive and well-informed coverage of foreign news makes nearly all British papers look very insular indeed. Beuve-Méry obviously relished difficulties, 'like selling a boring, expensive newspaper', as he once said. His pseudonym, Sirius, was reminiscent of the French term denoting remoteness of view-point, 'le point de vue de Sirius', and it is true that *Le Monde* often takes itself too humourlessly and regards common reality from too Olympian a vantage. The recent attack on it by a former reporter who charged it with secret subversiveness provoked a pompously self-righteous rejoinder signed by all the members of the team and the editor himself. For all its efforts at objectivity *Le Monde* has never claimed to support the conservative side of the great divide in France, and its recent insertion of political cartoons reveals a readiness to offer on occasion very slanted opinions on current events. Even this most trustworthy of papers needs to be read mistrustfully, but its courage, shown latterly in criticizing the French judiciary's many faults, and in publicizing the Greenpeace affair, is indisputable. Most recently the lengthy and divisive process of finding a successor to the previous editor has exacerbated the growing financial difficulties of *Le Monde*. Soon it will have to decide about changing its format (in order to use facsimile transmission for provincial printing) and about appearing in the morning (to avoid being late with news). It has massive debts and despite cuts still employs too many of the highest-paid staff in Paris. Its attempts to be less élitist in style have not yet shown much result.

The only other sizable daily not beholden to the Right is *Le Matin*, founded in 1977 and linked for a time to *Le Nouvel Observateur*. In 1985 its circulation dropped to below 100,000. Its change of ownership in 1986 might indicate a desire to distance it from the Left.

Some weeklies

L'Express and *Le Point*

As no serious Sunday press yet exists in France, there is a greater market than in Britain for weeklies, which have more time for reflection and a more sifted and glamorous presentation. *L'Express*, with a circulation of 500,000, is an interesting case of a journal starting out with a pronounced political conscience and gradually shedding or sophisticating it in tune with changes in the times. It first appeared in 1953, as a weekly supplement of the financial daily *Les Echos* (and despite the growth of its financial press, France still has no match for *The Economist* or *The Financial Times*). In 1955–6 it tried to transform itself into a daily and failed. In 1964 it changed to the news magazine formula. An editorial that year announced that the era of crusades was over. In the last decade or so, *L'Express* has revealed a taste for its own peace of mind, and the stimulation of its readers's cosseted bodies. Like its founding editor, Jean-Jacques Servan-Schreiber, it has generally striven to appear young, vigorous, non-conformist but 'with it', explanatory rather than partisan, and slick. It does very well for advertisers. Its public is composed mainly of *cadres*: the technocrat sector, youngish, well-equipped with and avid for more creature comforts and intellectual comfort. It has been said that *L'Express* aims at Americanizing politics in France. Certainly, its present appearance, a near carbon-copy of *Time*, suggests that this may be partly true. It goes in extensively for 're-writing' in the house style, and its articles present a pretty uniform idiom. It is easy on the eye and often on the brain. It was taken over in 1977 by the financier Sir James Goldsmith, and now proclaims itself Centrist. A recent editorial by Goldsmith (March 1986) settled on Chirac as representing the best hope for 'une France libre, prospère et heureuse'.

Le Point, with sales of 330,000, was founded in 1972 by several refugees from *L'Express*. It is largely non-oppositional, and in effect a near replica of *L'Express* in lay-out (intellectual/commercial incest, like hypochondria, is a French national sport). But with its practised policy of simplification, *Le Point* makes a point: too much indeed of the language of the French press is self-consciously inaccessible to the general public. Its youngish staff work on the principle of pooled ideas. It seeks to be the most 'Anglo-Saxon' (i.e. pragmatic) of the French weeklies. It successfully escaped when its parent company, Hachette, was taken over by the armaments manufacturer Matra. It is financially stable.

Le Nouvel Observateur

A much more individualistic production than *L'Express* is *Le Nouvel Observateur* (earlier called *L'Observateur*, then *France-Observateur*). It was founded with the intention of playing in the French press the role once taken by the *New Statesman* in Britain. It has always been firmly anti-colonialist and anti-Gaullist. Nevertheless it has shown itself unafraid to attack those it once favoured (e.g. Mendès-France), when it finds them compromising their stated beliefs. Like *L'Express* it lost a good many readers after the end of the exciting Algerian crisis. Yet in 1964 an editorial stated that, in the face of the Americanization of Europe and the alleged depoliticization of the public, *Le Nouvel Observateur* had opted to go against the current, convinced that a sufficiently large body of readers wanted to be informed and guided by a progressist journal dedicated to the democratic revival of France. This faith has proved justified, for this weekly steadily increases in circulation. After the events of May 1968 it rediscovered its old belligerence and today tends, sometimes to the point of silliness, to look for signs of revolutionary change in every walk of life: education, employment and literature, but also films, motoring and fashion. It boasts a team of idiosyncratic writers and a more than average number of tough, intellectual women columnists. Although some firms withdraw copy because of the frequent intransigence of its political stances, it carries a good deal of quality advertising, for its readership includes many well-off liberals. Its readership is young (20–45 in the main) and composed principally of *cadres moyens et supérieurs*, students, teachers, the liberal professions and trade union executives. Its rather pompously stated ambition (to remain 'un journal d'opinion, pur et dur') is being largely fulfilled. When it changed its format in 1972, to look more like *L'Express*, it sent a questionnaire to many political, academic and cultural luminaries, asking them what kind of paper they wanted it to be. Most replied: carry on as before, but avoid the trap of radical chic, *suivisme*. Its current circulation is 370,000.

Le Canard enchaîné

Le Canard enchaîné is the leading French satirical journal. It began as a trench news-sheet in 1916, dedicated to resisting the government's *bourrage de crâne* of the common soldier and citizen. It sought to unmask all official pronouncements, by lampooning the gaps between policy and practice.

Its title stemmed from the old word *canard*, meaning firstly any printed matter offered for public (especially popular) consumption, and secondly, false news. The only papers that the masses, if literate enough to read them, could afford throughout most of the nineteenth century were *canards*, as the high cost of proper newspapers reserved them for an élite. *Le Canard enchaîné* exploits this tradition towards a more honourable goal: 'the demystification of the man in the street'. Its professed policy is to provide 'a clownish but critical parody of the daily press'. To this end, its lay-out apes that of the normal daily and , though it appears weekly, its team's powers of improvisation ensure that its commentary on the news is always up to the minute. It aims to have the same relationship to the daily press as puppet shows have to the straight theatre. It tries to put into effect its slogan: 'La liberté de la presse ne s'use que si l'on ne s'en sert pas'. It mocks its trade partners for their ready self-censorship.

Its articles are specifically 'made in France'. It reflects what many Frenchmen like to think of as typical Frenchness: *débrouillardise*, *bon sens*, occasional *engueulades*. Neither *Punch* nor the *New Yorker* is a close equivalent. *Private Eye* is nearer, in its often schoolboyish thumbing of the nose at authority, though the *Canard*'s writers are mostly middle-aged or older, and their dissidence is less flashily contemporary. The *Canard* receives a heavy mail from readers: letters of support, rockets, snippets for that section of the paper devoted to the howlers and other idiocies of public pronouncements. This close contact of readers and journalists lends the *Canard* the air of a club. It is a club, too, in another sense: its comic tactics range from winking innuendoes to spoonerisms and thumping puns ('Ne disiez-vous pas, Monsieur de Gaulle, que les Français étaient des veaux? Ils ont veauté pour vous'). Among its many neologisms, it coined the highly useful 'bla-bla-bla' to describe hollow speechifying. With its circulation of 650,000 (three-quarters of that in the provinces), it clearly has, by French standards, a wide audience. It is most popular with school and university teachers, students and the less affluent members of the professional classes. Its editorial staff work as a co-operative, taking a share of the profits. Each has freedom of expression, but the chief editor retains the right to excommunicate. One of its leading columnists was once sacked for accepting the *Légion d'honneur*.

Its policy of accepting no advertising, either open or concealed, makes it unique in the French press. The result, however, is a rather grubby and old-fashioned appearance, which is perhaps part of its image as a rebellious old war-horse. Its standpoint is that of the *frondeur*, the defender of individual and minority rights. Its strong polemical tradition prevents its lending support easily, and it tends to oppose those in power, whether Right, Left or Centre. This was especially valuable in the last few years, when the Socialist government revealed itself to be every bit as self-righteously touchy about its press image as the preceding one had been.

Its satire is not exclusively political. It features a good deal of purely verbal humour and some analysis of cultural trends (it is very rude towards the whole concept of modishness). The tone is frequently that of an embittered but still virulent idealism. It is not an anti-social paper. The ideal is 'constructive anarchism'.

Often the rumours it reports are exclusive and well-informed (generally leaked by disgruntled insiders). There is traditionally a heavy restriction on official information in France. De Gaulle was a godsend: easily caricatured, his regal style inspired one *Canard* writer to describe his entourage regularly in terms of the court of Louis X1V, and Gaullist politics were in this way presented as a court entertainment in a France that had reverted to monarchy. The more faceless politicians of today present less striking targets.

In many ways, *Le Canard enchaîné* is outdated and sentimental (one of its heroes is Victor Hugo), but it undoubtedly reflects a native distrust of politicians and a strong desire on the part of most people to be left in peace by the 'powers that be'. The *Canard* has never been seized. One Prime Minister, urged to suppress a particularly outspoken issue, retorted that he had no desire to become a national laughing-stock. This peculiar kind of immunity goes with its status as an institution. Licensed fools, however, lose some of their bite, and governments can point to the *Canard's* untroubled existence as proof of their own liberalism, though this myth was recently punctured when the paper's offices were found to be bugged. Another drawback: regular readers note the strain behind the *Canard's* attempts to be funny about everything. News items are often milked dry. In this age of hidden persuaders, all the same, *Le Canard enchaîné*, like its cousins the geese on the Capitol in Rome, sounds an appealing alarm at every encroachment on freedom. In 1972 it was central to the publicizing of the scandals which disclosed corruption in high Gaullist circles. More recently its leaks about the gifts of diamonds to Giscard may well have cost him some credibility. It often specializes in publishing the tax returns of leading politicians. Financially, it has the last laugh: the *Canard* is the least lame duck of the French press. Michel Debré once said: 'Je n'aime pas *Le Canard enchaîné* car il m'a fait beaucoup de mal. Mais c'est un journal civique. Il est le seul journal en France qui exerce véritablement sa fonction.'

The regional press

Though the metropolitan press is not noted for recognizing its own distortions and omissions, in 1972 *Le Nouvel Observateur* published an article calling the regional press 'la presse du silence'. In response, provincial owners and editors protested, too much. Content analyses have in fact shown that regional papers studiously avoid raising important local issues in many cases. 'Pour l'infiniment petit', said the director of the Bordeaux-based *Sud-Ouest* (circulation 360,000), 'nous sommes irremplaçables.' When provincial papers fail to appear, statistics show that social, economic and cultural life in the catchment area suffers badly, and that attendance at funerals drops markedly. 'La nécrologie constitue la base de la vie d'un journal de province', as a *Sud-Ouest* editor said with a straight face. The regional paper is undoubtedly an agent of interconnection between scattered localities and individuals.

Pressures from all quarters, the commonly expressed but inadequately justified fear of upsetting advertisers, the notorious closeness of provincial community life, these are all reasons why the regional press treads carefully. In its defence it should be stressed that the Paris press lets the provinces down by talking more readily of national or foreign issues than of purely regional ones. Besides, the large provincial papers, because of their often monopolistic position, are perhaps right in trying to remain politically neutral. And for all its glaring shortcomings of moral cowardice, political conservatism, its care not to ruffle the hair of local bigwigs, the regional press at least talks of what interests its readers. It is helped in this service by its elaborate network of local correspondents, a luxury that the Paris dailies simply cannot afford. Indeed the provincials win both ways, for a good number of top Parisian journalists contribute articles to the regional press. However, with the introduction of modern technology, the Paris dailies can now add local pages to their standard editions and transmit these rapidly to the provinces, thus rivalling the regional press on its own ground. But the situation at present is that Paris papers seem to function mainly in the hothouse atmosphere of the capital, largely divorced from the provincial life led by the majority of Frenchmen.

The parallel press

1968 saw the resurrected phenomenon of the *journal mural* (a means of conveying information, slogans, insults, credos and morale-boosts among the rebels), which to many optimistic observers and participants was the writing on the wall for the old France. The often beautiful posters produced by the students of the Beaux-Arts demanded 'information libre!' Liberty of expression was indeed one of the main freedoms sought and temporarily practised by the insurgents. Since 1968 and until the late 1970s, this new press (called variously: parallel, wildcat, impressionist, underground, alternative or *gauchiste*) has had a remarkable and turbulent career. The sudden emergence of such papers and their often equally sudden extinction (they have been called 'exploding ephemera') were their facts of life, the second caused both by governmental measures of harassment and by internecine strife among the *groupuscules*. At their peak, sales of some reached 100,000.

Their innovation was principally to give a voice to the previously stifled protest of workers, servicemen, convicts, students, pupils and ethnic or sexual minorities. Readers were encouraged to participate directly via letters, the gathering and transmitting of news, the constitution of dossiers. Revolutionary press agencies were formed in order to co-ordinate this mass of material. What were at first mainly militants' newssheets, badly printed and arid in content, were often transformed into attractive, exciting and professional products.

Of them all, *Libération*, founded in 1973, is enjoying the longest life. Early in 1981, a split developed between those of its staff who favoured keeping it as it was – no hierarchy, rotation of jobs, identical wages for all, no advertising – and those who wanted a more competitively modern paper run with outside capital on truly professional lines. The latter won, and sales climbed to 70,000 (now 135,000). No doubt, as before, it will try to steer clear of all constituted organizations ('militants de la vie et non d'un parti', as many such journalists see themselves). It is a very attractive and buoyant paper.

In France, by law, any publication, even small or contentious, is guaranteed access to distribution and display, unlike in the Smith/Menzies chains in the United Kingdom. This might help to explain why many wildcat papers survived as long as they did. Some became blunter through repetition. Scatology was rampant. It sometimes seemed that, if the widespread manure could be reprocessed, by some natural organic method of course, and passed on to the ecological press, the gardens of communes might flourish. Another development of this press was strip cartoons in which even the heroes were grotesque (though this might have stemmed from slapdash draughtsmanship). All suffered from the debilitating fact of life that, to vie with the established press, they needed to emulate its organization: distribution systems, advertising, the hard sell. In fact, a type of short-circuit occurred, by which underground journalists wrote mainly for the initiated. 'Aspirant à réaliser la révolution par le plaisir, elle a souvent du mal à exister pour autre chose que son propre plaisir', as *Le Monde* once said. In addition to these newspapers, proper or improper, roneotyped sheets continue to serve a necessary function in barracks, factories, schools and universities for those disillusioned by traditional organs, parties or *syndicats.*

The anarchist press answers the needs of those sickened by endless doctrinal disputes, and it has strong links with the Women's and Gay Liberation movements. The aim of one such publication is typical of many: 'considérer chaque individu comme artiste afin d'éliminer l'artiste'. The motivation is often as much cultural or counter-cultural as political. Yet, just as no truly national daily yet exists in France, so no comprehensive paper unites all the variegated elements of the counter-culture, which are, in comparison with Anglo-Saxon youth, still relatively unemancipated. Of the contenders, the monthly *Actuel* (300,000 circulation), now more sophisticated, keeps up the tradition of healthy derisiveness.

The whole phenomenon of the parallel press clearly alarmed the authorities, which have sometimes resorted, in what seems like panic, to seizures and trials. Sartre (the 'lightning-conductor' of the new press), by accepting the function of director of, and therefore legal responsibility for, several *gauchiste* papers, tried repeatedly to prove that justice in France as regards the press has 'deux poids, deux mesures'. After he provoked the authorities to haul him in, the official response was a perfect example of Marcuse's concept of repressive tolerance: 'On n'arrête pas Voltaire'. All in all, however, this alternative press has acted as a constant thorn in the fleshy side of the Establishment. But it was Sartre himself who said soberingly, in 1970: 'Les journaux bourgeois disent plus la vérité que la presse révolutionnaire.' The capitalist press is in much less danger from the underground than from the wildcat wing of capitalism: free sheets, which magnetize advertising money.

Depoliticization

Like all young media, television is often credited with almost magical powers of influence. There is an undeniable threat to the written press from cable and regional television, and from new information systems available on home TV screens. None the less, as television and the radio are controlled by the State in France, the temptation to use both as conditioning agents has frequently proved irresistible. De Gaulle's big appearances on the little screen were in keeping with his general attitude towards the Fifth Republic: he could make direct appeals, bypassing such encumbrances as Parliament. Lately, as its unpopularity widened, the Socialist government undoubtedly laid an increasingly heavy paw on the media, though of course it made a welcome change to hear right-wing papers complain about such government malpractices; and politicians of all parties think that the media are against them. There is then all the more need for a vigorous, independent press to counterbalance official pressures. It seems likely that the audiovisual press has mainly shock value, and that people wishing to inform themselves properly on current affairs need to turn for commentary and extended explanation to the written word. In short, radio and television do not necessarily kill off the press, but rather stimulate the appetite for a serious press. What happens more often in fact is that most of the press feeds parasitically off the television; it bandwaggons.

The introduction of advertising on French television hit newspapers, but perhaps not so severely as the decline in 'small ads', due to the general economic situation. Furthermore, the monopoly system favours the big papers, and Paris dailies kill each other off more often than they succumb to competition from television. Television is dangerous, not only in that it steals advertising and thus weakens the press economically, but more in that, being a monolithic and largely unquestioned institution, it stifles thought.

It is difficult to deny that all forms of public communication in France – and this is where Gaullism and its heritage on Left or Right has most demoralized the nation – bear witness to the phenomenon of depoliticization: public apathy in the face of often crucial political matters. Since 1945, the Communist *Ce Soir*, the Socialist *Le Peuple*, the liberal *Combat* and the Gaullist *La Nation* have died. There are no extreme right-wing dailies at all, though the sales of the satirical weekly *Minute* doubled in the Paris area after May 1981 and now run at 200,000. It is openly racist and features personalized attacks on Socialists and Communists. Its heavy legal costs, the results of its scandalmongering, are met by its subscribers.

It can be argued, of course, that as the style of politics itself changes, so does public interest, but it is hard to distinguish what new forms of political awareness may have appeared. Many people are clearly bored with the increasingly formalized nature of politics in France, and transfer their energies to more private concerns (hence the rapid growth of the specialist press, the 'mini-media', dealing in hobbies). The *apolitisme*, especially of the regional press, leads naturally to conservative stances. And yet 'there is a monarchist way of reporting road accidents'. Every journal has a slant, and none more so than those that claim to be 'pure' newspapers. In these the manipulation of readers' attitudes is at its most surreptitious. Their style of reporting is often neither neutral enough to be 'information', nor intellectualized enough to be 'opinion'. It is governed by and it promotes *attitudes* (unconscious prejudices, fallacies, stereotypes). It has been claimed that educated Russians are better at decoding *Pravda* than western thinking people at reading between the lines of our own 'free' press. In addition to editorial bias, there is the matter of that loaded information, on which papers rely so heavily, supplied by press attachés and public relations officers: the whole question of the filtering and packaging of facts.

Proust spoke of 'cet acte abominable et voluptueux qui s'appelle: lire le journal'. Perhaps inevitably, the relationship of many readers with the paper of their choice is narcissistic. They gaze at their own face, hear their own voice, their own fears and desires, suitably embellished and projected back to them. There can be few people who read with the express intention, or even the readiness, to be jolted. Most of us can shut off what we do not wish to hear (conversely, attention, once polarized, can be acute). Few readers have time or patience to collate differing versions of the same news in different papers. As a result, opinions are often refuges, non-opinions. Today the temptation is not to *read* a paper but to 'spectate' it. The pages often resemble supermarkets, the new 'iconosphere'. The eclecticism of the present-day press, offering something to everyone, works against the notion of responsibility. The number and the variousness of readers are too great for any one line to be presented. While the weeklies can afford to be rather more committed, because they serve fairly faithful and homogeneous groups, the daily press as a whole is diversifying its contents; papers and magazines are getting closer together in style and material. Some of the more serious organs like *Le Monde* resist the contemporary craze for built-in obsolescence, by stressing the documentary function of the press (e.g. the publication of annual indexes of articles to facilitate reference back), but this is exceptional.

Sociétés de rédacteurs

Some of the most obvious shortcomings of the French press date back a long way. Over the past twenty years, the most hopeful signs of reform have come from within the journalistic profession itself, in which three warring factions predominate: the owners, the editorial staffs, and the technical operatives. The complexity of agreements and the marked individualism of the parties concerned have impeded the growth of honourable efficiency. The powerful union of printers has imposed high wages and under-employment of staff, by using archaic standards for calculating work loads. Although modern plant has been introduced, profitability has shown little increase, because the same number of men as before work it. In the 1969 troubles at *Le Figaro*, the technicians did not side with the editorial staff in its resistance to the owner's bid for complete control.

For three years recently, open war raged on *Le Parisien libéré*, a big-selling popular daily, between the owner Amaury and the monopolizing printing-workers' union (the *Fédération du livre*-CGT). There were broken agreements, sieges of premises, assaults on blackleg personnel, hijacking of pirate editions. Both the owner and his chief executive, Claude Bellanger, made great play of their Resistance records, although in this particular confrontation it was hard for outsiders to tell which side was the Maquis and which the oppressive occupying force. The owner presented his struggle as a democratic crusade against would-be totalitarian Communism and its attempts to control editorial matter, and to dictate the size of the workforce. The only clear results in three years of battling were the owner's decision to construct alternative printing-works and new distribution systems, and the drop in circulation by one half. In July 1976, Paris paper owners, including Amaury, and printers' unions settled their long dispute over technical modernization (photo-composition and computer typesetting).

A good many journalists refuse to envisage the press as simply a commercial proposition, and are haunted by theories about the corrupting power of money and by romantic visions of the press akin to knight-errantry. For them, papers should offer their readers 'daily refresher courses', an *éducation permanente*. To idealistic journalists, it is as scandalous that industrialists should control papers as it would be to most people if they controlled law courts or universities. And this statement by a powerful press lord, taxed with having sold out to big business interests, unwittingly illustrates what they are reacting against: 'Je ne me suis jamais vendu qu'à mes lecteurs.' The spokesmen for reform realize that the opponents of any proposed *co-gestion* in producing papers will raise the old alarmist bogyman of 'des soviets partout'. Few reformers are as radical as this. Some would settle for American-style foundations, which would run papers as limited-profit companies. The *sociétés de rédacteurs* that have been set up on *Le Monde*, *Le Figaro* and *Ouest-France* see themselves as active watch-dogs, ensuring that news is not treated purely as a commercial product and that editorial staff have a real say in all decision-making, but only at *Le Monde* do they have any true influence.

The common belief of such *sociétés* is that the press faces the same problems as society at large: in particular, the need to democratize the remaining autocratic structures. They recognize that part of their programme must include a better training for journalists themselves and university degree courses are well established at Paris, Lille, Strasbourg and Bordeaux. Refresher courses, especially in economics, about which many journalists are as under-informed as the general public, have also been established. In this whole area of reform, the French pressmen have outstripped their British counterparts, who have only recently begun actively to question the present functioning of the mass media and to propose needed changes.

One proposal made in *Esprit* is that *sociétés de lecteurs*, akin to consumer-protection groups, are at least as necessary as those of journalists. There is clearly a need for 'informational militants': self-appointed journalists who cross-check reports from news agencies or who raise hushed-up or forgotten issues. The biggest need is for plurality of viewpoints, though even pluralism should have its limits. Why, for instance, weep over the material difficulties of badly conceived and ill-run rags?

Conclusion

Edmund Burke spoke of the press as the Fourth Estate (and Keith Waterhouse less flatteringly of 'the 3rd form of the Fourth Estate'), alongside the judiciary, executive and legislative powers. What kind of force is the French press? It has been suggested that, like that of the Latin nations in general, it is more of a tribune press, which goes to the people instead of coming from it, or at least conversing with it. Hence the large amount of pontificating, the paternalism and the lack of attention given to readers' letters, which could act as a feedback and the start of a dialogue. One explanation, among many others, for the depolitization of the French press is the inhibiting historical example of *Le Petit Journal*. At the time of the Dreyfus Affair, it had the widest circulation of all French papers. It campaigned for Dreyfus; it lost half its readers. Consequently, there is a widespread reluctance to meddle or to shock, at least openly, for all papers try indirectly to direct opinion, by veiled allusions, undocumented sources, omissions or by effects of juxtaposition. Comment disguised as news is a constant ploy.

Perhaps the two features of the French press that most strike a foreign reader are, firstly, the *médisance*, the personal bitchiness, the bristly sense of honour common to French journalists of all persuasions; this derives in part from the importance granted to ideas, to ideologies. Secondly, there is the impression that French journalists, even mediocre ones, are soaked in history, politics and literature. Occasionally, this cultural formation proves too facile, turns to *déformation professionnelle*, and produces (like French lawyers, and like many of the readers who do write to papers) a kind of cheap subliterature, replete with rhetorical effects. Just as there is a long tradition of sedentary anthropology in France, so there is one of armchair journalism, which relies too much on printed sources or verbal inventiveness and too little on going to look for oneself. Perhaps a better result of a more articulate culture is that in *L'Humanité*, addressed among others to manual workers, can be found long words and cultural allusion beyond the imaginings of the British popular press. Even *France-Soir* publishes occasional serious articles. A lack of matter-of-factness can be a handicap but also a blessing.

Prophets see both the press and printed books as moribund phenomena. It might well be that papers will fairly soon become (as they started out) a privilege for the comfortable minority, because costs in future will be more closely matched by much increased selling prices. *Paris-Jour*, in that it had most blue-collar workers in its readership, was the most 'popular' paper in Paris before it died in 1972. After it closed, it seems that its readers did not switch to any other paper. It is sometimes said that Paris has room for only two morning and two evening papers. It would be snobbish to rejoice too much over the greater success of the quality press, for it is yet another indication of the separate orbits in France of the intelligentsia and the masses. René Pucheu offers a salutary reminder: 'La bêtise n'est pas un privilège des non-privilégiés.'

Bibliography

Agnès, Y. and Croissandeau, J.M., *Lire le journal*. Paris, Lobiès, 1979. Excellent on using the press as a teaching aid.
Albert, P., *La Presse*. Paris, PUF, 6th edn, 1982. A general study, short but accurate.

Archambault, F. and Lemoine, J.-F., *Quatre Milliards de journaux*. Paris, Moreau, 1977.

Bellanger, C. (ed.), *Histoire générale de la presse française*, 5 vols. Paris, PUF, 1969–76.

Bercoff, A., *L'Autre France: l'underpresse*. Paris, Stock, 1975.

Brochier, J.-C., *La Presse écrite*. Paris, Hatier, 1983.

Cayrol, R., *La Presse écrite et audiovisuelle*. Paris, PUF, 1973.

Freiberg, J.W., *The French Press: Class, State and Ideology*. New York, Praeger, 1981.

Jamet, M., *La Presse périodique en France*. Paris, Colin, 1983.

Jeanneney, J.-N., and Julliard, J., *Le Monde de Beuve-Méry*. Paris, Seuil, 1979.

Mathien, M., *La Presse quotidienne régionale*. Paris, PUF, 1983.

Pucheu, R., *Le Journal, les mythes et les hommes*. Paris, Editions Ouvrières, 1962.

Schwoebel, J., *La Presse, le pouvoir et l'argent*. Paris, Le Seuil, 1968. Good on the *sociétés de rédacteurs*.

Voyenne, B., *L'Information aujourd'hui*. Paris, Colin, 1979. A completely rewritten version of *La Presse dans la société contemporaine* (1962). The best general study.

The 'Kiosque' series published by Colin contains several fascinating studies of the press in action, for example, *La Gauche hebdomadaire*, *La Presse clandestine*, *Le Monde et ses lecteurs*, *Le Cas Paris-Soir*. It is currently being reprinted.

The monthly *Presse-Actualité* was, until replaced in 1986 by the more wide-ranging *Médiaspouvoirs*, a goldmine of up-to-date information. *La Documentation française* published in September 1983, nos. 4729-30, an excellent review of the whole question of the French press by P. Albert.

Nine

The broadcasting media

Neil Harris

Introduction

In recent years, the broadcasting systems of all the countries of western Europe have had to contend with the arrival on the scene of new, bewilderingly complex technology. Private pay channels, commercial TV and radio, direct broadcasting satellites and cable networks have come to stay; and governments have been forced to address themselves to the social, political and cultural implications of these new media. It has been necessary to consider the existing frameworks of radio and TV in the light of new developments, with particular emphasis on the role of public service broadcasting in the late 1980s. There is much debate everywhere; but nowhere in Europe is it of such moment as in France. The considerable governmental influence to be seen there in the workings of the media, where a head of broadcasting can say confidently 'a journalist should be French first, objective second', has made the successive administrations' handling of the new situation all the more interesting.

The arrival of the first Socialist government in France for many years has made the period 1981–6 one of exceptionally dramatic change in broadcasting. It can be argued that any government on its toes would have done as much; but the measures adopted have to an extent been deliberately chosen to highlight the *dirigiste*, hidebound approach of previous right-wing regimes, and to impress an electorate dismayed at seeing its country fall further and further behind its competitors. In fact, the old State-interventionist tactics have been seen to die hard. But the Right, back in power in 1986 with a precarious majority, seems on current evidence to be anxious to build on the achievements of these years, realizing that France must be seen to be a contender on the European and world media stages in the latter half of the decade and beyond.

Background

The BBC established its reputation as a free voice in the Second World War, and if in the light of post-war history it is impossible to say as much for the French broadcasting services, it is back to the same time that we must look to find the cause. In exile, de Gaulle realized the vital part radio could play in rallying Frenchmen to his cause, and once the war was over he lost no time in nationalizing the networks, thereby driving home the Gaullist message and expunging the collaborationist image created by the private radio stations in the war years. As television spread in the 1950s, de Gaulle proved himself as much a master of this new and even more powerful means of mass communication. His appearances on television, particularly as President, were virtuoso displays in controlling an audience and he even reserved some of his main policy decisions for his televised announcements. As long as he was able to exercise total control over the political content of radio and TV, he had no fear of a serious rival. Indeed, it was not until 1964 that a second State channel, Antenne 2, was created, and only 1973 before the more regionally-based third, FR3, came into being.

Not surprisingly, this absolute veto came in for much criticism. Gaullist assertions that such control was necessary to counterbalance opposition in some of the press did not cut much ice, since the rapid spread of television, and falling newspaper sales, had quickly made both radio and television more powerful and lasting means of putting over a message. In order as much as anything to placate their critics, the Gaullists created in 1964 the *Office de la radiodiffusion et télévision française* (ORTF). ORTF was ostensibly an autonomous body which assumed responsibility for programming; but many of the posts in the organization remained government appointments – was this then such a large step towards a broadcasting service free from State control?

Discontent with this lack of freedom, together with the problems of a cumbersome bureaucracy and unsatisfactory working conditions, reached its head, like so much else, in 1968. The ensuing 'liberalization' of the ORTF from 1969–72, the work of Prime Minister Jacques Chaban-Delmas, was fiercely criticized by many in the government; and the *Office* retained its unitary structure until 1974 when the incoming President Giscard d'Estaing, having based his electoral campaign on more flexible policies than those of his predecessors, rapidly (some say now much too rapidly) pushed through legislation breaking up the ORTF into seven independent companies, or *sociétés*. It was hoped that competition between these would prove beneficial for broadcasting at large, but the companies soon ran into financial difficulties. Furthermore the government, by making those at the head of the companies its own nominees, showed itself reluctant to grant real independence to these *filles de l'ORTF*. The very strong Gaullist presence in the administration no doubt contributed largely to this measure.

After 1981: the emergence of independent television

Like President Giscard in 1974, the Socialists saw the reform of broadcasting as one of their first tasks on coming to power. But this, the fifth reform of the service in twenty-five years, was to be the most radical yet. The new administration undertook to ensure that the public service (as they called it, significantly discarding the term 'monopoly') was protected from government intervention. In order to 'cut this umbilical cord' an *Haute Autorité* was created in 1982, a council of nine members, their mandate (doubtless intentionally) longer than that of the presidential term. The Authority took upon itself the task of appointing the directors of the *sociétés*, drawing up the 'cahiers des charges' which define the exact scope of broadcasting for each company, plus several other tasks which hitherto were handled exclusively by the government. Its personnel came from professions other than politics: the judiciary is represented, for example, and the Assembly and Senate as well as the President put up names for this council. The intention clearly was to set up a professional, independent body to act as a buffer between State and broadcasting services. In the reform of 1986, the Right has retained the council for the foreseeable future (although symbolically renaming it), and indeed has extended its powers. Despite certain vicissitudes, the Authority has been able to point to some solid achievements over the four years of its existence, not the least of which has been its role as watchdog at all elections in France, ensuring fair distribution of air-time for politicians on radio and TV – something which under previous regimes was by no means guaranteed.

The TV companies created by the 1974 reform continued to exist until very recently. Apart from TF1, Antenne 2 and FR3, there are *Télédiffusion de France* (TDF) (technical problems of broadcasting and maintenance of transmitters), and the *Société française de production* (SFP) (making of films, video production and marketing). It was intended that the new companies should commission programmes from the SFP, but they soon went their own way and the SFP ran further and further into debt. Twelve years on it still represents something of a millstone.

TF1 deliberately fosters a more popular image than its sister A2, which has more cultural aspirations, but it nevertheless ventures occasionally into more highbrow fare (its latest foray is an original film by Jean-Luc Godard). FR3 concerns itself to a certain extent with regional affairs, and has always been rather the poor relation (it only broadcasts for five hours a day). The channel has frequently been called 'pseudo-regionalist', as its outposts were ideologically responsible to Paris ('Ils n'ont de régional que leur adresse' said *Le Monde*). Despite moves to make the stations more independent and to encourage links with the community, they still do not seem to make much impact at local level.

After three years of government there was new and more visible evidence that the Socialists were out to change the television landscape for good. They announced the creation of a fourth channel for late 1984, a pay-TV to be called *Canal plus*, in which the powerful State-owned Havas advertising and media group was to have a controlling interest. The subscription (140F in 1986) is payable on top of the normal licence fee (541F in 1986 for a colour set), and there is extra outlay for a special decoding device, necessary since part of the output is scrambled in order to combat the piracy so widespread in the USA. The channel is on the air for twenty hours a day during the week, and round the clock at weekends. The material is firmly middlebrow: films and sports programmes for the most part. There is no original television material. The 'cahier des charges' stipulates that 60 per cent of all films shown must be of French origin, a popular move with the film industry and one designed to allay suspicion, familiar enough in France, that such an innovation would lead to an invasion of foreign (that is, American) culture. The then Prime Minister, Laurent Fabius, further calmed the film-makers' fears by assuring them that the same restrictions would apply to *Canal plus* in the matter of showing films as those in operation in cinema distribution, referring principally to the length of time allowed betwen a film's release and its appearance on TV.

In its first two years *Canal plus* has made itself into a success, notching up its millionth subscriber in May 1986. Those two years were worrying ones, however, for the channel's *exploitants* because, only a few months after *Canal plus* started, the government revealed that 1985 was going to be a watershed in the history of French television: independent television was about to become a reality. While the three State channels carried some advertising to boost their revenue, they could of course in no sense be seen as commercially-minded. The proposed new channel, *La Cinq*, which finally took to the air with great fanfare in February 1986, could scarcely be called anything else and was set to confirm the worst fears of those sceptical of the effect of such liberal policies. The franchise was won, after some bitter wrangling, by Italian TV magnate Silvio Berlusconi and his two French associates, both of whom were known Mitterrand sympathizers. Berlusconi built his huge empire in Italy on a television diet of game-shows, cheaply-produced music programmes, re-runs of old films and the like, and as there had been no time to prepare a detailed 'cahier des charges' he had more or less *carte blanche* as to programming. Since Berlusconi was alleged to be personally responsible for the disastrous drop in cinema attendances in Italy and the consequent virtual bankruptcy of the film industry there, French film-makers are naturally horrified that the same thing could be happening to them. The eminent film director Bertrand Tavernier described the move as 'a stab in the back', particularly indignant that it had been made by a government hitherto anxious to show its high cultural credentials.

No sooner had *La Cinq* got under way than another channel, TV6, was set up. This was a popular music and video channel, financed like *La Cinq* from advertising revenue, and run by the advertising agency Publicis amongst others. Both the fifth and sixth channels were known as *chaînes multivilles*, which indicated that they could not be received nationally; but whereas those running *La Cinq* were well on the way to realizing their intention of having the channel available to 80 per cent of French territory, transmission of the sixth was limited to certain urban areas (Paris, Lyons, Marseilles and Lille), and even there reception was sometimes difficult.

What enraged the opposition in all this had less to do with the quality of the programmes the channels were showing than with the government's timing. The President had clearly had his eye on the forthcoming *législatives* of March 1986 and had made, given the Right's own assurances in this area, a calculated pre-emptive strike. When Prime Minister Jacques Chirac, who is also Mayor of Paris, learnt that the engineers were intending to use the transmitters at the top of the Eiffel Tower (as the highest building in the city) to broadcast *La Cinq*, he put every possible obstacle in the path of TDF, including a refusal to allow negotiations with the Tower's trustees. The government then rushed through a law allowing public services such as TDF access to all monuments over 200 metres high. Chirac contested the law in the *Conseil d'Etat*, and lost. *La Cinq* would be on the air on time; but the bitterness remained and would soon be reflected in the new administration's attitudes towards the independent channels.

The *projet de loi* of 1986: the privatization issue

The measures put in train by the Socialists on taking office had led many to believe that political interference in the running of the broadcasting media was coming to an end. There were those, less convinced, who felt that the government, like its predecessors, would be unable to forgo applying pressure on networks over news and information. Certainly the practice of appointing government nominees to the key administrative posts was soon seen to be alive and well: in 1982 and 1983 men of pronounced Socialist sympathies were chosen as Presidents of TF1 and A2, in the teeth of the *Haute Autorité*. And in 1985 the popular newsreader Christine Ockrent resigned over what she saw as political meddling. We have seen that the government's move to create independent television was judged by the opposition to be an electoral device as much as anything, insurance against failure at the polls. But their own plans were more radical yet: in the run-up to March 1986 they announced plans to privatize two of the three State channels, calling into doubt thereby the very concept of public service broadcasting.

On gaining power the right-wing majority set about its task. It was apparent very soon that there were complex and delicate decisions to be made, with the job made no easier by exhortations from the right-wing press that the government should stick to its promises and hasten the legislation. The speed with which it was obliged to move left no time for any real debate to take place on the issue. The problems multiplied. For instance, there were major financial analyses to be made of the seven *sociétés* fragmented in 1974. It was felt in some quarters that no one of these companies could be tampered with without serious damage being done to some or all of the others; despite their nominal independent status, it was almost as if they constituted a closed financial system. Each of the three channels gives 500 million francs a year to TDF for broadcasting programmes, and TF1 and A2 each gives the SFP 600 million francs a year for production costs. Private companies interested in acquiring a channel would anticipate making significant cuts in these contributions: for example, the transmitters necessary at the moment to cover the *zones d'ombre*, those areas of France unable otherwise to receive transmission, would be rejected as commercially unjustifiable, so depriving between 5 and 10 per cent of French viewers altogether of non-satellite TV. A likely solution is that the government will take a protectionist stance towards the SFP and

TDF, perhaps obliging a private channel via its 'cahier des charges' to commission so much material from the SFP. This is all the more necessary as, in any case, the trend in recent years has been increasingly towards the purchase of cheap productions from abroad rather than concentrating on home-produced, cost-intensive material.

In May 1986 the government finally made up its mind as to which of the three State channels it was to privatize. Opinion had favoured either the 'minority' Antenne 2, or, less likely because much smaller (20 per cent of the audience), the regional FR3. But it was decided that it was the oldest of the channels, the *populaire de qualité* TF1, which was to go. This seemed to some at the time to have been a choice arrived at by someone with a list and a pin, but the new Minister of Communications, François Léotard, advanced persuasive reasons. TF1 produced less *créations* than A2, which made 215 hours of original material in 1985, including a popular serial along 'Dallas' lines, but homegrown, called 'Châteauvallon', a co-production with Channel 4. Also 75 per cent of films on the channel in 1986 would be French, including original work by the Polish director Andrejz Wajda. TF1 makes something of a financial loss, despite viewing figures which stand up well to those of A2. In fact A2 makes an almost comparable loss, but employs 130 less people. Another more symbolic but perhaps even more important reason for choosing the *soeur aînée* is that it is the one most closely associated with the old 'voice of France' approach to the media – it was on TF1 in 1949 that the first televised news magazine appeared, *Cinq colonnes à la une*. It will therefore be the choice most likely to convince the electorate of the sincerity of the government's attempts to create greater freedom of broadcasting.

Despite its reprieve the future of FR3 is uncertain; its statute is being examined and the government will pronounce on its fate by the end of 1987. Antenne 2 thus remains as the more important of the two public channels. The staff are already worried to hear their *Président-directeur* flattered at having his channel thought of as 'la chaîne publique de référence', a phrase on which they understandably put a rather sinister gloss. Almost as bad, they fear that A2 will become a stale vehicle for 'party political broadcasts, church services and

Nicaraguan basket-weaving'. And it is not even certain that the channel will remain forever public.

With the removal of one State network, it is reasonably certain that there will be a reduction in the licence fee, to about 450 francs, and that advertising on A2 and FR3 will be reduced. The new law abolishes the unpopular tax on VCRs, one major reason for their comparatively slow spread in France. But above all the extension of the powers of the *Haute Autorité*, here renamed the *Commission nationale de communication et libertés*, represents an important clarification of its future. As well as nominating the heads of the public services and several of their board members, the commission will have charge of the frequency allocation of any new private channels, and will impose any operating restrictions it deems appropriate. Any cable network must receive authorization from the CNCL.

As far as the new commercial channels are concerned, their future is no more clear cut than that of their State counterparts. The franchises of *La Cinq* and TV6 were summarily revoked after only a few months, with the minister starting out by forbidding the former to show any films, its staple fare. Its part-owner Silvio Berlusconi has already started proceedings for breach of contract, promising 'the legal battle of the century'. The French authorities are standing firm at the moment, declaring that Berlusconi henceforth must deal with the constituted body, the CNCL. The survival of TV6 is in doubt, as the government apparently does not intend to relaunch a 'multiville', preferring to use the frequencies instead for local stations, particularly in the Paris area. The predictable attitude of the Right here is to attack the most conspicuous fruits of the Socialist policies.

At TFl itself there has been naturally much bitterness. One staff member declared that it was 'like selling off the Comédie-Française to ICI or Versailles to IBM'. The decision provoked a major strike and the first street demonstration since 1974; the main fear of course is of job cuts. Those in important posts have been the main targets for the predictable mudslinging since the news emerged; familiar accusations abound of excessively biased commentaries and of news deliberately *gauchi*. Prime Minister Chirac, in response to one allegation of preferential treatment on a political discussion programme, warned that everyone on the channel 'would be advised to watch his step', a disingenuous remark given the government's insistence that no witch-hunt was intended. This was itself undermined by the fact that the right-wing press has drawn up a list of about twenty-five journalists it wants immediately sacked. All in all, there are worries that a return may be imminent of the strident *contestataire* relations between politics and broadcasting that characterized the 1970s, particularly unwelcome given the current highly volatile situation. At least between 1981–6 conflict, though present, was more muted.

Meanwhile the customers are already queuing up in large numbers, headed by the ever-growing *multimédias* like Robert Hersant's *Figaro* group, James Goldsmith's Groupe-Express and Hachette-Matra. Large organizations with experience in the audiovisual field, such as the *Compagnie luxembourgeoise de télédiffusion* (CLT) are also in the running. They were not at all pleased to learn that there is a certain amount of dissension within the government as to the selling-off method. Some ministers initially favoured a complex auction system, others public flotation, but the current formula – 50 per cent of shares for the main *exploitants*, 40 per cent for the public, and 10 per cent for employees – is anathema to such as Hersant, who sees himself as very much a *patron*. This may be one reason why, given the sudden availability of *La Cinq*, some groups seem more interested in taking over that already commercially-oriented enterprise. TF1, with its essentially middle-of-the-road format, already resembles to some extent a commercial channel. However the powerful *médiavores* are no doubt unimpressed by, in the Minister's words 'the challenge to private finance to redress the channel's difficult financial situation.' *La Cinq* is at least a going concern. It remains to be seen how its purchaser will deal with the newly-empowered commission, who will certainly favour the *mieux-disant culturel* among the candidates more than ever before, a break with the long-standing French tradition whereby a 'cahier des charges' is prepared first, for which bids are then entered. The decisions made by the CNCL will be entirely subjective, and it will not be accountable to the *Conseil d'Etat*. This extra independence brings the commission more into line with an organization such as the British IBA, to which it has somewhat inaccurately been compared in the past.

It may be that no organization, however large, will have the financial muscle to take on TFl single-handed. At the moment an official audit is going on there and elsewhere in the broadcasting system, and its findings will certainly bring round many hitherto worried about privatization. The channel is over-manned: four people do the work of two. A rival channel can deliver a twelve-minute *reportage* for 3.5 times less what it costs TFl. And there are 200 hours of documentaries commissioned by the channel which are gathering dust on the shelves. Some attribute such inefficiencies to the situation pre-1982, when the presidents of the channels were appointed *en conseil des ministres*, with a week's grace before the next meeting at which it was not out of the question he would be replaced. Small wonder, then, that in the absence of a firm hand on the tiller disorder should reign at lower level.

National radio

No comparably wide-ranging reforms have been made to the three State-controlled national radio stations, operating under the collective title Radio-France. The President of Radio-France is the only one who will continue to be appointed by ministers. France-Inter, the main news network, is still seen very much as a government mouthpiece but, despite such a handicap and stiff competition from elsewhere, it is the only large station to have increased its listening audience since 1984. This may be thanks to some enterprising recent experimentation with its *grilles*; its staff is aware that it cannot allow itself to be too narrow in its appeal. Its avowed aim is indeed to reach the largest possible audience, and so it ranges over a wide field, from light entertainment to interviews with eminent figures in the political and cultural worlds. These interviews are usually, despite the station's apparent function as *porte-parole*, lengthy and probing, although perhaps more searching of the subject's personal life than of his policies.

France-Culture and France-Musique, the other two State stations, are as their names suggest designed to cater for more highbrow tastes. The fact that there are two 'cultural' stations indicates the importance still placed on high art on the media in France (Bernard Pivot's Friday evening book programme *Apostrophes*, on Antenne 2, has for some time been one of the most popular on television). Defenders of the public service in the current debate hold up France-Culture as an example of what would almost certainly disappear if market forces were allowed to operate unchecked on the airwaves. It presents broadly-based fare, using radio for *composition sonore* and experimenting with combinations of music and drama. For this, it has the resources of the excellent *Atelier de création radiophonique*, an enviable asset for any radio company. The station is also noteworthy for its championship of young novelists' work. For its part France-Musique limits itself largely to more conventional music broadcasts, but leaves scope for experimentation and devotes a considerable amount of time to the promotion of new music. The two networks see themselves as *petites cousines*, occasionally pooling their resources in order to cover the same event (perhaps the Aix festival, for example). However, such enterprise is often counterbalanced by carelessness over simple things: on one occasion, for example, France-Musique broadcast an extended classical piece, covering two sides of a record, which began and ended halfway through because the second side had been played first. Accidents happen anywhere, of course, but it was surprising that the mistake went unnoticed for three-quarters of an hour.

Finally Radio-France has a world service, Radio-France Internationale, which it has been keen to expand. A new short-wave transmitter was opened in French Guyana in early 1985, serving Latin America and the Caribbean, where many Francophone peoples live. Its next objective is the geopolitically important area of South East Asia, and over the last three years it has begun to attract interest in South America. RFI's ambition is to be received worldwide by 1987.

The chief rivals to Radio-France are the commercial stations Radio-Luxembourg (RTL), Radio Monte-Carlo (RMC) and Europe-1 in the Saar, all known as *périphériques* as they broadcast from outside French territory. As these all offer news less subject to government pressure, they have unsurprisingly proved more popular, by and large, than the State networks, with

Europe-1 being most listened to for news. There is a curious anomaly, however, with regard to the *périphériques*: although they are all commercial in terms of their ethos, progamming and dependence on advertising revenue, the French State none the less until very recently had shares in all three, in the case of RTL via Havas (which also controls *Canal plus*), and in the case of Europe-1 and RMC via the *Société française de radiodiffusion* (SOFIRAD). The government took them over gradually as the stations' need for French co-operation became evident, particularly in the matters of offices in Paris, transmitters and cables on French territory. Before 1981 it was common for the President and ministers to claim air-time on the *périphériques* at crucial moments, for example, immediately before elections. The departure of some of the people in important positions in these companies after May 1981 may be seen as a continuation of the same kind of political pressurization. In March 1986, just before the parliamentary elections, the government announced that it was turning the very popular Europe-1 station over to full private ownership, selling its controlling interest to the French publishing house Hachette-Matra for about £50 million – clearly a move designed to do for radio what the creation of commercial channels had done for TV, and timed to extract maximum advantage at the polls. One result of the transaction is that Hachette, having branched out into radio, will expand further into TV; there are reports that it is interested in one of the remaining State-owned networks, perhaps Antenne 2. The move into TV is seen by the powerful press barons as a natural extension of their operations.

Local radio

Latterly Radio-France has made a point of stressing its policy of decentralization, setting great store by 'the interplay of local and national networks', according to its President, Jean-Noël Jeanneney. In its first year the Socialist government created fifty-six local stations as well as increasing technical assistance in the form of radio workshops. Its concern is a natural consequence of the enormous growth in popularity of local radio in France, which by mid-1986 has taken over one-third of the total radio audience. During the restrictive 1970s pirate radio flourished, and efforts by the State to jam illegal operators, while effective in some cases, appeared increasingly unable to stem the tide. As with television, the Socialists (whose leader François Mitterrand had actually been served with an arrest warrant for broadcasting on a station subsequently seized by riot police) made freedom of the airwaves an important part of their election manifesto, and in 1982 the ban on private local stations on the FM band was lifted.

An immediate jostling for airspace ensued. The recently formed *Haute Autorité*, whose responsibility it was to allocate frequencies and regulate transmission capacity (maximum range 30 km), was all but submerged with requests for licences; and in practice, even after reducing the number to manageable proportions – only a limited number of frequencies being available – found it well-nigh impossible to enforce its rulings. (This situation remains in 1986: the outgoing *Haute Autorité* had 250 *dossiers* for the Paris region alone, with a maximum 21 to grant.) Between 1982–4 the scene was chaotic, not least because even those stations allowed air-time were not permitted to finance themselves through advertising. Most were forced to lead a very precarious existence, relying often on voluntary contributions; and although it was pointed out to the government that if it allowed its own State TV to take a certain amount of advertising it seemed illogical to prevent private local radio stations from doing so, it was not until 1984 that the ban was lifted, giving rise to a further explosion in numbers. The State-controlled TDF was placed in charge of broadcasting over 100 local radios which not long before it had been engaged in jamming.

Even then, the anarchic conditions prevailing on the airwaves were hardly appealing to those who mattered most, the advertising customers. To try and make themselves more attractive here, many stations have adopted the obvious solution: amalgamation and growth. Some networks even have satellite ambitions. A popular formula involves the formulation of one central *tête de pont* station to make programmes, which are then broadcast over numerous stations in other parts of France. Thus simultaneous publicity spots are guaranteed without precluding messages of local interest.

One such is 'Nostalgie' radio based in Lyon, which already

has a 30-year success record and has signed a contract enabling it to be heard in 100 towns in France via satellite by the end of 1986. Financially this would put it on a par with the *périphériques*. Robert Hersant has pointed out that 90 per cent of the publicity revenue on the FM wave band is of local origin, and that any station of moderate size with national aspirations risks losing its main source of income. Indeed, certain military frequencies on FM are shortly to be made available for the *périphériques* themselves to enter the lists; Hersant, a great believer in national radio on FM, already has at Neuilly some of the most modern transmitting equipment in Europe.

A network which has made a success of its limitations is Radio Vallée de Seine, which has expanded considerably without losing its local roots. Set up in the euphoric if penurious days of 1981 the station, based in Rouen, met with immediate success, listeners and advertisers alike being impressed by the unusual quality of the programmes as well as the professional approach. Now RVS covers Rouen, Le Havre and Caen, with the possibility in the near future of including Dieppe, Etretat and Fécamp: that is, just about all of Normandy. Its administrators consider the creation of national networks on FM a step backward, even when possible; they claim advertising must come from local sources, and professional ambition must balance regional needs. The similar success of ROF (*Régie ondes et fréquences*) set up by the press group *Ouest-France* and Havas indicates that a like combination of limited aims, broadcasting ability and commercial acumen yields results.

Satellite and cable

De Gaulle's reluctance in the post-war years to allow independent TV to develop had consequences for the whole of the telecommunications industry. The French telephone system, for example, was for a long time hopelessly archaic. Slowly governments woke up to the fact that the technological revolution was upon them and was clearly irreversible. The Socialists on their arrival enthusiastically embraced the idea of modernization, pouring enormous amounts of money into development projects (currently France and Germany are three years ahead of Britain in the matter of direct broadcasting by satellite). Partly these are joint schemes with other countries, necessarily so given the expense involved and the crowded European airspace, with the satellite operation providing the clearest example of the perils of this kind of collaboration. Luxemburg had plans of its own for a DBS satellite in the early 1980s, but after some delicate negotiations the CLT was persuaded to give up these ideas in favour of a share in France's own satellite, TDFl. Then CLT, apparently certain that its track record in Europe was sufficient guarantee of the use of two of TDFl's four channels, began to show less interest in financing it, and finally the French government was forced to look elsewhere for investors. CLT was in any case by now concerned that any newly-created private stations in France might poach its own protected publicity resources. The affair illustrates the problems inherent in a costly technological venture involving foreign companies who have their own (and their government's) financial interests at heart.

In November 1985 the French government announced the franchises for the four channels of TDFl. One was to be an English-language channel run by Robert Maxwell, giving him a potential audience of 20 million throughout western Europe, and putting him into competition with Rupert Murdoch's Sky channel, which already reaches 4.5 million homes. Another was allocated to the owners of *La Cinq* to boost its transmission area in France, a third conceived as a 'cultural' channel run by a European consortium featuring Pierre Desgraupes, a former head of Antenne 2. The fourth would either be given to Silvio Berlusconi or be run as a German-language channel by RTL. Unlike lower-powered satellites which must use the existing cable network, TDFl will be available directly provided viewers are equipped with a reception dish. Elsewhere there are plans for the satellite to service up to 100 private local TV stations, possibly affiliated to two national private networks. Since 1985, however, TDFl has run into technical difficulties, and will not now be launched until early 1987. And to put things back to square one, the new government has decided to cancel all existing applications for a concession on TDFl until the *projet de loi* has gone through Parliament. Robert Maxwell, like Berlusconi, has threatened to go to law, but as a lure proposes to create a satellite news service based in Paris, made in English but broadcast in different languages via TDF1.

France was similarly behind other countries in the matter of cable. Belgium and Holland have been extensively cabled for some years, and Germany has a £20 billion scheme in hand. Although cabling plans (or satellite plans for that matter) did not feature on the Socialist manifesto in 1981, they soon set about the task with zeal and determination, incorporating cable as a central element in their programme for industrial renewal. The new fibre-optic cable techniques allow provision for many inter-related audiovisual services, and an enquiry in 1984 found that cable was the only viable long-term system to satisfy professional users as well as the casual viewer. As much as anything, the employment opportunities it represents make it an important investment for the future. The Left believed, using an argument strongly reminiscent of the Gaullists' in the early 1960s, that the advent of local TV via cable would counteract, by recreating plurality of opinion, what it saw as bias in the press. Then the arrival of independent television in 1985 seemed to cut the ground from under the feet of the cable industry: would anyone be interested in subscribing to something they could sample elsewhere for free? In the analogous case of *Canal plus* the worries proved, after an uncertain period, unfounded. It remains to be seen what long-term effects cable will suffer.

While in Britain the government has tried to attract private investment to the cabling programme, in France, characteristically, the State not only built but will continue to own and operate the equipment. There are already rules devised to protect French production: one-third of revenues must be used to finance original material; there must be a maximum 30 per cent foreign programming; and at least 15 per cent of programmes must be of 'a local nature'. Given that fibre-optic cables are capable of carrying up to fifteen channels, to avoid unnecessary duplication it has been recommended that public and private groups combine to organize channels on thematic lines. At this stage, of course, given that all is once more in the melting-pot, it is unclear who will be in charge of the channels. But the government is pressing ahead with its plans to lay down as much of the cable infrastructure as possible, and is confident of achieving its target of 1.5 million homes switched into the system by 1987, rising to half the country by the 1990s, the whole at a cost of 5.5 billion dollars.

Conclusion

The organization of the networks in Britain is often put forward by the French, with a certain baffled admiration, as an example of how public and private broadcasting services can co-exist with mutual profit. Those who believe in the preservation of a public broadcasting system in France insist that it is only through its continued presence that standards can possibly be maintained at all; it should be there as a standing reproach to the commercial networks. They argue that this presupposes a reasonably loose interpretation of the term 'public service', feeling that 'le ghetto culturel' on the one hand is as bad as 'la savonnette commerciale' on the other. The public, even after years of witnessing blatant State interference in broadcasting, remains unconvinced that complete liberalization is any more of a miracle-working formula than nationalization; always naturally conservative in times of upheaval, it is clearly anxious not to lose totally its terms of reference. It seems likely, though, that the distinction between public and private is destined to become increasingly blurred. The Minister of Communications has said that the axiom 'public funding for the public service, advertising revenue for the private' is rapidly becoming obsolete. In fact it has long since been so, but official acceptance of the situation at least suggests that the government is facing up to reality.

'Le petit monde de la télévision a perdu ses frontières mais gardé ses illusions', a media commentator said recently. French broadcasting in all its forms, State radio perhaps apart, is in a state of transition, one for which it has been ill-prepared by its long hibernation. Certainly those who work within the system can no longer harbour the illusion that their voice is uniquely authoritative, but it should be possible to use this as a source of strength. What they hope for above all is a settled environment ensuring them the largest possible measure of independence, something which in the past in France has been very rare. Once the dust has settled (the government estimates that it will be two years before the effects of the 1986 reform become apparent) it will be possible to see whether there is sufficient will-power on all sides to make the best of the opportunities offered.

Bibliography

Those wishing to keep up-to-date with the fast-moving events in French broadcasting may consult the books and periodicals kept in the library of the Independent Broadcasting Authority in London. Technical information can also be found there.

Thomas, R., *Broadcasting and Democracy in France*. London, Crosby Lockwood Staples, 1976. A detailed exploration of the subject, giving an outline of 1974 reforms.

Kühn, R., 'France: the end of the government monopoly', in R. Kühn (ed.), *The Politics of Broadcasting*. London, Croom Helm, 1985. An examination of the effect of the measures taken by the Socialist government 1981–4.

Kühn, R., 'France and the new media', in R.Kühn (ed.), *Broadcasting and Politics in Western Europe*. London, Cass, 1985. A cogent analysis of France's attempts to address new satellite and cable technology.

de Tarlé, A., 'France: the monopoly that won't divide', in *Television and Political Life*. London, Macmillan, 1979.

Good background material can be found in:

Caillavet, H., *Changer la Télévision*. Paris, Flammarion, 1979.

Ténot, F., *Radios Privées/Radios Pirates*, Paris, Denoel, 1977.

Cazenave, F., *Les Radios Libres*, Paris, PUF, 1980.

The following all appeared in the summer of 1986; gossipy, polemical, partisan views of broadcasting in France by men who have all held high-ranking posts within the system. They are best described as carefully-timed *témoignages*.

Mourousi, Y, *Il est temps de parler. . . .* Paris, RMC Flammarion, 1986.

Cavada, J.-M., *En toute liberté*. Paris, Grasset, 1986.

Chapier, H., *Je retourne ma veste*. Paris, Lafon-Carrère, 1986.

Lestrohan, P., *Cocoricotélé: tabou*. Paris, Marabout, 1986.

Polac, M: *Mes dossiers sont les vôtres*. Paris, Balland, 1986.

Contributors

JOHN FLOWER, MA, Ph.D., Professor of French, University of Exeter. Main interests: French literature and history of ideas, literature and politics from the late nineteenth century to the present day. Publications include *Intention and Achievement: an essay on the novels of François Mauriac* (Oxford University Press), *Georges Bernanos: 'Journal d'un curé de campagne'* (Edward Arnold), *Roger Vailland, the Man and his Masks* and *Writers and Politics in Modern France* (Hodder & Stoughton), *Literature and the Left in France since the Late Nineteenth Century* (Macmillan and Methuen), *Provence* (George Philip). Editor of the *Journal of European Studies*.

ANDRÉE SHEPHERD, L. ès L., Agrégée d'Anglais, Lecturer in English, University of Tours. Main interests: twentieth-century French and English sociology and politics. Publications include a study of the occupation of French factories in May 1968, *Imagination in Power* (Spokesman Books), a translation of Serge Mallet's book *The New Working Class* (Spokesman Books), and contributions to the *Encyclopédie de civilisation britannique* (Larousse) and *Littérature anglaise* (Bordas). Research in progress on the New Left in Britain.

MALCOLM SLATER, MA. B.Sc. (Econ), LL B, Lecturer in French Studies, University of Bradford. Main interests: French foreign policy; European Community politics. Recent publications include *Contemporary French Politics* (Macmillan).

RICHARD McALLISTER, MA, Senior Lecturer in Politics, University of Edinburgh. Main interests: the politics and policies of the European Community; central-local relations in west European states. Author (with D. Hunter) of *Local Government — Death or Devolution?* (Outer Circle Policy Unit, London), and of contributions to books and to journals including *Common Market Law Review, Journal of Common Market Studies, Futures,* and *The New Atlantis*.

BRIAN FITZPATRICK, MA, Ph.D., Lecturer in History, University of Ulster. Main interest: French Right in the nineteenth century. Publications include *Catholic royalism in the department of the Gard, 1814–1852* (Cambridge University Press), and several articles.

ALAN CLARK, BA, Ph.D., Senior Lecturer in French, University of Canterbury, Christchurch, New Zealand. Main interests: French literature; intellectual, social and political history of the twentieth century; ideas and policy of the French Left; the history and politics of New Caledonia. Publications include: *La France dans l'histoire selon Bernanos* (Lettres Modernes), an edition of Valéry Giscard d'Estaing's *Démocratie française* (Methuen), an *Anthologie Mitterrand* (Methuen), and numerous articles on French foreign and Pacific policy.

MARGARET ARCHER, B.Sc. (Econ), Ph.D., Professor of Sociology, University of Warwick, and Chairperson of the ISA's Publications Committee. Main interests: the development and change of educational systems, European social structure, and macro-sociological theory. Publications include *Social Conflict and Educational Change in England and France: 1789–1848* (with Michalina Vaughan; Cambridge University Press), *Students University and Society* (Heinemann), *Contemporary Europe: Class, Status and Power* (edited with S. Giner; Weidenfeld & Nicolson), *Social Origins of Educational Systems* (Sage), *Contemporary Europe: Social Structures and Cultural Patterns*, (Routledge & Kegan Paul) and *The Sociology of Educational Expansion: Take-Off, Growth and Inflation* (Sage).

WALTER REDFERN, MA, Ph.D., Professor in French Studies, University of Reading. Main interests: French literature and in particular the novel from the eighteenth century to the present day. Publications include *The Private World of Jean Giono* (Blackwell), *Paul Nizan: Committed Literature in a Conspiratorial World* (Princeton University Press), *Queneau: 'Zazie dans le métro'* (Grant & Cutler), *Puns* (Blackwell), *Georges Darien: Robbery and Private Enterprise* (Rodopi), and an edition of Sartre: *Les Mains sales* (Methuen).

NEIL HARRIS, BA, freelance teacher and translator, formerly Tutorial Assistant in French, University of Exeter. Main interests: French literature since 1800, Stendhal, and the relationship of music to literature.

Index